Gender, Work and Community After De-Industrialisation

Identity Studies in the Social Sciences

Series Editors: **Margaret Wetherell**, Open University; **Valerie Hey**, Sussex University; **Stephen Reicher**, St Andrews University

Editorial Board: **Marta Augoustinos**, University of Adelaide, Australia; **Wendy Brown**, University of California, Berkeley, USA; **David McCrone**, University of Edinburgh, UK; **Angela McRobbie**, Goldsmiths College, University of London, UK; **Chandra Talpade Mohanty**, Syracuse University, USA; **Harriet B. Nielsen**, University of Oslo, Norway; **Ann Phoenix**, Institute of Education, University of London, UK; **Mike Savage**, University of Manchester, UK

Titles include:

Will Atkinson
CLASS, INDIVIDUALIZATION AND LATE MODERNITY
In Search of the Reflexive Worker

John Kirk, Sylvie Contrepois and Steve Jefferys (*editors*)
CHANGING WORK AND COMMUNITY IDENTITIES IN EUROPEAN REGIONS
Perspectives on the Past and Present

John Kirk and Christine Wall
WORK AND IDENTITY
Historical and Cultural Contexts

Janice McLaughlin, Peter Phillimore and Diane Richardson (*editors*)
CONTESTING RECOGNITION
Culture, Identity and Citizenship

Ben Rogaly and Becky Taylor
MOVING HISTORIES OF CLASS AND COMMUNITY
Identity, Place and Belonging in Contemporary England

Susie Scott
TOTAL INSTITUTIONS AND REINVENTED IDENTITIES

Margaret Wetherell (*editor*)
IDENTITY IN THE 21ST CENTURY
New Trends in Changing Times

Margaret Wetherell (*editor*)
THEORIZING IDENTITIES AND SOCIAL ACTION

Valerie Walkerdine and Luis Jimenez (*editors*)
GENDER, WORK AND COMMUNITY AFTER DE-INDUSTRIALISATION
A Psychosocial Approach to Affect

Identity Studies in the Social Sciences
Series Standing Order ISBN 978–0–230–20500–0 (Hardback)
978–0–230–20501–7 (Paperback)
(*outside North America only*)

You can receive future titles in this series as they are published by placing a standing order. Please contact your bookseller or, in case of difficulty, write to us at the address below with your name and address, the title of the series and the ISBN quoted above.

Customer Services Department, Macmillan Distribution Ltd, Houndmills, Basingstoke, Hampshire RG21 6XS, England

---

Gender, Work and Community After De-Industrialisation

A Psychosocial Approach to Affect

Valerie Walkerdine
Cardiff University, UK

Luis Jimenez
University of East London, UK

palgrave
macmillan

First published 2012 by
PALGRAVE MACMILLAN

Palgrave Macmillan in the UK is an imprint of Macmillan Publishers Limited, registered in England, company number 785998, of Houndmills, Basingstoke, Hampshire RG21 6XS.

Palgrave Macmillan in the US is a division of St Martin's Press LLC, 175 Fifth Avenue, New York, NY 10010.

Palgrave Macmillan is the global academic imprint of the above companies and has companies and representatives throughout the world.

Palgrave® and Macmillan® are registered trademarks in the United States, the United Kingdom, Europe and other countries.

ISBN 978–0–230–24706–2

This book is printed on paper suitable for recycling and made from fully managed and sustained forest sources. Logging, pulping and manufacturing processes are expected to conform to the environmental regulations of the country of origin.

A catalogue record for this book is available from the British Library.

A catalog record for this book is available from the Library of Congress.

In memory of Rosemary Walkerdine.

Contents

Acknowledgements

Many people have been involved in the making of this book. First of all, we should thank the Economic and Social Research Council who funded the research with two separate grants (RES-148-25-0033 and RES-000-22-247). The first of these was part of the programme on Identities and Social Action, where we were surrounded by other wonderful academics doing fascinating and important research. The programme was headed by Margie Wetherell, who gave us a great deal of support and always believed in the research and its importance.

The people of Steeltown were generous with their time, and their belief in what we were trying to do. As well as the enthusiasm of many ex-steelworkers, the local MP was brilliant, as were the people from the local council, who asked us to address one of their council meetings. We cannot name many of the people we would wish to acknowledge because of the need to safeguard their identities and that of the town, but they went a long way towards helping us in our research, as did the ex-steelworkers who ran the local archive and those now tasked with regeneration.

The School of Social Sciences at Cardiff University has always supported this research, and we thank the many staff and students who discussed it with us on many occasions. Françoise Davoine and Jean-Max Gaudilliere took a great deal of trouble to read and comment on a draft of the book with their usual insight and generosity. Francesca Ashurst helped in constructing the Bibliography, and David Studdert was always helpful and spent much time discussing concepts of community with me. Lisa Blackman gave a great deal of encouragement with an article for *Body and Society*, which formed the basis of one of the chapters. It became so much better for all her input. To all, our heartfelt thanks.

Introduction

Hiraeth

(n.) masc. The sense of loss that comes from having been separated from one's home; missing the feeling of being home, of having a place.
And there, the weeping willow trees
Bear the old harps that sang amain,
The lads' wild anguish fills the breeze,
Their blood is mingled with the rain.

– Ellis Evans

The legendary lore of the Welsh...beautiful words expressing a somber sadness, an ache, a hiraeth. The Welsh long for home, yearn for the Wales of the past...the Wales of warriors and peace, the days of danger and beauty. But this home has long since vanished under the rule of a foreign force, and the few left to remember it live in a community threatened by linguistic and cultural extinction.

– Jessica Boynton (http://people.emich.edu/
jboynton/research/welsh.html)

It was Melanie, who comes from the Rhonda, an ex-coal-mining area of South Wales, who first told me about the song called 'Myfanwy'. It is a song of lost love and is a favourite of Welsh male-voice choirs. This, she told me, is what came into her mind when she read about my work in Steeltown, an immense loss and longing that for her linked with the Welsh word 'hiraeth', a term for the loss of home and country/landscape that stretches right back to the English conquest of Wales. As I downloaded and then listened to the hauntingly beautiful song sung by a male choir, the traditional choir of working men from the valleys of South Wales, I began to understand the immensity of the loss that was being mourned. It was not simply the loss of steel and coal, if that were not enough, but the centuries-old loss that it connected to semiotically and affectively, the body's longing for home, to be at home, to be at home in one's land, a land conquered, impoverished and plundered for its raw materials. The ever-present melancholy of the loss, evoked for everyone by the haunting music, captured all those losses inside its simple longing. Felix Guattari (1989) called such songs 'existential refrains' – refrains that brings forth a deep feeling of loss and longing because they evoke the loss of that land that defines us, where we once felt at home and safe, the existential territory.

The story of Steeltown, a town in South Wales built on iron and steel production, is in many ways the story of the importance and then decline of heavy industry in many parts of the globe. But it is also specific. The word 'hiraeth' tells us in all its simplicity that this is a land of loss and longing, and of fierce pride and resistance. This is a proud but conquered people who have tried over centuries to fight back but have had to deal with the consequences of the loss that has afflicted them all and continues to afflict them. This story then is about how the people of one town experienced, felt, found ways of coping and living with the huge insecurities that beset it during and after the industrial times and then struggled with the closure of iron and steel production, which had existed for 200 years, leaving a large gaping hole not only in the centre of the town but also in the already fragile employment situation in the area. The South Wales valleys were the premier site of coal mining in Wales until they were closed after the bitter miners' strike against the decision of the Thatcher government to close the pits in 1984. This was the death knell of heavy industry in the area, an area now with very high levels of unemployment, heavy reliance on benefits and considerable deprivation. This can only get worse as funding is withdrawn by the Westminster government.

Although the Welsh Assembly Government has paid great attention to regenerating Steeltown and the surrounding area, the issues dealt with in this book are poorly understood in policy and government terms, yet in our view they are absolutely central to an understanding of how the people of towns like Steeltown can face the future. As we show here, the effect of cumulative losses is complex and does not stop with the generation of those made redundant but can be seen in the next generation, the young people of the town.

In this volume, we look at how the people of Steeltown lived and supported each other over two centuries of iron and steel production, producing creative ways of living with uncertainty that made them find methods to help each other feel safe and at home. In this context, we explore what happened after the steel works closed in 2002; what happened for the men, for the women and also for some of the young unemployed men of the next generation. We approach this using a psychosocial approach, attempting to understand how the affective and emotional experiences of these issues were produced as a response to the social history and present of which they were a part. In our view, the issues faced by the townspeople are common to experiences shared by people in de-industrialised communities everywhere and give us a crucial insight into ways of being and producing communal support, and of the terrible aftermath of closure, with its toll exacted on everyone, all of which deserve to be much more widely understood than they currently are. Indeed, we argue that the issues we raise are crucial to an understanding of what has happened to and what is experienced by many people today whose lives have been blighted by industrial decline and closure.

This book is the work of two of us, but we have experimented with voice. The issues that we raise and the research that we carried out evoked many feelings in both of us. These are central to our way of working and so it was imperative for us to find a style of writing that conveyed that. For this reason, we often use the first-person singular without declaring which of us – which 'I'– is actually speaking. We hope that the reader will thus be able more easily to engage with our own affective response to the research and to the people we met.

This book comprises nine chapters. Chapter 1 explores the history of Steeltown and attempts to situate the closure within the experience of the setting-up of the town and the experience of the people becoming 'labour' – a workforce – which was then subject to the vagaries of fluctuating commodity prices and therefore profit, the introduction of political economy and the Poor Law Amendment Act of 1834. In understanding the effects of the 2002 closure of the works, we argue, we must understand the effectivity of the previous 200 years and the production of a climate of chronic insecurity.

Chapter 2 brings that history more up to date by presenting the introduction of neo- or advanced liberalism and understanding the implications of this for communities like Steeltown.

Chapter 3 presents ways within the social sciences of understanding communities like Steeltown, looks at past work on de-industrialisation and makes a case for the centrality of affect to the study of community. In developing an account of affect, we utilise work on embodiment, particularly psychoanalytic work on the skin and the development of ways of coping with chronic insecurity both for a single body and for the development of a community body. We explore practices and ways of relating, as well as the spatial and temporal aspects of the town, as affective relations come to operate as a way of creatively buttressing the community against the ongoing effects of chronic insecurity.

In Chapter 4, we take this argument further by exploring the literature on trauma as a way of engaging with the effect of the catastrophic closure of the steel works in 2002. This closure meant that ways of relating and affective practices developed over the last two centuries were no longer as effective, since they were centrally connected to the rhythms of the works.

Chapter 5 investigates the centrality of masculinity to understanding how the hardness of the men was key to the survival of the community throughout the times of steel production. We explore the centrality of the fantasy of what that masculinity signified as well as how it was embodied as both pain and pleasure, and the significance of a strong gendered division of labour.

In Chapters 6 and 7, we take this analysis further by exploring the effects of the closure on the next generation, particularly a group of unemployed young men. By talking to them, we discover that they are afraid of closing the gap between masculinity and femininity, a fear shared by many in their parents' generation. We explore this as an effect of the intergenerational transmission of historical trauma, that is, the effect of the loss of heavy industrial work as a loss of protection by the men, who can no longer save the town against the juggernaut of globalisation. We specifically relate this back to the period of chronic insecurity of the previous 200 years to understand the central significance of history in the understanding of intergenerational transmission.

Chapter 8 brings us to the women and to femininity. Their heroic struggle to keep the community going can appear somewhat eclipsed by the suffering of the men, but we show how understanding what the women do, and how they are trying desperately to keep things going and to keep a fantasy of a heroic masculinity alive, despite its impossibility, keeps them caught in a pincer movement in which no one can quite move because of the absolute desperation to keep things the same. The chapter explores the central issue of change for the women when they can barely manage to put food on the table for their children and keep their families together.

Chapter 9 concludes the book by attempting to look forward to con-nect what has happened in the past to ways of thinking about the possibilities for subjectivity and collectivity in the future. It does so by linking the work of Bracha Ettinger, described in Chapter 8, with forms of work organising inspired by the radical analyst and political activist Felix Guattari.

1
Two Hundred Years of Iron and Steel

It is utterly indifferent to the English bourgeois whether his working-men starve or not, if only he makes money. All the conditions of life are measured by money, and what brings no money is nonsense, unpractical, idealistic bosh... The relation of the manufacturer to his operatives has nothing human in it; it is purely economic. The manufacturer is Capital, the operative Labour. And if the operative will not be forced into this abstraction, if he insists that he is not Labour, but a man, who possesses, among other things, the attribute of labour-force, if he takes it into his head that he need not allow himself to be sold and bought in the market, as the commodity 'Labour', the bourgeois reason comes to a standstill. He cannot comprehend that he holds any other relation to the operatives than that of purchase and sale; he sees in them not human beings, but hands, as he constantly calls them to their faces.

– Friedrich Engels, *The Condition of the Working Class in England in 1844*

Capitalist production, when considered in isolation from the process of circulation and the excesses of competition, is very economical with the materialised labour incorporated in commodities. Yet, more than any other mode of production, it squanders human lives, or living-labour, and not only blood and flesh, but also nerve and brain.

– Karl Marx, *Capital: A Critique of Political Economy*, Vol. 3 (1863–83)

Steeltown is situated at the head of a long valley in what was formerly South Wales' major coalfield. Until recently, it was quite geographically isolated, with poor transport links. The first time I saw the town, a small community nestled at the northern end of the steep-sided valley, I was struck by the emptiness, the huge flattened area that had once been the steelworks. The eye wandered over what was a vast space, and it was hard to conjure up an image of a large works with its belching blast furnaces lighting up the town.[1] After the closure, ambitious plans were made to build a hospital, housing and other facilities on the site and, although in 2008 a train service connecting Steeltown with the capital was opened, the townspeople remain sceptical.

This scepticism is understandable when one learns how much the people have been let down over the years. The research reported in this volume engages with the psychosocial and affective effects of that closure, effects that might not easily be noticed but that have a tremendous significance for how we understand the impacts of de-industrialisation.

There is a tendency in the popular imagination to think of these communities as having a kind of salt-of-the-earth stability, a kind of timelessness in which the settled nature of the communities has hardly changed over time until the closure of a mine, a works, a factory. Thus, deindustrialisation is presented as something that disrupts that stability and fundamentally changes relations. While it is clear that the changes introduced by the decline of the manufacturing base in the United Kingdom, globalisation and neoliberalism did indeed have a massive impact on the lives of working people, it is incorrect to assume that they had predictable lives until that point.

One fine autumn day I met the ex-steelworkers who volunteered to maintain the Steeltown archive, which is housed in an overcrowded room on an industrial estate on a hill overlooking the town. In the course of some animated discussion over a cup of tea, the men gave me huge amounts of material from the room in which all the steel archives are kept. From that material, which includes two local histories, I pieced together an account of the 200 years from the opening of the original ironworks in 1790 until its closure in 2002. What became distressingly increasingly obvious was that during those two centuries, there was very little stability. At most, there were short periods of a few years when life was a little more predictable. I shall elaborate on this in Chapter 2. What the archive material presented me with is the central idea that when the townspeople look back to the period of the steelworks with nostalgia and affection, it is not because life was unproblematically good. What I aim to show in this chapter is that in fact life was very difficult for generation after generation, and that far from stability, what people had to cope with was chronic instability and insecurity. What became obvious to me when confronted with the present and how people were talking and feeling in the context of the time after the closure of the works was that it was impossible to engage effectively with the present without understanding how that present was possible, how the bodies and the practices of those people with whom we had been working had been honed, shaped, disciplined.

Understanding the constitution of the present and how it is made possible has always been at the heart of a Foucauldian project (cf. Henriques et al., 1984). What I found in Steeltown was, in my view, profoundly shaped by the disciplinary regimes of the past. These serve to make the bodies of men and women, as well as the complex affective practices of community. More than this, they shape the transmission to the next generation, a generation of young men and women, stuck like glue to Steeltown (at least those who have not moved away). These young people seem to long for a lost past, are unable to move and become the target of attacks by the older townspeople for, in the case of young men, taking jobs considered too feminine, which produces powerful and painful conflicts between generations.

So, the past in the present is central to my method and understanding – not so much because I want to understand a social history of Steeltown but because it is necessary to understand how the present is constituted. Thus we can understand the present, as we will see, through the material that current occupants of Steeltown give to us, but in order to understand how this present is possible, I have used archival and secondary sources in an attempt to find the contours of the past as it appears in and constitutes the present affects and practices. We will see how the bodies of the inhabitants of Steeltown are honed by the demands of steelwork and the practices of caring for steelworkers. The present is not simply a lost past but also represents a massive change from heterogeneity to homogeneity and some of the highest unemployment in the United Kingdom. In this sense, it is necessary to think not only of the past but also of the present and equally of the future. How can we map that future (Guattari, 1989)? It is this method that I see as fundamentally psychosocial in the sense that we cannot understand what I will describe as chronic insecurity without engaging with its provenance.

I feel that this gives us a real insight into how certain psychosocial aspects became central to the story of the survival of the townspeople because they had to find a way of coping with and overcoming that insecurity. This they did, and they did so amazingly. Thus my short historical sketch will concentrate on setting out both the insecurity and the development of ways of coping with it.

Until the late eighteenth century, what became Steeltown was a farming area and the town did not exist. It was independent and Welsh speaking, with relatively poor subsistence farming but a sense of freedom, and with some people owning their own farms. Though the local landowner, with his eye on the main chance, leased a tract of land to a company that set up an ironworks at the head of the valley in 1790. The Industrial Revolution brought huge changes to the area. The demand for iron and later steel transformed the area physically, from a beautiful if remote valley to what was described as an industrial wasteland, but it also gradually created a community and later a town, Steeltown, with housing provided for workers. The settlement became a community over time and during the period of iron and steel production from 1790 to 2002, it saw a huge influx of people, some relative wealth but also terrible poverty, pain, hurt and crises of various kinds, as well as religious nonconformism, and political and trade union action. This history created Steeltown and forged its people over generations. But in 2002, the steelworks finally closed forever and within a month, the company had razed the enormous site to the ground. What had stood at the centre of the town, with belching furnaces, noise and activity, became an enormous flat space, a nothing where something had once been.

In telling the story of some aspects of what happened to the townspeople after the final closure, it is important for us to put this in the context of what went before. This particular story is about how, on a practical and emotional level, a community was formed and managed to survive in very difficult circumstances. In thinking about what happened to people and how they coped after the closure, we need to understand also how they coped before the closure. In particular, what did one generation pass on to another in terms of ways of coping and being? This is a central and serious point that has largely been ignored and is not well documented. When people have to cope with adversity again and again over generations, not only do they find strategies for surviving, but the body, the mind, the social organisation, all must reflect the ways of dealing with that hardship, and this is passed down from one generation to the next. Nowadays, we are used to the idea that we are expected to talk about painful experiences and any number of psychology professionals are marshalled after major disasters. But small disasters and major disasters alike produce in the body affective responses of which we may or may not be aware: bodily dispositions, chronic illnesses, ways of being and defending against the anxiety, hurt and pain of what is experienced. It is now widely acknowledged (Gant and Hopper, 2008; Garland, 1999; Hopper, 2003b, 2009; Stern, 1997) that what we call intergenerational trauma (Davoine and Gaudilliere, 2004; Urlic, 2004) is transmitted from one generation to another, without the next generation necessarily even knowing what it is that causes the anxieties they experience. This is because they have been transmitted from the previous generation often silently because the experiences of the parent generation are so painful that they cannot bear to talk about them. These intergenerational dynamics can be very effective because they operate in psychosocial ways as a kind of affective and collective continuum, in the sense that a continuous series of events can blend into each other gradually and seamlessly, making it hard to say where one ends and the next begins. Yet they still manage to transmit something affectively, so that the next generation may feel anxieties that they cannot name and that in a sense they experience as their own but that do not belong to them – they belong with the actual material hurt experienced by previous generations. For Steeltown, the modes of everyday relations and practices linking people together was established over time and was threatened on many occasions, until at last the central linchpin that held the town together was destroyed.

But what if, all over the world, such issues confront people in different ways, again and again? What if the small and large histories always operate to produce ways of coping in all of us and we all transmit them to the next generation. What if we do not need a war or genocide to experience this but only what Gail Pheterson (1993) called ordinary everyday humiliation? In other words, what if the experience of small and large historical events, of everyday pain, anxiety and hurt, itself always passes from one generation to the next, being transformed along the way? What if ways of living and being together always bear the hallmarks of what has to be endured? If this is so, then to understand the effects of the closure of the steelworks, we need to understand what the community had to endure from 1790 and not just after 2002. Only then can we understand what broke when the steelworks closed and what its consequences were for people's lives and ways of coping and moving on. In particular, I want to consider the fact that communities like Steeltown for two centuries and more were at the mercy of the vagaries of the global iron and steel trade. When we explore the history of the town, we see that sometimes there was a demand for iron and steel, sometimes the price went up and sometimes it went down, sometimes there was no demand or iron and steel were supplied more cheaply from elsewhere in the world, or there was a depression, recession or war. Steeltown, like most industrial communities, lived with this constant uncertainty and was at the mercy of this ever-changing and unpredictable global situation. Would there be money, food, work? There were good times and bad times, better pay versus soup kitchens. On top of this, the work was dangerous – perhaps not as dangerous as the mines, but dangerous enough. How does a community cope with this ongoing uncertainty? Our contention is that it copes by building certain kinds of practices, ways of being and ways of handling emotion that produce a sense of continuity to act as a buffer against uncertainty. However, this way of being, which has withstood much, is severely tested when the source of work for the town disappears altogether, though this is not the first time – the works closed twice before, as we shall see. Of course, it would be easy to say that the experience of this hardship over several genera-tions produces creativity and resilience, but these are easy words to say and in saying them we tend to gloss over what created them – a mass of people in thrall to the trade of commodities like iron and steel, whose lives are tossed on the heavy and stormy seas of international capitalism. We forget what created stability for upper- and middle-class lives and we tend to pathologise or over-romanticise the ways of coping that commu-nities like Steeltown came up with. This is what we want to open up in this volume. In presenting some aspects of the history of Steeltown, we aim to think about what had to be endured and how.

In this first chapter, I obviously cannot undertake more than a small historical sketch, but the aim is not to tell the history of Steeltown so much as to understand what the people experienced over several gen-erations and what the implications of this are for understanding what went on after the closure.

In thinking in this way, it is necessary to point out that the aim is to place the people of Steeltown in history and to understand the embod-ied effects of experiencing that history on the bodies of generations of inhabitants. So, the aim is not to make the inhabitants into victims, to fuel resentment or to pathologise by using quasi-therapeutic language. It is important to state this because there have been a considerable num-ber of critiques of the use of emotions in social research from a number of social, cultural and political theorists (see, for example, Ahmed, 2004; Berlant, 2000; Holland, 2007; Squire, 2001; West-Newman, 2008). In my view, most of these fall wide of the mark because they fail to engage with how people live and experience the historical events they live through and because there is often a split between notions of solidarity, resilience, resistance (good) and victimhood, trauma, pain and pathol-ogy (bad). My argument is that these are not really able to be split in this way – between the active and passive. The view of history that I am proposing understands that our affective experience of events, be they large social histories or small family ones, for example, are intertwined in complex ways; and that it is that complexity and the affective and social organisation that ensues that I want to understand because what happened in 2002 built on forms of social organisation and coping that have been set down to cope with the continual difficulties experienced over a 200-year period.

In placing the inhabitants of Steeltown in history, we are also making a larger point about psychosocial relations in general. Although modernist approaches have tended to remove the history, concentrating only on family dynamics, we argue that it is impossible to understand what people have suffered and the affective, psychic and social effects of this without understanding what conditions had to be endured. In other words, we are arguing against a version of human nature that adds on unconscious and affective processes and attempts to understand the affective and unconscious effectivities of the specific forms of historical experience – as Davoine and Gaudilliere (2004) put it – where the large histories meet the small histories.

The beginnings of Steeltown

> The history of [Steeltown] and other working class communities is one of a struggle to retain jobs, to defend working conditions and to provide public services which add decency and dignity to people's lives.
>
> I witnessed such courage in the 1984 miners' strike and our forefathers shared similar experiences in the earlier part of the twentieth century. The sacrifices made then and in more recent years were to defend our communities.
>
> ...Unemployment, bad housing and an industrially scarred environment have all taken their toll.
>
> – Local MP in foreword (reference restricted)[2]
>
> Equally important is the social revolution in which its new industrialised people, uneducated, unrepresented and dominated by the demands of industry were, through years of change, that were sometimes turbulent, firmly welded under the impact of political, religious and educational influences into an independent, democratic and politically active and well-knit community.[3]

So here we have the sense that it was industrial struggle in adversity that brought the people together and out of that shared struggle were forged a set of relations. Early settlers had a hard life and food supplies were uncertain in the harsh winter. Before the ironworks was established there was an agricultural community, but the soil was not good and conditions were harsh, so there was considerable poverty. The Industrial Revolution was what started the community as people strove for a better life. A local historian,[4] on whose account of Steeltown I rely in large measure, says that people were also independent and free, and the land ripe for exploitation; and that this changed what the people had to experience and bear.

The Industrial Revolution produced a demand for iron. Coal in the local valley and surroundings provided the basis for its production. So gradually the Industrial Revolution came to the South Wales valleys. The issue is to think about the effects of the transformation of an agricultural poor but independent people into an industrial workforce. In quoting Marx and Engels to introduce this chapter, we see how they both set out the distress and pain produced by the exploitation of working people and in addition how the bourgeoisie understood labour as simply one component of the production of profit, with a need to treat people as an abstract, expendable aspect of the mode of capitalist production. As a young man in Manchester, Engels was deeply troubled by what he saw, and he went on to support Marx financially in his attempt to theorise the economics of capitalist production through the production of surplus value through labour, and to understand how work and production could happen otherwise. In developing an alternative economic model, he wanted to pay attention to the way in which workers become simply understood through and reduced to the abstract concept of 'labour', which then becomes understood as one component in the production of profit. By reducing work to 'labour', the industrialists could simply see this as an element in the production process, so that, for example, when demand for steel went up, more labour was needed, and when down, less. The human consequences of becoming 'labour' were, as we shall see, not only not considered but deliberately ignored, since the principle aim was the production of wealth. Thus, our interest here is to think about what it was like to live life on what Carolyn Steedman (1996) called the borderlands, or what we might now call 'precarity' (Neilson and Rossiter, 2008) in the sense that there was an absence of stability and one had constantly to adapt to and cope with change brought about by shifts in the need for 'labour'. As we will see, conditions were never stable for very long and shifted from quite good to absolutely appalling frequently for two centuries.

Although in many ways Marx and Engels started with the unbearableness of the conditions of working life, they did not dwell on what we might now call their psychosocial consequences. This is understandable because in concentrating on exploitation, alienation and ideology, they were trying to build an alternative. They wanted to mobilise workers to recognise themselves as having different interests from their bosses and therefore to come together as a distinct 'class' to fight for a revolution or a complete change in the economic mode of production that did not make work an expendable aspect of the production of wealth. In doing this, there was more emphasis on what might not be seen by working people, who might view things the wrong way round, as in a camera obscura of ideology, in which their differences from bosses and their exploitation was less visible to view, and who might therefore be prevented from understanding and fighting for an end to exploitation. It is also in part related to the type of social theory and concepts available at that time. For example, the notion of 'sociology' was not coined until 1847 by Auguste Compte.

However, one consequence of this was less emphasis on the experience of embodied suffering rather than the failure to see and the possibility of seeing for political action. Thus, my concern is not ideology but embodied suffering – the effects on bodies of chronic instability and insecurity over generations and the attempts to find ways to cope with this. This topic has been very largely ignored, though perhaps the one person to have approached it is Raymond Williams (1973) with his concept of 'structures of feeling'. Although his work is quite enigmatic, it does at least engage with the circulation within sociality of ways of feeling rather than ways of seeing or telling.[5]

What is problematic in this debate is that there has been a polarisation of discourse and experience/agency. In particular, beyond a sense of phenomenology, there has been no sense of the embodied effects of the suffering and indeed fighting, anger, agitation, resistance produced by this history. I believe that the effects are profound and that we need to understand them and their legacy today. In this sense, then, I wish to go beyond that opposition active/passive or structure and agency. Of course, the people create a sense that they can do things – but if that agency is created in and through a sense of jointly shared and embodied experience and safety, then it falters when things change and so threatens the possibility of creativity.

To give an example of what I mean, we might cite the local historian's argument that there had to be an adjustment to industrial time with the beginning of the works. He argues that people had a more relaxed sense of time in agriculture – sheep could be left for a day but blast furnaces could not. Therefore the drinking and relatively freewheeling culture had to be tamed, the experience of time changed and sobriety had to be the norm, hence a ban on drinking and the absence of pubs in the community. In this sense, he is showing us how the embodied sense of time shifted dramatically from a sense of an agricultural rhythm to a greater need for regulating the body according to the demands of an industrial clock, which also demanded a body ready for work and, so, sober (Adam, 2004). This shift would have taken time and effort – the body had to be disciplined. What followed from this slow and perhaps difficult change was the development of organisation built around the new notion of time, with start and finish times for work.

The 200 years of history shows us a community in the making in the sense that it was gradually formed by successive owners of the plant who provided at first rudimentary housing and then more and better housing, and eventually houses built on land leased by the company with roads and amenities being provided too, but it was very much a 'company town'. In this it shared characteristics with company towns the world over. There was at first only a company shop, and the raison d'être of the town was the works. So, gradually the material aspects of the town were created. Conditions of work were at first very harsh and women and children were among those employed, with the company being one of the last in the country to stop this practice, despite legislation. What is noticeable throughout the history are periods of extreme hardship and poverty, poor conditions, lay-offs, strikes, disasters, growing union activity and militancy. So we get a picture of instability in which a people were at the mercy of capitalism, in which demand for Welsh iron and steel shifted, leaving the employees and their families to bear the consequences.

Certain government enquiries looked at the education and morals of the town and area because it had been a hotbed of Chartist uprising as several thousand people had marched on Newport in 1839. In fact the desire for political and industrial reform through Chartism and the demand for trade unions grew rapidly in the 1830s. They were understood as a 'radical protest against the industrial exploitation and political slavery of the working classes' (reference restricted). The local historian argues that the division between haves and have-nots was particularly wide in the area. Workers suffered a 12-hour working day, the work was very hard, food was poor, and child and female labour was common.

Insanitary conditions were an issue, with no proper walkways, so that in wet weather people went ankle deep in mud. However, it was noted in Emund Head's report on the 'Sanitary Condition of the Labouring

Classes' (Poor Law Commission Office, Somerset House, 9 July 1842) that the interior of the houses was spotlessly clean and well maintained. However, there were three outbreaks of cholera in 1832, 1849 and 1866, and it was not until the 1880s that drains and sewerage were provided, followed by piped water in 1878. There were also outbreaks of smallpox, typhoid and scarlet fever. Infant mortality was high and life expectancy was short.

This was a company settlement and it was the company that provided housing by and large. The disposition of the housing was crucial:

> the cottages usually faced onto a lane between them and the gardens, known as 'the bailey'; it was a meeting place for the whole row, and a fertile field for gossip. (reference restricted)[6]

This same phenomenon was discussed by townspeople in the early twenty-first century, as we shall see in Chapter 3, so the arrangement of the houses in the 1800s provided the basis for modes of sociality that lasted well over one hundred and fifty years. Gradually, the company ceased building houses and offered leases to builders and building clubs. There was still no recognised centre and people were reliant on company stores. This also related to a 'long pay' system in which people were paid in kind, with goods only available for purchase at the company store.

Political economy and the Poor Law

In this section I want to situate what happened to the people of Steeltown within the context of the development of political economy and the approach to the relation between the creation of wealth and the production of poverty. What is important about this is that if we situate the experience of the people within the context of the history of global capital, the discourses, policies and practices that emerged in the nineteenth century set up the regulation of working people in particular ways. Thus, when the local historian tells us that the Poor Law Amendment Act of 1834 and the creation of the workhouse caused widespread terror and hatred among the local population, we need to understand just how this related to the experience of employment and unemployment during this period. Basically, there existed forms of poor relief that were developed at parish level from 1601, but these were stopped by the 1834 act in order to stop poverty caused by pauperism or indigence. Thus developed the idea that the citizen through habits of idleness and indigence was responsible for poverty and must be punished by the workhouse. Thus unemployment, which was, of course, endemic and subject to fluctuation in relation to the demand for iron and then steel, became terrifying with its threat of being sent to the workhouse. I want to place this within the context of the emergence of political economy, that is, the science of the production of wealth. Marx and Engels made a point of demonstrating how work becomes 'labour' and the systematic way in which everything is subservient to the creation of profit, that is wealth. It is not surprising that, within this context, the non-working poor should become a target. Anything that was understood as a drain on resources was a hindrance to the production of wealth. The aim therefore was to make non-work as unpleasant as possible in order to keep people in work, whatever the conditions. Thus, it is not surprising, as the local historian[7] suggests, that the people of Steeltown were terrified. As Arribas-Ayllon (2007) argues,

> In line with mercantilist beliefs that hunger and want increased industry, Townsend argues that it is the lot of the poor that hunger should compel them to labour. Hunger, after all, is not only 'a peaceable, silent, unremitted pressure, but, as the most natural motive to industry and labour, it calls forth the most powerful exertions' (p. 24). The error of the poor laws is to remove this natural spur for hunger and destroy the natural motive to 'labour and industry'. And yet the mechanism of hunger is more absolute and more efficient than that of 'legal constraints' which is accompanied by 'too much trouble, violence and noise'. The imperative to relieve the poor contradicts the objective of setting them to work if it means circumventing the natural law of want. Townsend summarises the problem of provision for the poor as thus:

> Now a fixed, a certain, and a constant provision for the poor weakens this spring; it increases their improvidence, but does not promote their cheerful compliance with those demands, which the community is obliged to make on the most indigent of its members; it tends to destroy the harmony and beauty, the symmetry and order of that system, which God and nature have established in the world. The improvident among the poor have been advancing in their claims: they now begin to understand that they have a legal right to all. (1971, p. 36)

In other words, it was felt necessary to make people compelled to work because they needed to eat. Spending money on the poor was also felt to be a mistake because it dissipated wealth and so this led to the creation of the workhouse.

In his 1817 volume *The Principles of Political Economy and Taxation*, Ricardo, a wealthy stockbroker and one of the founders of political economy and, indeed, economics, introduces the labour theory of value, which basically sees the value of labour as central to economics:

> if the reward of the labourer were always in proportion to what he produced, the quantity of labour bestowed on a commodity, and the quantity of labour which that commodity would purchase, would be equal, and either might accurately measure the variations of other things: but they are not equal; the first is under many circumstances an invariable standard, indicating correctly the variations of other things; the latter is subject to as many fluctuations as the commodities compared with it... Is not the value of labour equally variable; being not only affected, as all other things are, by the proportion between the supply and demand, which uniformly varies with every change in the condition of the community, but also by the varying price of food and other necessaries, on which the wages of labour are expended? (Ricardo, 1821, p. 4, cited in Arribas-Ayllon, 2007)

The closest we come to an economic conception of poverty is in theory of wages. Given that classical political economy now effects a bifurcation of labour, it has a 'natural price' and a 'market price' (Arribas-Ayllon p. 38). The natural price of labour 'is that which is necessary to enable the labourer... to subsist and to perpetuate their race without, either increase or diminution' which depends not on the quantity of money he may receive in wages, but the quantity of 'food, necessaries and conveniences' that his money is capable of purchasing. Under this schema, poverty is, for Ricardo, the condition in which the market price of labour falls below its natural price: 'poverty deprives them of those comforts which custom renders absolute necessaries'. Variations in the price of labour are said to be subject to two causes: the supply and demand of labourers, and the price of the commodities on which the wages of the labour are expended. In Ricardo's *The Principles*..., we find a thoroughly 'demoralised' sphere of economic activity that is no longer conditioned by the sphere of exchange, and the haggling and bargaining of workmen and masters, but by a scientifically rendered domain governed by a distributional mechanism. The major modification here is that poverty ceases to be a moral, humanitarian or sentimental crisis of relations between the rich and poor, but is instead a logical and collective phenomenon; after all, the variations in the natural price of labour depends on 'the habits and customs of the people' (Arribas-Ayllon, p. 40).

In Ricardo's theory of wages, we find a convergence between a new economic rationality of labour and Malthusian statements that hold that wage levels are dependent on the ratio of population to capital, capital being the means of employing labour. Ricardo invokes Malthus's geometric maxim to show that as population increases, capital has a tendency of increasing more rapidly, in which case 'wages during the whole period would have a tendency to rise, because the demand for labour would increase still faster than the supply' (1821, p. 40). However, as population increases and land of worse quality is cultivated, the tendency of capital diminishes since the productive powers of labour also decrease. Hence, there is a tendency for the rate of growth of capital to decrease while the rate of growth of population remains constant:

> under the most favourable circumstances, the power of production is still greater than that of population, it will not long continue so; for the land being limited in quantity, and differing in quality, with every increased portion of capital employed on it, there will be a decreased rate of production, whilst the power of population continues always the same'. (Ricardo, 1821, p. 41)

Ricardo was closely aligned with Thomas Malthus, who also wrote about political economy (1820, 1827). They both stated that poor relief was in direct opposition to the principles of political economy because it diverts money from capital investment and thus has an effect on production, plus it increases the numbers of the poor and the population rises, which is a drain on resources and thus upsets the dynamism of the economy, thus ultimately increasing the numbers of poor people and making the rich poor. Thus gradual diminution of poor relief was advocated in order to make the poor more self-reliant. This was the workhouse. Thus poverty was to become a condition that was to be understood through the figure of the pauper. The pauper was idle and had to be made to work. Thus, gradually those out of work became subject to pathologisation in the sense that poverty became understood as the result of a moral absence, which had to be corrected. In this sense then, the inhabitants of Steeltown had much to fear and no wonder they were terrified of the workhouse. They were already subject to the categorisation as the abstract 'labour', which made them at the mercy of capitalists and the production of profit, so that their conditions of work and their ability to house, feed and clothe their families was subject to intense unpredictability. With the Poor Law Amendment Act, they further had to fear not only the workhouse but also the sense that lack of work leading to poverty was produced by idleness and was a moral category, not the result of circumstances completely outside their control. Thus, I am trying to paint a picture of the terrors, uncertainty and pressures that would have created huge anxieties in the lives of these workers and their families and that shifted and changed but rarely improved.

The workhouses were constructed using the principle of Bentham's (1875) panopticon, much discussed by Foucault (1977), where inmates simply had to imagine themselves to be watched in order to regulate their behaviour themselves: the implication of being observed is enough for inmates to observe themselves, in which case subjection is simultaneously an act of self-disciplining.

Bentham took the classic workhouse and made it into a programme in which people could 'improve' themselves. Every establishment was to become self-financing, with the workhouse operating as a disciplinary machine in which people learnt the proper conduct that was expected of them for things to work efficiently. This was to become a 'laboratory for conducting experiments on human conduct' (Foucault, 1977). The monitoring and calibration of conduct would serve to remoralise the soul of the pauper. Thus the aim was to recreate the conditions of wage labour and so provide the clear lesson that work for subsistence was the only alternative to the terrible conditions of the workhouse, thus acting as a deterrent for potential paupers, as the local historian makes clear when he tells us how terrified people were of it.

Arribas-Ayllon tells us that the 'New Poor Law of 1834 is pivotal in the history of liberal government. Before 1834, liberal government drew on the apparatus of the workhouse, with its Benthamite principle of less eligibility, and its Malthusian thesis of natural scarcity, in order to establish the minimum conditions for wage-labour.' But after 1834, the new approach stressed an ethic of personal and family responsibility, with a national 'labour market', in which the potential worker became labour and therefore existed within a market for their labours, with the necessity to work for whatever wages were available in order to avoid the workhouse.

As Engels says:

> But these wise Malthusians were so thoroughly convinced of the infallibility of their theory that they did not for one moment hesitate to cast the poor into the Procrustean bed of their economic notions and treat them with the most revolting cruelty. Convinced with Malthus and the rest of the adherents of free competition that it is best to let each one take care of himself, they would have preferred

to abolish the Poor Laws altogether. Since, however, they had neither the courage nor the authority to do this, they proposed a Poor Law constructed as far as possible in harmony with the doctrine of Malthus, which is yet more barbarous than that of laissez-faire, because it interferes actively in cases in which the latter is passive. We have seen how Malthus characterises poverty, or rather the want of employment, as a crime under the title 'superfluity', and recommends for it punishment by starvation. The commissioners were not quite so barbarous; death outright by starvation was something too terrible even for a Poor Law Commissioner. 'Good,' said they, 'we grant you poor a right to exist, but only to exist; the right to multiply you have not, nor the right to exist as befits human beings. You are a pest, and if we cannot get rid of you as we do of other pests, you shall feel, at least, that you are a pest, and you shall at least be held in check, kept from bringing into the world other surplus, either directly or through inducing in others laziness and want of employment. Live you shall, but live as an awful warning to all those who might have inducements to become superfluous.'

As we have seen, demand for iron and steel, and the price it fetched, varied so the availability of work also varied, and as we will see, the fluctuation in wages and even the availability of work was entirely subject to the demands for iron and then steel in the national and international markets and therefore was entirely subject to the fluctuations of international capitalism. That workers could not expect stable and fair conditions to prevail but in fact always to fluctuate was absolutely central to the necessity to produce a self-regulating workforce who would avoid the workhouse by having to accept and adjust to this variation, taking whatever work they could get for whatever wage was available, whether it was considered fair or not. To keep the workers and their families keen, workhouses were built so that they had to work for whatever wages and conditions were on offer to avoid the workhouse and, moreover, even though it was accepted that supply and demand fluctuated, poverty was seen as idleness, a habit of mind and conduct, but it functioned as a way of keeping people terrified about the future, a future that was not under their own control in any way. My particular concern here then is to understand the effect of that terror about the future, the experience of uncertainty and how it produces forms of organisation and modes of coping with this.[8] One example of such an organisation is the Friendly Societies, which were set up by workers and communities to provide a pay-in scheme that would provide financial support in times of illness and unemployment. Thus, one of the arguments I want to make is that the only recourse to endemic uncertainty the people had was to attempt to create structures that provided self-help and stability. I think we can begin to see just where the idea of the community as 'tightly knit' may come from.

Malthus also argues that marriage was encouraged as a form of stabilising influence so that a man had to try to provide for this family. What we will begin to see is the influence of chapels, which provided both communal support and political rhetoric but also enforced a harsh morality, which helped to cement this stability. So, according to Malthus, population is considered to have the capacity to increase in geometrical ratio while subsistence is said to increase in no more than arithmetical ratio (Malthus, 1798, p. 14). The effect of the difference between the two rates of increase establishes a tendency for population to outstrip the means of subsistence that is necessary for its support. In addition, given that such a tendency is constrained by practical circumstances, Malthus argues that some manner of checks exist that limit the increase in population approximately to the level of subsistence. Having established this tendency and the existence of such checks, the final part of his thesis is an enquiry into the nature of the checks that ought to be practised to avoid a situation of scarcity and misery.

> The labourer who earns eighteen pence a day, and lives with some degree of comfort as a single man, will hesitate a little before he divides that pittance among four or five, which seems to be but just sufficient for one. Harder fare and harder labour he would submit to for the sake of living with the woman that he loves but he must feel conscious, if he thinks at all, should he have a large family, and any ill luck whatever, no degree of frugality, no possible exertion of his manual strength, could preserve him from the heart-rending sensation of seeing his children starve, or of forfeiting his independence, and being obliged to the parish for their support. (Malthus, 1798, p. 67)

Malthus persistently underscores marriage as the institutional embodiment of an obligation of the man to support his family. Moral restraint becomes the only acceptable alternative for the male who suspects he is unable to fulfil this obligation. For women, the prospect of rearing a child outside wedlock receives the fullest condemnation of the society she has needlessly burdened.

In opposition to the above doctrines was the emergence of liberal philanthropy at the end of the nineteenth century – charity schools, hospitals, almshouses and benevolent societies – which came to represent an alternative system of moral relations to that of the Poor Law (Ashurst, 2010).

It is in light of this that the development of what is usually referred to as a 'close-knit' community was absolutely central to survival because it provided the possibility of some form of stability and a sense of continuity of being within the context of no external stability.

Political activity: Chartism

> Such is the state of the British working-class as I have come to know it in the course of twenty-one months, through the medium of my own eyes, and through official and other trustworthy reports. And when I call this condition, as I have frequently enough done in the foregoing pages, an utterly unbearable one, I am not alone in so doing. As early as 1833, Gaskell declared that he despaired of a peaceful issue, and that a revolution can hardly fail to follow. 1n 1838, Carlyle explained Chartism and the revolutionary activity of the working-men as arising out of the misery in which they live, and only wondered that they have sat so quietly eight long years at the Barmecide[9] feast, at which they have been regaled by the Liberal bourgeoisie with empty promises. And in 1844 he declared that the work of organising labour must be begun at once 'if Europe, at any rate if England, is to continue inhabitable much longer.' (Engels, 1892; accessed as http://www.marxists.org/archive/marx/works/1845/condition-working-class/index.htm)

Chartism was a movement for political and social reform between 1838 and 1850. It was possibly the first mass working-class labour movement in the world and took its name from the People's Charter of 1838, which stipulated the six main aims of the movement as:

1. A vote for every man twenty-one years of age, of sound mind, and not undergoing punishment for crime.
2. The ballot – to protect the elector in the exercise of his vote.
3. No property qualification for members of Parliament – thus enabling the constituencies to return the man of their choice, be he rich or poor.

4. Payment of members, thus enabling an honest tradesman, working man, or other person, to serve a constituency, when taken from his business to attend to the interests of the Country.
5. Equal Constituencies, securing the same amount of representation for the same number of electors, instead of allowing small constituencies to swamp the votes of large ones.
6. Annual parliaments, thus presenting the most effectual check to bribery and intimidation, since though a constituency might be bought once in seven years (even with the ballot), no purse could buy a constituency (under a system of universal suffrage) in each ensuing twelve-month; and since members, when elected for a year only, would not be able to defy and betray their constituents as now.

Life was hard in Steeltown during this period, but the townspeople had to bear it because the alternatives, such as the workhouse, were even worse. Thus, it is hardly surprising that two different forces took root within the community: nonconformist religion, and radical politics and trade unionism. With regard to the former, the churches increased in strength and influence from 1851, offering Sunday schools and becoming, the local historian tells us, a chief agent in educating and civilising the masses. There were also temperance movements, which aimed to curb drunkenness. Hardly surprisingly, many workers seeking relief in alcohol, which, of course, acted in opposition to the production of the diligent and not indigent worker.

Since the vote was not given to workers but only to the middle classes in the Reform Bill of 1832, many working people turned to Chartism for a programme of political reform, supported by many nonconformist ministers.

According to local records, several thousand men marched to Newport (the port town on the Severn Estuary) from the valleys in 1839, though many were arrested. Since government spies were everywhere, planning was secret and afterwards many escaped prison by maintaining absolute silence. Again, I want to point to something that, as we will see, becomes central to ways of being in the late twentieth century: you don't talk about certain things outside the family.

According to the local historian[10], trade unions were slow to form in Steeltown. He puts this down to the high demand for iron and therefore high levels of employment. It was the miners who first formed unions in the area. The Iron-makers' Union took off in a period of industrial depression from 1870 to 1886, when employers tried to reduce wages, as they did in the pits in the area. The Iron and Steelworkers' Union was set up in 1872 and there was a great strike in 1898 in the local coal field, with much distress and poverty suffered during it and only a slight increase in wages achieved after 22 weeks of striking.

Imagine how people in a community stick together to support each other in such circumstances, how they survive hunger and fear, and how they gain a strength that they can carry inside them through the dark times to protect them and their fellow citizens. It is during such periods of uncertainty and adversity that a community finds ways to become self-supporting in order to cope with suffering and to survive.

So, by the end of the nineteenth century, we see a town in which there is constant uncertainty brought about by the conditions of labour and the development of political economy with its stress on the need for a flexible workforce and constantly changing wages and conditions to accommodate international fluctuations in the production of wealth. This alone is enough to produce suffering, but, in addition, the Poor Law Amendment Act introduced the terrifying workhouse, which was to hang as a threat over those without work, but also acted to regulate worker behaviour such that those who were self-regulating – industrious rather idle – could become the 'deserving poor'. The conditions in the workhouse were terrible, and children there were frequently taken away from their parents and made to become apprentices in the most appalling conditions, or sent overseas to the new colonies, in equally dire conditions (Ashurst, 2010). Thus, on the one had we have a clear example of the effectivity of the production of workers as abstract 'labour', with clear examples of Foucault's sense of disciplining the population (Foucault, 1977) and of his concepts of the self-regulation and self-formation necessitated by liberalism. However, my concern here is not to think simply about how the relations of power/knowledge/desire (Henriques et al., 1984) constitute the figure of the worker, but to think about how that was experienced. On the one hand, the chronic uncertainty must have produced attempts to be able to bear the suffering. Modern work on trauma shows us that chronic anxieties such as those experienced by the Steeltown workers during this period have effects on the body that can be passed down through the generations.[11] In particular, as I argue in Chapter 3, very basic to human existence is the sense of safety central to a feeling of continuity of being. I argue that the conditions experienced by these townspeople would have made an unproblematic sense of continuity of being extremely difficult and that the strength (tight-knittedness) of the local community would emerge as a way of attempting to produce a sense of continuity and safety not provided by external conditions.

Marx and Engels stressed the importance of the political awareness of the conditions of all labouring people that made them into a class who could recognise each other and therefore come together and fight. E P Thompson tells us that this already built on previous attempts to organise that existed for the labouring classes (Thompson, 1963). However, I am proposing that within Steeltown and similar industrialised communities, the provision of nonconformist religion, of Friendly Societies and of other self-help arrangements, and the development of communal ways of looking after each other were also ways of creatively dealing with the lack of certainty and continuity. This, I suggest, is why such communities can at once be branded as both radical and conservative.

The twentieth century

To give the bare bones of what happened in Steeltown in the early twentieth century, the iron and steel industry modernised rapidly between 1899 and 1912, leading to a 50 per cent increase in the town's population between 1901 and 1911. Trade unions became more powerful and Labour became the dominant party. The demand for social reforms and a better distribution of wealth was at the root of miners' strikes in 1898 and 1912 and the railway workers' strike in 1911. While iron and steel were obviously needed for the First World War, there was a collapse of the post-war industrial boom in 1921–2. This severely affected the coal and steel industries in Wales and England. The Conservative government made the decision to develop newer industries related to home ownership and consumption. This left the old industries and the industrial areas of South Wales and the north of England flailing and depressed, after what seemed like a deliberate policy not to support those industries. Churchill was chancellor of the exchequer in 1924. His policies on the economy in general resulted in further unemployment, and his budget measures were also seen as assisting the generally prosperous rentier banking and salaried classes (to which Churchill and his associates generally belonged) at the expense of manufacturers and exporters, who were known then to be suffering from imports and from competition in traditional export markets (Henderson, 1955). In fact the iron- and steelworks was closed in 1929 and demolished in 1936, but in 1938 a new strip mill, the first in Europe, was erected on the site and was repeatedly extended and re-equipped to maintain prosperity in the district. In the early years of the twentieth century, a new manager was brought in and because of an increase in dividend and the onset of the Boer War, the plant could be modernised and production was strong.

However, the dumping of cheap imported steel made profits lower than they could have been and there was a great deal of debate about tariff protection. However, the Liberal government supported free trade and so the steelworks was once again under threat. Thus, the years 1907 to 1911 were lean years for the British steel industry because of decreased home sales and lack of expansion to overseas markets.

The 1911 closure

> Three thousand men were rendered idle including not only furnace men and steelworkers but also quarrymen, coke oven workers, and engineers. For ten months they suffered great hardship; at the time there was no unemployment benefit, and when savings were exhausted Poor Law relief for their families was barely enough for the necessities of life. (reference restricted)[12]

This closure happened with little warning and the community suffered terribly until the works was reopened in 1912 after deputations from the workers and a new sheet mill was completed in 1913. This closure was brought about because the owner felt that not enough profit was to be made from steel and therefore wanted to concentrate on coal. This demonstrates, of course, the concern with profit and the lack of heed for workers, which is so well outlined by Marx and Engels.

The local historian[13] helpfully provides us with a portrait of the daily life of the community from 1900 to 1920. This is important in establishing the rhythms that became the bedrock of a sense of security. The works hooter sounded hourly from 6.00 to 9.00 a.m., then at noon, 5.00 and 6.00 p.m. From 5.30 a.m. until 7.30 p.m., the sound of boots filled the air as workers went to the works and the pits and night workers came home. By 8.00 a.m., building workers started work and by 8.50 a.m. the bell rang for school. Shops stayed open till late at night. However, the local historian[14] adds that death and disablement were common and the community organised concerts as benefits and all rallied around bereaved families. A man would hand his wages to the woman of the house, who gave him spending money and managed the family finances. Although health and longevity gradually increased over the years, hard work for both women at home and men at the works or down the pit took its toll and both died relatively young. Infant mortality was high, though much reduced as a result of improved sanitation following the provision of better health and benefits in 1950. The area was strongly trade unionised with 100 per cent of workers in iron and steel and the pits in unions. The workforce was to undergo more boom and bust when the steelworks prospered in the years of the First World War, then after the war the price of steel rose, resulting in expansive schemes of welfare and provision for the staff. However, by 1922, the price of steel had collapsed and the company made heavy losses every year from then until 1926. After 1923, its losses were consistently heavy and, according to Gray Jones, in 1929 during the Depression, the plant was permanently closed. With already high unemployment in 1923, by 1929, one in three men were out of work.

In 1927 there was also a pit disaster in Steeltown, with considerable loss of life. Two years later in October, the steelworks closed, though the sheet mill was kept working. In 1931 the government finally introduced tariff protection, which meant that steel could finally be produced more cheaply than imported steel. However, the Steeltown plant was not reopened despite massive unemployment. In 1934 the government established a Commission for Distressed Areas and introduced new benefit regulations. These were designed to reduce payments to the long-term unemployed. There were nationwide demonstrations in 1934–5 and finally the means-tested benefits were withdrawn. In 1936 a new strip mill was built, with massive clearing of the old infrastructure. In 1938 it began operating. It worked continuously through the Second World War and was repeatedly developed until 1961, after having been nationalised in 1950. This brought prosperity to the town.

> As for the people, they have the neighbourliness and dependability of a close-knit community so characteristic of the South Wales valleys. (reference restricted)[15]

Post-war developments

We might imagine that there was consolidation and relative stability after the Second World War, but this was hardly the case. Although there was strong demand for steel in the years immediately following, and although the industry was nationalised briefly by the post-war Labour government, this was not to last. Nationalisation occurred in 1949, but the Conservative government denationalised the industry again in 1951. First, the plant needed constant updating to keep up with new technology being used elsewhere, such as in the United States. This investment in plant took place mostly during the 1950s and vastly increased productivity. However, by 1958, the government announced the development of a new strip mill in Newport, south of the valleys.

At this point, rumours about the fate of Steeltown began to circulate. Profits began to fall in 1961, which resulted in lay-offs. This followed a series of serious accidents at the works, resulting in loss of life. Because of competition from elsewhere and lacking further investment, the company announced 1500 redundancies in 1962. Despite record output in 1963, rumours about closure persisted. In October 1964 the *Sunday Times* published an article that quoted a government steel development plan, suggesting that there was overcapacity in world steel markets and that production should be concentrated in large plants to exploit economies of scale. This meant that Steeltown might not survive beyond 1970. This caused considerable distress as well as endless speculation in the town (reference restricted)[16]. Despite this, the works brought in record production levels in 1964. The Labour government renationalised the steel industry in 1967. Again, record outputs were achieved up to 1967, but by 1969 the investment in the works was considered unsuitable for the current situation, which included using imported rather than local iron ore. By the end of 1969, the plant was making a loss. Thus, the people of Steeltown once again had to cope with uncertainty about their future. This kind of anxiety is well documented and can produce a sense of terror that one is going to cease to exist (see Chapter 3).

In the 1970s, £45 million was invested in order to develop a tinplate mill and to increase production by 35 per cent. Other areas were gradually closed down. Even so, the plant failed to make money. In December 1971 the government published the Iron and Steel Bill, which was intended to help the industry become profitable again by reducing its capital to a level more in line with the earning power of its assets and to allow borrowing to permit investment in plant. Record outputs continued. In 1972, Steeltown lost 4500 jobs. A modest profit was returned the following year. However, despite some large profits, the international situation with respect to the demand for and price of steel meant that iron and steel making in Steeltown ceased in 1975. While tin plate continued to be manufactured, British Steel lost £1102 million between 1975 and 1979. The reasons given were inflation, the poor market in the United Kingdom and Europe, and particularly the strong pound. The losses also included £50 million because of road hauliers and railway strikes. Despite this, the tin plate sector made a profit (reference restricted)[17]. There was a long stoppage due to strike action in 1980, when the government wage offer was rejected by the unions because they felt that it amounted to a drop in earnings in real terms and they held out for more. In the financial year 1980/1, British Steel lost £668 million. The workforce was again reduced in 1982, with further losses and a problem produced by the rise in the price of tin. The effect of the 1984 miners' strike was also felt badly in the steel industry and although there was record productivity, this only resulted in decreased losses. In 1986/7 the corporation began to make a profit, making it one of the few profitable integrated steel producers in Europe. At the end of 1987 it was privatised. In the 1990s, however, profits began to fall again and increased costs combined with lower selling prices reflected world economic conditions. Again, jobs were lost and by 1992 there was a loss of £51 million. In August 1995, part of the Steeltown tinplate works was closed with a loss of 168 jobs. By 1996, record profits were being made, but by 1999 the company was once again making a loss, this time related to an economic crisis in the Far East and the strength of the pound. In June 1999, British Steel merged with a Dutch company to become Corus. However, in April 2000 the company made a loss and the permanent closure of the Steeltown steelworks in 2002 was announced. The site closed in July of that year and by August the huge site had been razed to the ground.

Insecurity

If the reader feels a little giddy from the roller-coaster presentation of all these changes, imagine the effect on the town and its people across the generations for a span of 200 years. It is our proposal that the terrible uncertainty under which the inhabitants of Steeltown lived for so long could not help but provide a constant anxiety – never knowing what was to happen next, whether life would be the same or safe, whether there would be employment or not and what would happen if there was no work. Such uncertainty must have affected not only the bodies and minds of the workers and their families but also the social organisation of the town. Of course, it is easy to say that such experience brings strength, resistance and resilience. Indeed the latter idea has become rather fashionable. But our aim in this volume is to think about the complexity of the effects across generations and their implications for what happened in the community after the closure.

We have seen that conditions were harsh and uncertain during the whole two centuries. However, this uncertainty produced the development by the people of ways of coping, surviving and resisting that were built around the focus of the steelworks. We can say that the production of work is set against the threat of poverty, not only because the condition of being poor is terrifying but because there lingers a sense of the management of poverty, the regulation of the workhouse and therefore the threat of the condition of indigence or idleness. Having to keep on working regardless is something that, as we will see, comes up quite frequently in our material. No wonder, then, if the consequence of not working is a very harsh disciplinary regime. Much better to hone the male body, to make it strong and apparently invincible, to celebrate it, to build strong resistance and strong trade unions; and, of course, to build a strong supportive community, built on mutuality. Here then we can see the effectivity of the modes of disciplining that the history of iron and steel – the history of labour and exploitation – produces. It is the contention of this book that we can understand this effectivity in two ways. The first is in the production of modes of being, which we can witness in practices of the self and community, the bodily dispositions and the fantasies of what one should be and would like to become or is afraid of being. Second is in the anxieties and affects, an affective economy, if you will, that is also the consequence of the experience of the disciplining and exploitation. A community was created over the period in which it took a long time to build up patterns of mutual support and organisation that were central to life. While taking a couple of centuries to cement, it was taken away quickly.

In the 200 years, people had no alternative but to cope. This demand on them lives within the body and is passed on as profound anxiety, which lives within the whole social body. We need to understand what had to be suffered and survived, and how; and what were the consequences, both good and bad. This is vastly under-researched in our individualised and de-historicised psychology. While terms like 'resilience' are bandied around (Hansard, 2001; Welsh Assembly Government, 2002) it overlooks the emotional costs, the pain and defences necessary by valorising coping as a way of solving problems, thus continuing the liberal practice of placing the responsibility for this situation at the door of the workers and their families, rather than the economic and political system which created it. If this is the case for Steeltown, how much is it also there for many communities all over the world? How far is it passed down generations of ordinary people whose 'strong communities' toppled much longer ago?

In the next chapter, we will explore how the tenets of liberalism were rekindled in the emergence of advanced liberalism (Rose, 1999) or neoliberalism, and how this meant that life after the closure of the Steeltown works was lived.

2
Advanced Liberalism

Introduction

In Chapter 1, we saw that the people of Steeltown had endured chronic insecurity for 200 years. This was produced by the fluctuations in the international iron and steel market and the effects these had on the possibilities for the production of wealth in Britain. The making of the workers into an abstract category, 'labour', enabled them to be understood as simply replaceable elements in the production of wealth. In order to ensure the maximum amount of wealth creation, a system of political economy was developed in the nineteenth century in which poverty had to be minimised. This minimisation of poverty meant the conversion of the poor or unemployed into the pauper, who would be held responsible for their poverty through habits of indigence and idleness. This was cemented through the introduction of the workhouse in which paupers had to undergo a regime of very harsh work. This placed in people fears of the workhouse, which meant that they would recognise the need to accept any wages and conditions of work, rather than be able to stand up for fair pay for their work. It was this classical liberal doctrine that meant that people had to be responsible for governing themselves in order to make wealth creation in unstable global conditions possible. This was countered by the work of radical political movements, such as Chartism, theorists, such as Marx and Engels, who developed a theory of capital, and social reformers, such as philanthropists, who attempted to counter the inhumanity of political economy. By the Second World War, many revolutionary movements had attempted to create a different economy that created stability for workers, and it was in this context that the post-war Labour government tried to develop socialism through a swathe of nationalisations of basic industries, including steel. However, nationalisation failed because, as was obvious in Chapter 1, it was impossible to create stable conditions for workers when the nationalised steel industry was still at the mercy of international capitalism in the form of fluctuations in prices and demand for steel. It was this in turn that created the conditions in which politicians of the Right would argue that since commodities like steel could be manufactured more cheaply elsewhere, advanced industrial economies should switch from manufacturing to finance. What at first was posed by Margaret Thatcher and Ronald Reagan as monetarism (Frazer, 1982) made possible a return to and development of doctrines of nineteenth-century liberalism, which became known as advanced or neoliberalism. This was made necessary because the decline of heavy manufacturing, mining and steelmaking meant that there were far fewer long-term workplaces. Work was often outsourced and short-term work became common. It is not surprising therefore that the nineteenth-century doctrines once more became useful in presenting the need for workers to regulate themselves. It was necessary to make workers responsible for their conduct and work because it was no longer possible to provide the stability attempted by the protosocialist post-war governments. In order to secure wealth in this context, 'labour' had again to be flexible and workers had to accept what conditions were created by the market and thus, again, chronic instability. Thus, while neoliberalism was certainly not a copy of nineteenth-century liberalism, it was made possible by the concepts derived from political economy. While insecurity, as we have shown, was hardly new for the workers of Steeltown, the works had become a central pivot around which forms of social support had grown and been cemented in the 200-year period. What was catastrophic about this change was not the insecurity itself but the loss of a central object around which those practices could take place. In this chapter, therefore, we set out the tenets of advanced liberalism and go on to give a background to the changes facing the workers after the closure of the works in 2002.

In preferring the term 'advanced liberalism' over neoliberalism, Rose (1996, 1999) signals the ways in which neoliberalism is not so much a 'new' form of liberal government, as we have seen, but rather a hybrid, refigured or intensified form. His genealogical account of advanced liberalism avoids thinking in terms of a simple succession 'in which one style of government supersedes and effaces its predecessor' (1999, p. 142). Rather, he observes the ways in which forms of governance became more complex, opening up new lines of power and truth. Within advanced liberalism, the 'social state' gave way to the 'enabling state', and was no longer responsible for providing all of society's needs for security, health, education and so on. Individuals, firms, organisations, schools, hospitals and parents must each and all take on a portion of the responsibility for their own well-being. The social and the economic were seen as antagonistic, which meant that economic governance was desocialised so as to maximise and facilitate the entrepreneurial conduct of an individual who should be responsible for their biography (Rose, 1999). This was achieved through the restructuring, deregulation and privatisation of the economy and the labour market as well as the restructuring of welfare provisions that are seen as producing passivity and dependence (which are anathema to the production of inspirational, entrepreneurial and competitive subjects).

This restructuring of the economy and the labour market constituted a programmatic ambition of neoliberal government for the subject to self-actualise through their own labour, produced through discourses that at once presented the subject as 'free to choose' and freedom to be entrepreneurial on the one hand and punitive practices on the other, which were popularised in the many forms of disciplining presented on television, such as proper child care, habits of home and self-improvement, and keeping a clean house (Ouelette and Hay, 2008). Work was positioned and promoted as the best way to improve one's situation, and although the workhouse disappeared, the sanctions for non-work became more punitive and also focused on the habits and behaviour of the benefits claimant. Civic responsibility was refigured as the imperative to improve one's lot through the selling of one's labour on the market. There was no longer seen to be a conflict between the self-interest of the economic subject and the patriotic duty of the citizen: the subject fulfils their obligation to the nation/state by pursuing economic well-being for oneself and one's family, for one's employer, company, business or corporation. As Rose sees it, freedom is refigured as freedom from want (which might be provided through the benefits of the welfare state) into the capacity for self-realisation, obtainable only through individual activity. 'Hence an economic politics which enjoins work on all citizens is one which provides mutual benefit for the individual and the collective: it enhances national economic health at the same time as it generates individual freedom' (Rose, 1999, p. 145).

In the name of better and more efficient government, the state must govern less, and the economy be optimised through the entrepreneurial activity of autonomous actors (individuals and families, firms and corporations). Once responsibilised, individuals are to govern themselves within a state-secured framework of law and order. Individuals, rather than governments, were understood to be best able to exercise rational choices among the field of rational actors and institutions that comprised the economic networks in which they were enmeshed. In this way, suggests Rose (1999), a new articulation of the relation between government, expertise and subjectivity took shape. Government was restructured in the name of economic logic, and the goal of economic government was to create and sustain the central elements of economic well-being – such as the enterprise form and competition. Within such a refiguration of the relation between government, the individual and the market, the relation between the social and the economic was also refigured. All aspects of social behaviour were thought of along economic lines 'as calculative actions undertaken through the universal human faculty of choice' (Rose, 1999, p. 141). This notion of enterprise proposed a specific human actor, 'no longer the nineteenth century economic subject of interests but an entrepreneur of his or her self' (Rose, 1999, p. 142). All human actors to be governed were conceived of as individuals active in making choices in order to further their own interests and those of their family, and were to be potentially active in their own government. The powers of the state were thus understood as directed at empowering entrepreneurial subjects in their quest for self-realisation. Within this framework, the worker was not simply supposed to sell their labour power but to fashion themselves in a manner that included thoughts, desires, ambitions and actions of a rational economic, entrepreneurial subject.

In this way, neoliberalism understood both the social and citizenship as primarily concerned with the economy. It promoted an 'autonomization of society' through the 'invention and proliferation of new quasi-economic models of action for the independent conduct of its activities' (ibid., p. 27). As a technique of 'rolling back the state', neoliberalism constructed models of action based on economic enterprise and extended them to various areas of social life that were formerly excluded from it. Institutions previously constituting the welfare state (schools, public utilities, hospitals, charities, police, etc.) were increasingly required to operate according to a competitive market logic within a newly invented system of institutional re/forms and practices. Neoliberal forms of government generalise an enterprise form to the conduct not only of organisations previously seen as non-economic but also of individuals (Burchell, 1996).

In this way, neoliberalism intensified the nineteenth-century liberal endeavour to construct a relationship between government and the governed that depended on the ways in which individuals are expected to assume the status of being the subjects of their lives, on the ways in which they fashion themselves as certain kinds of subjects, and the ways in which they practice their freedom. As a result, the concept of the citizen was transformed, or refigured. The passive citizen of the welfare state became the active citizen with rights, duties, obligations and expectations – becoming the citizen as active entrepreneur of the self. This is not, argues Rose, simply a reactivation of liberal values of self-reliance, autonomy and independence as the necessary conditions for self-respect, self-esteem, self-worth and self-advancement, but rather an emphasis on enterprise and the capitalisation on existence itself through calculated acts and investments. So, individuals were expected to take part in their self-governance through acts of socially sanctioned consumption and responsible choice in the shaping of a lifestyle. This extended also to the psychologisation of work (Walkerdine and Bansel, 2009), in which workers were also supposed to display certain kinds of psychological and personality attributes. We can see its central location within recruitment literature, for example, which refers much less to skills needed for a particular job and more to the type of person or personality needed. For example, see the following extracts from two job advertisements found on the Internet in 2010:

> This is completely different to any advertising sales you will have encountered. If you have a passion for sport, the desire to achieve, but above all the willingness to work hard and reap the rewards, then this is the job for you.
>
> The following traits are essential:
>
> **Insatiable Appetite for Sales:** You will be target driven with the ability to upsell and close when the time is right
>
> **Buckets of Ambition:** You will have the potential to be a future leader as you advance your travel sales career
>
> **Globetrotters:** You will have a passion for travel and an incurable case of the travel bug
>
> **High Flyers:** You will have achieved a minimum of two A Levels and the demonstrated ability to grasp new skills quickly.

These advertisements stress the importance of desire, as well as ability in and a passion for sport or travel or 'an incurable case of the travel bug'. They also stress the wish to achieve and close deals. These are presented as personality and character trait based as much as they are skills based. In this sense, we see the need to be a particular kind of person rather than to have specific skills. Thus we could argue that workers are no longer alienated from their labour as in the classic Marxist argument. Marx understood the factory worker as being alienated from the craft of the production of an artefact. Now, workers do not even have a simple relation of alienation – it is something else because they often have to embody what their company is selling, though it could be understood as a kind of super-alienation in which the worker can only approach the product of their labour through the position of the consumer, as we will explore later in this chapter. Paul du Gay's (1996) research on workers in the retail sector argues that they become part of lifestyle consumption because they have to become part of the 'personality' that the store sells. One of the interesting aspects of this is that this kind of work demands characteristics previously associated with the feminine. The much vaunted lifestyle – shopping for anything from fashion to houses to holidays – presents the relationship between production and consumption quite differently from that of previous generations of workers. Although post-war workers were presented with the possibility of buying cars and fridges, they were not offered a variety of ways to make money in order to consume. If consumption is presented as the central locus of identity, work simply becomes one site for making money to consume, not the site of identity itself. Because both shopping and looking good have traditionally been feminised concerns, it is not simply that the new worker is feminised but that the relationship between work and play, production and consumption has become feminised. This, as we shall see, has particular significance for the men of Steeltown.

This condition of freedom and autonomy as lived through consumer identities aimed to produce subjects amenable to the specific, multiple and intersecting policies and practices of governance through which they were discursively produced as free and autonomous.

In addition to this, global markets mean a shift in manufacturing from the global north to the global, the decline of the manufacturing base in Britain, the rise of service industries, the rise and fall of communications industries, and particularly changes in types of contractual relationships from jobs for life to casualisation. There is also a marked gender shift, especially from male manual work to traditionally feminine service industries. This has huge repercussions for the Steeltown workers, as we shall see.

The imperative to be free

If we follow the arguments made by Rose and others, we would assume that what the ex-steelworkers would have to do is to remake themselves as neoliberal workers. This would mean that they would take on the responsibility of making themselves fit for the available work and that this would require both psychological work and an entrepreneurial spirit, as well as a strong aspirational sense. As we have seen in Chapter 1, this is not the first time that responsibility has been shifted to the workers via quasi-psychological discourse. In the nineteenth century, the development of political economy and the opening of the workhouse demanded a responsibilisation of sorts to avoid such a fate, with the demand that workers accept any conditions of work to avoid the charge of indigence. In the twenty-first-century context, however, there is no central ongoing work and most of the heavy industry has disappeared in an area of extremely high unemployment. How then did the workers and others in the community fare at finding work? Did they remake themselves or become guardians of their own biographies? Did they turn into entrepreneurs? Their ways of coping, as we shall see throughout this book and as we began to see in the last chapter, depended on a great deal of cooperation, mutuality and solidarity in order for people to support themselves through very harsh times. Yet, the very discourse of neoliberalism assumes that all of this has broken down, that people need to find new patterns of association and that in the absence of long-term work, they need to make themselves competitive in the new market, which will open up ways of being that were hitherto impossible. This is particularly noticeable in the work of British sociologist Anthony Giddens (1991), who describes the way in which the decline of traditional community ties – for example, of class and gender relations – means that people have to live what he describes as a 'reflexive project of the self', in which they have a succession of narratives through which they tell their life story. To sustain the self without ties that tell us who we are, this new freedom has to be lived, according to this account, by having a strong ego, resilience to withstand the sense of lack of context, of belonging. Giddens was a major architect of the Third Way (Giddens, 1998, 2000).

In the new political project, developed by both the Conservatives and Labour, in the context of globalisation, neoliberalism as a form of governance worked with the assumption that old forms of community and class relations had broken down and that what was needed was a new form of being and new modes of associating, propped up by volunteering (Brown et al., 2000; Fyfe and Milligan, 2003; Lewis, 1999; Morison, 2000).

In the United Kingdom, Blair's Third Way welfare reform agenda emphasised the importance of fostering an active civil society with voluntary associations as its organised vanguard (Giddens, 1998). Other observers have linked the rediscovery of volunteering in the capitalist world to a more general 'crisis of liberal democracy' (Brown et al., 2000, pp. 56–7). Alienation from and indifference to political institutions, concerns over the erosion of citizenship and declining social capital have all prompted the re-emergence of the 'discourse of civil society' (Cohen and Arato, 1992), in which voluntarism is viewed as having a pivotal role in rekindling a sense of civic responsibility and enhancing social cohesion (Dekker and van den Broek, 1998). Thus, voluntary associations appear to be increasingly identified in policy and academic discourses as some sort of a panacea to many of the problems faced by neoliberal states. They are not only crucial to strategies of welfare pluralism but also viewed as 'place[s] where politics can be democratized, active citizenship strengthened, the public sphere reinvigorated' (Brown et al., 2000, p. 57).

As well as Giddens, the Blair government also turned to Robert Puttnam's analysis of what he called social capital (Puttnam, 1995, 2000, 2002). Indeed, Puttnam also documents the decline of social capital with data of many varieties in US locations. In his work, he observes how many traditional civic, social and fraternal organisations – typified by bowling leagues – underwent a massive decline in membership while the number of people bowling had increased dramatically. Puttnam makes a distinction between what he calls two kinds of social capital: bonding capital and bridging capital. Bonding, he argues, occurs when people socialise with similar people; for example, those of the same age, same race, same religion and so on. However, he also argued that in order to create peaceful societies in diverse multi-ethnic communities, people needed also to have a second kind of social capital: bridging. This refers to what people have to do when making friends with people who are not like them. Puttnam argues that these two kinds of social capital – bonding and bridging – strengthen each other. Consequently, with the decline of bonding capital inevitably comes the decline of bridging capital, leading to greater ethnic tension. Puttnam's work assumes that social capital is a possession that declines (bonding capital) but that what he calls bonding capital (oh, the irony of calling it capital!) we show in this volume as affective relations that allow the possibility of survival in harsh and insecure conditions. We also show that the idea of creating a bridge to different 'others' is not a simple act of voluntarism through which communities coexisting in difference are produced, but is experienced as terrifying insecurity, which produces certain profound effects, none of which equate to a simple ability to integrate with new 'others'.

In work that Walkerdine, Davies and Bansel carried out in Australia between 2002 and 2004 (Walkerdine and Bansel, 2009), this shift appears obvious within accounts presented to us in interview by a range of workers from Sydney. In these conversations, a psychological narrative was central to all accounts. Indeed, the younger the participant, the less likely they were to mention social or external factors as having any bearing on their progress in work. So, for example, a secretary in her 30s talked about giving 150 per cent in her job because she had very high standards. She attributed this to her feeling that her father expected high standards and that she never felt good enough. What is important in this situation is that she described the way in which her bosses constantly gave her more and more work because, it appears, she was capable of and willing to give 150 per cent. In other words, she was coping with amounts of work that are well beyond the bounds of a working week, but rather than talk about exploitation, she talked about her psychological history. Thus, the relation between the secretary and her bosses was figured in terms of a narrative of her need for high standards on the basis of childhood experiences with her father. This elides the exploitative aspects of the relation with her bosses and, by eliding and refiguring them inside a personal narrative, no room is left for anything other than a personal and psychological response to the situation. So, the issue for worker subjectivity becomes the way in which we understand the breakdown of traditional communities, families, location and the introduction of what Beck and Beck-Gernsheim (2001) call reflexive modernisation. The debates cohere around a subject – a person who is not located in a place, a job or a role but who is free to make constant choices and to make constant change. This is the classical subject of liberalism in the context of the global market and, of course, contrasts quite markedly with the situation produced in Steeltown over two hundred years. Along with a number of others (Beck et al., 1994), Giddens (1991) argues that the reflexive project of the self that accompanies these profound social changes involves a freedom from traditional positions and roles and therefore opens up new possibilities of being. The subject therefore needs to be both flexible and mutable, multiple and changing, but also to have a strong resilience to withstand the loss of traditional supports.

Neoliberalism in Steeltown

How then did the inhabitants of Steeltown react to these changes? The local economy had undergone significant structural change in recent decades, with a major shift from the traditional coal, iron, steel and heavy industry in general to light-manufacturing occupations and service sector employment. This shift was accompanied by a sizeable reduction in the number of jobs available and a very high level of unemployment with resultant outward migration (Welsh Assembly Government, 2010).

Official statistics reveal that at borough level, the percentage of manufacturing work in the area was 28.2 per cent, which contrasts with 13.7 per cent for the whole of Wales and with 10.7 per cent for the rest of the United Kingdom. Similarly, the proportion of service work has risen to 67.4 per cent of total local (borough) economic activity and this figure contrasts with 79.1 per cent for the whole of Wales and 85.5 per cent for the United Kingdom as a whole. The area faces acute and widespread deprivation. A large proportion of its residents experience multiple and interconnected disadvantages, such as being raised in poverty or council care, poor health, low educational achievement and high levels of unemployment (ONS, 2010).

The long history of community support and trade unionism provided a strong base for a mutualist rather than individualised way of doing things. Indeed, we can say that strong commitment to mutual support and lack of desire to be better than others was a strong aspect of the working-class ethic, which helped the inhabitants deal with the situation in which they found themselves and fight for better conditions for all. As we will see in Chapter 3, this did create the possibility of resistance to advanced liberal discourse among older workers, especially those made redundant. However, it must immediately be said that, of course, no workers were immune to the changes wrought by the closure – no central employer, no heavy industry, poor wages and mostly service jobs. However, older and young workers did tend to talk about those changes in different ways.

Older workers were more likely to attempt to deal with the change by expressing the need to make other things more important than work, such as looking after ageing parents or staying in the same place. Particularly those who had reached retirement age (55 and above) as well as those near that age, most of whom took early retirement at the age of 50 and managed to get a pension as ex-steelworkers, tended not to see themselves simply as mere rational economic subjects/agents needing to be constantly updated and reskilled. Instead, their overall affective responses were not limited to the aim of seeing themselves as bearers of exchangeable forms of cumulative capital that they could rationally sell and trade anytime according to the demands of the labour market. Rather, we found evidence that some of these men reflected on their current circumstances in such a way that they came gradually to think critically about the rigidity of the available notions of their working-class masculinities. By this we mean the hardship and exploitive nature of their manual work and how as men they are often perceived merely as categories of income while they are supposed to be stoic and uncomplaining about these and merely conform and aspire to be a good efficient worker and consumer. The men's reflections also incorporated critical reading of some of the limits of the neoliberal discourse of plastic change and choice, which, combined with their experiences of redundancy and retraining, also provided them with further experiential references that enabled them to reconsider the relative importance of work and the wage form as only one part of their subjectivity. For example, some men felt that staying close to their families and local affective networks was important for them since, as we shall see in Chapter 3, without this they would feel lost and adrift. Thus, they were less likely to see themselves through a new discursive lens, though were not immune, as we shall see in Chapter 4, and certainly did make moves that could be understood as neoliberal and entrepreneurial, which of course became endemic, since new forms of work often demanded that they were created by the individual or that funding was sought to support new activities.

Throughout our interviews with the ex-steel men and their families, it became clear that for many, daily life became much more difficult. Many men were earning one-third of their previous salaries, and some were unemployed and living on benefits, so often faced difficulty in coping with their and their family's most basic needs. Some of these difficulties ranged from the most prosaic realities of struggling to be able put food on the table to not being able to turn up to interview appointments because they did not have enough money to pay for their transport. In this context, it was not uncommon to hear how many of these families could not contemplate keeping their children in education after the age of 16 because, although some courses were free and others partially financed, they could simply not afford the related costs (e.g. food and transport).

While some of the younger people had previously been in workplaces that had already experienced restructure, closure and redundancy, their time in the steelworks tended to follow a family tradition. In that sense, young men in the town could usually find work that did not demand any degree of academic qualifications on leaving school at 16. We found that all the younger men (30–45) seemed to embrace change and the impact this had on their masculinities, however stressful. By contrast, the older men (50+) seemed to resort instead to masculine ideals of regaining respect and appreciation, being acknowledged and financially supported for the hard manual work they had done for many years, and having the right to a life less stressful and more fulfilling in their own terms; for example, by staying closer to and revaluing their families and friends as key sources of support while at the same time maintaining their accustomed masculinities barely changed (as retiring men facing older age issues). All groups contained examples of serious health impacts, such as massive heart attack, major depression, alcoholism and arthritis.

It was the young people who expressed neoliberal sentiments most. One man at 21 had bought an investment property. Other young men in work were already keenly aware of work instability. For example, Mark was knew that the company he was working for, which was not related to steel production, could also soon close down and relocating to Slovakia because of production costs. Workers had been told by their current employers that if they wanted to avoid that happening, the only way to save their jobs would be to agree to work extra time with no additional payment.

> If I say yes to this reduction in our pay it means working an extra four hours a week for no extra pay err pay freeze indefinitely so it would be the same wage as what I'm on now, probably until the place shuts which would mean with income tax, and everything rising each year, my wage would probably be going down rather than going up which obviously is . . . wrong, you know, nobody wants to lose money each year, they want to get more money each year, so a lot of people need to look at their own individual needs and see whether or not they want to work the extra hours and lose money each year or to see now and they'll probably announce in a couple of months that it will probably our plant in Steeltown that'll close in no less than 1 year from now.

When asked about his options and plans in case his company closed down, he replied:

> I don't know at the moment I'm, I've just sold my house so I'm not in desperate need of money at the moment sort of thing. So I could

actually afford to take a couple of months off or whatever and then take my time to look for another job, cos obviously other peoples' circumstances change umm. I'm single at the moment, living with my parents so. This house it belongs to my parents, yeah. They're still paying a little bit off, there's not much left on it, but, like personally I haven't got big outgoings each month so I don't exactly need to rush out and get a job tomorrow sort of thing . . . My sister's a full-time mother, she's got three kids and she lives with her partner. My brother's unemployed at the moment living with his girlfriend and, that's about it.

I haven't actually thought about sort of the next path to go down sort of thing. I'll probably wait then for the decision to come back which from a personal point of view I think it is going to be the Steeltown plant that closes, umm and then I'll probably start looking down possible paths to go, any further training that may be required, or maybe going back to college see what sort of extra qualifications you can pick up, but I'll probably wait until the decision is made before looking

At the moment I'm currently happy doing the job that I'm doing so I don't know maybe if when I start looking I'll think oh I wouldn't mind trying that and maybe go down that road and if I don't like that go back and sort of keep your options open and see what's around at the time

Basically I'm in charge of a certain area of the machine shop where I've got to make sure the machines are running, they're producing the parts correctly umm, they're produced on time, look after the operators who run the machines, just that basic side of it.

But many others, especially some unemployed young men, as we shall see in Chapter 5, remained committed to heavy industrial work and their main concerns were avoiding poverty. There is little sense of a regulation of a self who can actually transform themselves and so succeed in a portfolio career. In other words, as Walkerdine and Bansel (2009) argued, the responses to globalisation are quite specific to place and cannot simply be read from the modes of governance. Some of the Steeltown ex-steelworkers did see themselves as having undreamed of opportunities and some of these can be understood as entrepreneurial, as we show in Chapter 5, but what we aim to show is how complex the response was to the changed conditions in the town.

Generations of men have gone into the steelworks, so it is very common for redundant workers to talk of their pride in following the path taken by their fathers. We can recognise that in Steeltown, redundancy was managed as a collective experience, both in terms of a group of men from the same place all doing the same work and facing a mass closure, and because of the intervention of the trade unions. The collective unions decided that it was impossible to fight the closure and adopted a strategy of supporting workers in finding other employment. In particular, they encouraged workers to think of ways in which they might build alternative work on their interests and encouraged them by paying for retraining. This act alone had an enormous impact on the ways in which the shift was experienced and the opportunities for employment that were opened up. The workers who made the most successful transition all took up this suggestion. It could be argued that the unions prepared the workforce for a neoliberal workplace – their strategy was to encourage them to think about building a new career on leisure interests.

This was a much criticised approach because it effectively accepted rather than fought the inevitability of the closure but attempted to prepare the men for the new world of work. Notice how the union emphasised that men might develop their leisure interests or hobbies as the basis for finding work, and that this mirrors the adverts we discussed earlier that stressed things like a passion for sport and travel.

The fact that many men faced this closure together did make the experience less isolating than it might have been, but it did not negate the long-term effects on the town. The loss of income, the disappearance of the central works and all the businesses and shops that related to it, the shift of the workers into different jobs with no central employer, the need to find work elsewhere – all these and many more factors took their toll, as we shall see later. In Chapter 3, we shall explore the ways in which the interviews revealed how the community was held together in the time of the works. This relates directly to the issues of insecurity discussed in Chapter 1 and shows us in much more detail what was lost and had to be coped with when the works closed. In this respect, it makes our understanding of the governmentality of advanced liberalism more complex because it allows us to recognise the centrality of affective experience and relations in producing the responses to the changes both in the mode of governance and the aftermath of the closure, with the huge changes this brought to the local labour market and therefore to the lives of the inhabitants of Steeltown.

3
Communal Beingness and Affect

> Nothing is secure. Nothing is secure at all. That's the sad thing about it. You can't relax. People are just stressed by the thought that I could be at work today and tomorrow it's closed, which they have in the Valleys. It's on the news. They've gone to work and the doors are locked.
>
> – Christine, Steeltown resident

Introduction

In Chapter 1, we saw that the inhabitants of Steeltown had to cope with chronic insecurity for over two hundred years and then the works closed and everything changed, ushering in more insecurity but without a central employer in changed work conditions, as we explored in Chapter 2. What it is important to convey is that far from witnessing a stable community with full employment and then a wrench and shift to neoliberalism, we are talking about a community that has a long history of chronic insecurity. As Christine says above, nothing is secure – but nothing has been secure for two centuries. In this sense, in many ways then, the closure of the steelworks and neoliberalism present perhaps less of a shift than one might imagine and, rather, intensification of the same – that nothing is secure. So, we are arguing in this chapter that the community developed over that two hundred years ways of coping and supporting each other that provided some sense of security, a sense in particular of continuity of being to counterpoint what was not provided by the economic and work conditions. It did so in the only way that people could – by finding and creating ways to support each other. So what we need to understand is not a break from security, but the ongoing chronic insecurity and the loss of ways of providing mutual support and solidarity that were developed during the time of the steelworks. Only during the post-war period of the welfare state did things get better, but successive governments were not able to control the demand for steel and so nationalisation did not provide the security that the townspeople needed. What we are striving to understand here is how that support manifested itself and that this formed a central way in which affective support was given that enabled a vulnerable people to survive terrible conditions over generations. In other words, this mutual support was affective and social, or psychosocial. In our view, the importance of this cannot be overemphasised but such issues have largely been ignored in debates about de-industrialisation (Bailey, 2003; Bailey and De Ruyter, 2007; Charlwood, 2006; Leys, 2000; Singh and Zammit, 2003), which have been rather superficial in their treatment of subjectivity. However, in addition to this, we argue that what happened in 2002 was a real crisis because although the iron- and steelworks had shut before, it had always reopened and in this case reopening was not possible – the works was razed to the ground within one month of closure. This meant that the means of support that had developed over the long period of the works, and which was based on the central significance of the works within the town in many ways, could no longer function properly. Thus, what was threatened was not only a continuity of work but a continuity of being. We contend that it was not the works itself but the ways of coping with insecurity that had produced the possibility of ontological security for those who stayed in the community. That ontological security was now threatened because the practices that made it possible, based around the works, were falling apart. Thus a crisis was provoked for the community.

In this chapter I discuss the ways in which the community produced a sense of ontological security and at what cost. I then go on to think about the crisis provoked by the closure and how to understand its psychosocial significance. In doing this, I refer to a variety of literature on suffering and trauma. What have developed within psychological, social and humanities fields are a number of approaches to crisis that attempt to understand the effects of both ongoing suffering and a particular event (in this literature often war or genocide). I want to think about how far this literature could be useful in understanding what happened in Steeltown and its lasting psychosocial effects across generations.

The research that we undertook in Steeltown began with a series of psychosocial interviews of ex-steelworkers and others in the town, undertaken from 2005 to 2008. Psychosocial interviews use a narrative framework, setting up a conversation between researcher and participant, enabling a dialogue about the experience of the situation after the closure of the works. The technique uses a very open framework aimed at finding what the issues are for the participant in their own words (Hoggett et al., 2006, 2010; Stopford, 2004; Walkerdine and Jimenez, 2006; Walkerdine et al., 2002). It also uses a series of interviews to gain deeper insights and to be able to follow up points made on previous occasions. This makes for a very rich set of material. We can think of the process of engaging with these interviews as stimulating an affective response within the interviewer, which is then checked against other data and developed into a tentative way of reading and theorising. In these interviews, a number of themes began to emerge that dealt with loss in relation to the community life before the closure. It was in speaking of the absence of certain features of life now that we were able to learn something of what life was prior to the closure. In understanding this, we began to see that the community offered sets of routines, ways of being and doing things, that made the inhabitants feel secure and supported.

What I encountered were often nostalgic descriptions of life as it had been, contrasted with incredible feelings of loss of those ways of being in the present. I slowly gained the sense that the ties that were being described were of tremendous importance for the sense of life or of continuity of being within the community, that the possibility of being for the residents was deeply tied up with how the community was held together and so held them, and that this could be described, among other ways, as an affective process. This chapter begins to think about these issues and specifically how to think about affect and community.

Affect

The tradition of work on affect that I have found most helpful in the development of this work comes from two sources: British and American object relations psychoanalysis and some French psychoanalytic work, as I will go on to describe. The use of affect within psychoanalysis begins with Freud but was later developed by Melanie Klein and what came to be known as 'object relations'. In particular, the work that I found useful was developed through studies with children, and some of it pays particular attention to what is communicated through the body, both of the patient and the analyst and the centrality of the body in object relations. I have chosen this work above and beyond phenomenological work, for example, because although in many ways this tradition is strongly influenced by phenomenology, it goes beyond this framework (Guattari, 1989) to explore how certain embodied experiences can produce feelings of great anxiety. In this way, the work does not have a strong differentiation between what is felt on and in the body and what we might call an affective state. Nor indeed does it differentiate between actual physical sensations; for example, of spilling out, with a sensation of the body spilling out of the container of the skin, which is certainly experienced as very real even though the skin has not been broken. This is central to a psychoanalytic approach.

In my previous work on affect (Walkerdine, 2007), which explored children's video-game play, I referred to understandings of affect developed by the German psychologist Wundt in the nineteenth century (2009), together with psychoanalytic approaches. For example, Wundt understands affect as sensation plus ideation. When we add an understanding of unconscious processes to this, we understand that sensation and ideation are linked through phantasy. In this sense, affect means we look at three aspects of affect – the sensation, the ideation of that as pain, for example, and the defence against the pain, which is the fantasy of pleasure – that pleasure is the pleasure of control or being somewhere or someone else in video-game play. I am suggesting that this triple way of thinking about the centrality of affect to new media is absolutely essential to our understanding of the pleasures afforded by video games and the ways in which they make subjectivity possible. In the case of video games, the player has not only to phenomenologically experience virtual space through haptic and visual sensation but has to imagine themselves in that space. This involves phantasy of being a character, for example, and so is more complex than a simple phenomenological reading (Hansen, 2004). This is not to say that a different kind of phenomenological reading might have an important place within the account I am developing, as I shall go on to suggest. However, it is important to note that just as children playing video games had to imagine and fantasise, so we can suggest that there are central aspects of what psychoanalysis calls unconscious phantasy in the social relations of community. However, it might importantly be noted that some schools of psychoanalysis have stressed the ideational at the expense of sensation. This is what I think is shifted quite significantly in the tradition of work to which I will refer. Equally, critics such as Deleuze and Guattari (1984) have argued that psychoanalytic approaches remain trapped within the logic of family. However, I will refer to a tradition that places material and affective processes as central. I want to suggest that the closure of the steelworks ruptures a sense of the community's continuity of being in a catastrophic way, which are felt and experienced in a wide variety of ways. Not only do I think that it is important to think about affect in this way, but I also suggest that affective processes need to be much more strongly foregrounded in work with communities.

Studying community

There is a long tradition of debate within the social sciences about whether it is possible and desirable to use the concept of community (see e.g. Studdert, 2006). While it is clear that early studies of community within sociology tended to understand community as something stable and fixed within a location (see Pahl, 2005 for a review), more recent work has emphasised the importance of social networks (cf. Savage, 2008). However, while this approach recognises the centrality of relationality (Studdert, 2006), it is mathematised and formulaic and does little to understand how relationalities operate except by specifying that certain linkages exist. Pahl (2005) calls this 'communities in the mind', as it allows us to think about the 'personal communities' that represent people's senses of their social networks and relationships. Similarly, Anderson (1983) assumes that communities are essentially 'imagined', while Liepins (2000) had a fourfold classification of community. Useful as these aspects may be, they do not engage at all with affective relations. Studdert (2006) argues that standard sociological accounts deny communal beingness of any role in the construction of subjectivity or beingness. I will argue that communal beingness (and indeed becoming) is central to an understanding of community.

It is perhaps not surprising that in all of these approaches there is no mention of emotional ties or work and the psychological is reduced to 'imagination' or 'community in the mind' and, in any case, the psychological is reduced to 'mind' with a strong demarcation between subjects and objects (Latour, 1993). In other words, we understand that people have a sense of belonging, we can track their patterns of association, but the limits of the sociological imagination seem to stop there. In his critique of sociological conceptions of community, Studdert (2006) uses the work of Hannah Arendt (1958) to argue for the central importance of interrelationality. However, unlike social network approaches, Studdert's reading of Arendt recognises that 'webs of relations' actually construct 'whos' at their centre, rather than simply assuming a simplistic concept of a stable pre-existing subject who is simply linked to others. Maffesoli (1996) proposes a concept of sociality in which small socialities based on a notion of tribes are created out of a coming together around particular points of reference. While Maffesoli argues for a new tribalism and a sense of something new and beyond locational communities, nevertheless he is alone in proposing that these tribes are linked through affect. However, his work argues that affective ties create new patterns of community, whereas I wish to argue that affective relations are part and parcel of the most 'traditional' of communities, aspects that have not been foregrounded in previous approaches.

I want to argue for the centrality of affect for understanding how people sharing a locality might be held together; in other words, how communal beingness might work and how the interrelationalities of which Studdert speaks may be understood as, among other things, affective. These interrelations can be understood phenomenologically as actions, movements, feelings, objects, places and intersubjective bonds. These are amply described by the participants in this study, as we shall see. However, as the psychoanalytic work I am going to discuss makes clear, such embodied affective relations are also experienced psychically. That is, intersubjective bonds bring feelings of being held, contained, alive. This may help to stop feelings of the fear of being uncontained, unsafe or dying, all of which came up obliquely in the interviews we conducted with the Steeltown residents. So, there is a level of fear, anxiety, pain, pleasure and desire that is embodied and that exists as part of any description of the phenomenological. It is this which I am going to concentrate on in this chapter. We could also refer to work on the rhythms of life (Lefebvre, 2004), taken up by Henriques (2010), who argues that affect works through a number of affective practices, not all of which pass through subjects. In a study of Jamaican dancehall, Henriques argues that the 'vibe' that can literally be understood as musical vibration circulates through the practices of the sound engineers, the dancers and the DJs and not simply through the emotions of the participants. The vibe of the music creates rhythms that link to a number of other rhythmical sources, such as heartbeats and circadian rhythms. So, when I ask how people are held together, I wish to draw on psychoanalytic approaches that do think about the notion of bodily containment. At first I will look at this in terms of embodied relations in infancy, but we will discuss how we might think of the communal body as holding in a similar way.

The skin as a boundary

The work that I want to discuss concerns what, in psychoanalytic terms, is understood as very early experience of bodily separation from birth. Esther Bick (1968) is the person credited with bringing the tradition of infant observation to child psychotherapy and who first emphasised the importance of the skin in early object relations. She argues that the experience of skin was twofold: the experience of feeding for a baby was an experience of a nipple in a mouth and of being held close by a warm body, with soothing words, and so on. Bick proposes that these two experiences offer a sense of 'being held', that is, a sense that the body is not going to disintegrate but is held and therefore is solid. She proposes that this experience is essential for an infant to begin to feel a sense of an interior that is contained by their own skin. This is usually referred to as 'containment' and relates therefore to an embodied relational process and a sense that this literal holding, both by the body and in the mouth, is a feeling of being both filled up and held. These experiences provide a sense of emotional holding, so that through them a sense of being emotionally contained results and provides the bedrock for being able to experience oneself as whole and therefore as safe. Thus, we can say that this is at once relational, embodied and unconscious in that it paves the way to being able to think, or for a distinction between thinking and feeling to be made (cf. Ogden, 1986). At this point, there is no repression and no thought but only feeling and affect. This state is described as un-integration and prefigures the possibility of becoming a separate being, with a sense of integration. What we might describe as the psychic emerges from this. It is a controversial aspect of psychoanalysis because it describes the very first experiences that are not languaged, but it formed an absolutely essential basis of psychoanalytic work with children in Britain. In that sense, affect is prelinguistic and deeply embodied. Where something goes wrong, Bick describes what she calls 'second skin phenomena', in which un-integration persists and the baby tries to seek an object – a light, a smell, a voice – that would allow it to experience a sense of being held together. Thus we can say that this experience is extremely frightening and can be experienced as being uncontained in some way, such as spilling out of the boundaries of the body, and it threatens annihilation. This tradition of work was further developed by Frances Tustin (1981), who used it as the basis for understanding autism. The tradition of work differs from traditional British Kleinianism and has been espoused by Mitrani (1996, 2001) in the United States and by child psychotherapists at the Tavistock Clinic (Urwin, 2002) in Britain. In France, this work has been developed particularly by Didier Anzieu (1989).

Thus, it is argued that the psychic skin is just as important as the physical skin because it provides for us an affective sense of our boundaries. In that sense, the psychic skin is dependent on first of all experiencing the holding of the physical skin. To give an example of what can go wrong at this level, sensations of the body as uncontainable, leaking, spilling and so on would accord with unconscious anxieties about the affective containment of the primitive ego, which is why Anzieu refers to this as the 'skin ego' (or 'ego skin' in some translations). Thus our experience of our bodies in space is both perceptual and sensate in the phenomenological sense but also emotional and unconscious. Literally our feelings are both through the senses and through the bodily memories of containment that provide the absolutely basic building blocks of the possibility of subjectivity and therefore of an experience of subjects and objects. The sensation that one does not have boundaries, or has unstable boundaries, can be very frightening indeed. In this approach, the early containment of anxiety through literal holding is what allows an infant to feel that they are within their own skin, so to speak, to feel that they do have affective boundaries that correspond to physical ones. Thus, what is communicated by the caregiver is a complex relation of literal holding to psychic holding or containment. It is this, these authors would argue, that provides a sense of continuity of being in which a young child is gradually able to replace literal physical holding with a sense of being whole and continuous.

So, we have a state of containment of primitive anxieties through the production of the relational process of integration and its failure as un-integration. This is quite different from disintegration. Disintegration is a process of breaking down the sense of containment through trauma (i.e. a sense of integration or being held is lost and so a sense of annihilation and falling apart happens), but in un-integration, the integration itself has never happened. However, Winnicott (1958) argues that a state of un-integration is a healthy state of being at rest, which can be returned to by the infant, a sort of safe falling apart, which is the precursor to the capacity to be alone. Bick argues that failure to contain terrifying anxieties could result in the development of a muscular shell or a muscular holding, designed to hold everything in, which she calls a second skin. Another related defence is adhesive identification (a concept generated by Bick and developed by Meltzer) in which the infant clings to the surface of an object in order to gain 'a rudimentary degree of safety to combat massive anxieties about catastrophic anxieties in the coherence of the body-self that it is feared could result in the spilling out of the self into boundless space' (Meltzer, 1974; Willoughby, 2001).

Although this tradition of psychoanalytic work understands these experiences as central to the human condition, and as originating in infancy, it is one of my concerns to recognise that it is history – the history of chronic insecurity – that we are talking about here. In other words, although the work that I am citing has a developmental ontology that focuses on infancy, I am using it to explore the affective experience of chronic anxiety in particular historical circumstances within communities. I am not wanting to place emphasis on mothering practices as causal but to point to the embodied ways in which anxiety might be transmitted across communities and down generations. In later chapters, we will explore psychoanalytic work that makes that history central and does not work with a Kleinian view of the unconscious. But at this point my particular aim is to be able to acknowledge the central experiences associated with chronic insecurity, which are those that relate to un-integration and disintegration. I want to think about how these experiences might be chronic and passed from one generation to another and so how the community members found ways to cope with the anxieties that these feelings produced – the fears of annihilation – and dealt with them creatively by finding ways to support one another. For we cannot but imagine that such experiences as those that the townspeople endured for over two hundred were ones that created massive anxieties that threatened the certainty that they could keep on existing. Thus, we are seeking to understand how the community built up ways of shoring themselves up against such overwhelming feelings and fears.

Can a community hold its members?

In what ways can we think about the relations of a community such as Steeltown as providing a community body that reacts in a similar way to that described above? Anzieu (1984) argues that 'groups suffer from not having a body and consequently imagine one' (p. 214). This fantasy of a body provides an organising principle and a nostalgic dream of symbiosis between its members that provides a containing envelope delimited and protected by an ego-skin. In the following sections, I argue that the steelworks community provided such a dream of symbiosis and an ego-skin, with the works as a central object, supported by aspects from the feeling of the community as a family, to the organisation of time and space and the ways of keeping people in the community and shutting others out. Anzieu (1989) argues that 'groups constitute a psychic envelope in which 'each group member may internalize in the place of an overly rigid or inadequate ego-skin' (p. 253). In what sense can we say that Steeltown constituted a community with an inadequate ego-skin?[1]

Like most small communities formed around a workplace, such as steel or coal production, the community was formed by people moving to the area from England and Ireland during the first period of iron production towards the end of the eighteenth century. We could say that what we have first is an unintegrated mass of people who formed a sense of communal beingness through their shared experience of setting up and living in the steelworks town and of making steel. This is well documented by local historians, as discussed in Chapter 1. The conditions of work over generations were harsh, with poor pay and conditions and frequent hardship. Steelmaking was a dangerous occupation and accidents were not uncommon. In addition to this, uncertainty was the key. Over the course of 200 years, the global demand for iron and then steel fluctuated, so that the workers were at the mercy of this and other issues connected with the iron and steel trade and the global economic position. So, over generations it could not be known whether times would be good or harsh. The works shut twice before finally closing in 2002. The community weathered the depression with terrifying levels of unemployment and poverty. In other words, this community was in thrall to global capitalism and the townspeople were like pawns on a chessboard. Gradually, strong unions were formed that fought for better conditions of work and pay, though latterly, before the final closure, concerns about redundancies and closure were endemic. In other words, what we have here is a long history of difficult and dangerous work, which must produce an anxiety about annihilation and the necessity to produce ways of coping that could produce a sense of continuity and security to counter the extreme uncertainty of the employment situation. According to the reports generated in interview, this is what people did. While I cannot reach back over generations, I can supplement my present-day account with historical records as we have done in Chapter 1. While the psychoanalytic accounts discussed above begin with terrors in infancy, Anzieu's own work with groups suggest how similar phenomena are at work in groups. Moreover, we need to put this account into history. Anxiety about containment and continuity is, I suggest, made absolutely endemic by the large historical events of industrialisation and de-industrialisation. Those large historical events produce what Davoine and Gaudilliere (2004) call small histories, that is, the personal and collective community histories about ways of coping affectively with these conditions. It is in this way that I suggest that these insights from psychoanalysis are most helpful. My suggestion then is that a second skin could be said to hold the townspeople in a rigid containment, which did provide a profound containing function, and a strong sense of continuity of being. But there was a cost to this, which was a strict set of rules about conduct, a resistance to outsiders and the inability of people to leave the town. In other words, I am suggesting a strong protective membrane, further ruptured by the trauma of the steelworks closure, thus bringing the overwhelming anxiety and threat of annihilation to fruition. In Anzieu's terms, we could see the steelworks itself as a central object. It was geographically placed at the centre of the town and people recount the central and iconic importance of the lights, sounds and fire as central sensory aspects of the effect of the works on the town. But it was also a psychic object in that it could be said to contain all the projections of the townspeople: the steelworks provided the possibility of life for the town. By that I mean that it existed as a material object and an object of fantasy[2] – it was, after all, the source of life when it was operating and of extreme hardship when it closed. By object of fantasy, I mean that it provided not only a material object but a sense that this very works was the object that sustained the possibility of life and work and thus would have a very rich place within the fantasy life of the inhabitants. After its closure, it was razed to the ground within one month of closure and so what was left was a huge material and affective empty space where there had once been an object.

Willoughby (2004) argues that group second skin phenomena can include a clinging to an object with poor toleration of outsiders. 'Toleration of otherness within second skin systems is difficult given the nature of the prevailing survival anxieties' (p. 192), which he suggests leads to the expelling of dissenters in order to save the group.

In the interviews with Steeltown residents, a number of issues were raised that relate to the concerns outlined above. Residents talked consistently of Steeltown being like a family, they had a great fear of outsiders and they found it impossible to contemplate moving away. In addition, they articulated strong rules about what could and could not be spoken about with workmates and inside and outside the family. I will go on now to exemplify these aspects.

The organisation of space and time

As Deleuze and Guattari stress, we exist in time, so that an understanding of place, Massey (2005) suggests, cannot simply be as a slice through time, the way that it has traditionally been understood by geographers as rather static. This is particularly important here because the looking back to a time of relative safety seems to represent a sense of shoring up a continuity of being as against the ravages of time – the incessant redundancies, the constant threats to steel production, the problems of getting by on poor wages – that existed for many generations. The disposition of rows of terraced houses served to facilitate a certain kind of affective relation between inhabitants. I discuss it here because I think that, like the centrality of the works, the organisation of the housing establishes that certain ways of relating were facilitated by this dynamic spacing of the houses. Susan, a woman in her 30s, told me about her childhood growing up in Steeltown. In particular, she recalled the disposition of the houses and the temporal/spatial relation to them:

> ... then they were all at home but they all then got to know each other.
>
> With the street where I grew up you had your houses in a row, then you had a back road, I called it and then you had your garden. A back road which was about two cars wide. And obviously then your coal-bunkers were round the back. So the back road was like where everyone congregated. You'd go up the garden to peg your washing out and what have you, you'd see next door or two doors down. 'Oh hi ya' and then you'd have a natter with them. They don't sit out the back in the summer, we don't have a game of cricket out the back in the summer, um everyone would get, you know, we'd draw hop scotch out the back in the summer, but today most houses then their gardens are attached to their house and then they're fenced off. So, unless you're sort of six feet tall you don't see anyone from next door.
>
> And a lot of the house in M..., every...there's only two streets in M...that haven't got the back road, every street has got the back road, then their garden, their garden is not actually attached to their house, you got this back road and then the garden, so I think that was why I always felt that our village then was, was so close.
>
> But now with as I say newer houses I don't think people tend to see, you know, you go out in your garden and you peg your washing out but you won't see her next door because, because you can't see over the fence, because where I live now is like that, I mean gardens and my fence and my fence and my fence is about 5 foot, so you know if I nip in the garden to put stuff in the bin, or if I peg my washing out I don't see anyone, because I can't see them.
>
> So I think that has something to do with it.

What is noteworthy about this for me is the careful description of the arrangement of the houses with their back roads, gardens and low fences. The back road and the terraced houses produced the spatial disposition that was added to by low fences over which residents could talk.

So, as she says, people congregated and 'nattered' or played cricket in the summer. We see also her opposition between then and now – the present high fences and the absence of sharing produced by a sense of privacy occasioned by higher fences over which no one can see each other.[3] Indeed, as we saw in Chapter 1, the local historian (noted that houses were built like this and with this intention in date 'the cottages usually faced onto a lane between them and the gardens, known as 'the bailey''; it was a meeting place for the whole row, and a fertile field for gossip'. As we noted, this arrangement of the houses in the 1800s provided the basis for modes of sociality which lasted well over one hundred and fifty years.

Thus, we might say that one aspect of the former 'modes of communal beingness' was the disposition of houses and the height of the fences, which made possible particular ways of being together. If we look further at other aspects that Susan mentions, we see that as a young child, she felt included as a potential woman in the temporal and spatial rituals performed by the women when they talked to each other outside their back doors. Thus this performance of femininity – the affective practices of the women in which they used the space to talk to each other and offer emotional support – is one in which, as a girl, she was able to join in. Now, again, the absence of the space signals for her a loss of this kind of affective communication:

> Yeah, that's right. Yeah, yeah people did share more with you whether it was personal problems, you know, I can remember my mother and my next door neighbour and her mother. Because she lived next door to her because it was like all little clusters of family, you know, they'd come in, in the evening, or if it was a nice night they'd sit out the front with their little chairs and what have you and you'd talk about really personal, and I used to sit there as a little girl, and listen to it all. And they used to find it really amusing, that, that I wanted to sit there with all the older ladies. I mean I was only 8 or 9 and I'd be sat there listening to them thinking oh and now and again I'd chip in you know. Um, but some of the things they talked about I would never dream of talking about with my neighbours today.
>
> *Interviewer*: Like what?
>
> Financial worries, relationship problems.
>
> Even, even maybe if they were having sexual problems with their husband or what have you, you know. It wouldn't be anything rude or anything like that. But it would be like oh God there's something wrong with him lately you know he won't leave me alone and but I don't...I wouldn't be able to speak to my neighbours like that

because its just 'Hello, how are you' you know and that's about as far as the conversation goes. I don't really say a lot else to them. I mean I get in from work, get out the car, go in the house, OK, a lot of them do take parcels and things for me. And I mean the street was 30 houses long but everyone knew each other. I always felt that everyone liked each other as well because like I say their husbands worked hard, they were out all day.

So, also the husbands out all day and the wives at home created its own subcommunity of women, with her statement that the women would 'peg your washing out and what have you, you'd see next door or two doors down. "Oh hi ya" and then you'd have a natter with them.'

In that sense, we begin to see how the industrial mode of production, with its central works and terraced housing, together with historical specificities of the family wage, with the women at home, produces a particular sense of a time and space in which femininity is performed: in which washing is pegged out, people natter and emotional issues get discussed and a particularly gendered affective community is maintained, in which, for example, Susan learned what it meant to be a woman. The embodied dispositions are here clearly conveyed by the games of cricket, the putting out of the washing, the sitting on the little chairs to have a natter. These are facilitated by the kind of housing, the paths at the backs of the houses, the gardens and the low fences, producing a feeling that 'our village was so close'. Everybody in this remembered scenario is close, is part of a unit, and allows us to think about what the term 'close-knit community', so often applied by social researchers to Welsh communities (e.g. Mcdonald et al., 2005), actually means. So, we have shared spaces, shared activities, emotional sharing, all of which produce a sense of being knit together, a sense strongly conveyed by Studdert's use of the idea of community as interrelationality. The relations are sets of temporal sequences, spatial relations, embodied affects and performances that are strongly gendered, which for Susan creates a profound sense of loss in their absence. Of course, we could argue that her memory is nostalgic, but that would surely be to miss the central importance of the production of the sense of closeness and the bewildered loss at its absence. How to do neighbourliness, she worries, later in the interview, when the fences are so high now and when people's patterns of work are so different from each other. In that sense, I suggest that Anzieu's idea of the group as a psychic envelope is here conveyed clearly. In one sense, we could understand this backwards glance as nostalgic as we note that in Susan's memory the season is summer in which everyone could sit outside, rather than a harsh winter. However, this should not cloud the fact that she is describing a profound sense of change in which she is moved from a more communal form of daily life to one in which she feels isolated. In this sense then, I want to understand the spatial organisation of the houses and the temporal use of the space outside them as a form of holding that offers intense affective containment and that has become a kind of 'community ego-skin', which has since been experienced as lost in a most painful way. This loss is directly associated with the shift in the rhythms of life associated with the closure of the steelworks.

Thus, we see an organisation of space, and also of time, that is profoundly gendered. The men go off to work at set times and the women look after the home. This has its own rhythmical and comforting quality to it (Ogden, 1989), as Susan tells us. All of these aspects taken together provide a sense of 'going on being' (Winnicott, 1958), and one that is ruptured by all the changes that have followed from the closure of the works and the changes in the labour market. Yet, while Anzieu, Bion, Hopper and others consider the affective implications of group relations in ways well supported by these data, we need to avoid a reductionism that minimises the centrality of the paths, houses and fences, and the practices that accompany them.[4]

Community as family

The particular form of closeness described by residents is often described as a family within the interviews. At first, we thought this was being used as a metaphor, but as the work progressed we came to see that it was being used literally in the sense that it was a kind of informal extended family in which others outside the family regularly provided quasi-familial support, as in the following example given by Susan:

> As with me yeah, you know, when my Mum was in and out of hospital a lot, you know, and my father was still trying to work shifts in the steelworks. To keep the money coming in, my next-door neighbour she was like a mother to me.
> You know, I'd just go straight in her house, there would be tea on the table for me and my brother, you know, she'd give us clean clothes, she'd go ...
> She'd go in our house ...
> Yeah. I mean, I always said she was like a second mother to me.
> But that's the way we were.

Um, you'd just walk in, in each other's houses, you'd leave your door open, you know, if times were hard you'd help each other out, you'd give someone a lift, you'd take em to the shops, you'd help em if they were sick, you'd cook em some dinner or, you know. But today, I don't feel like you've got that, you can walk down the street now and maybe you won't bump into anyone you know.

Martha echoed this sentiment:

So the attitude of people in [Steeltown] is fantastic we're like one big family, it's sort of we're all belonging to one another.

If 'we are all belonging to one another', and neighbours are like mothers, we see that the close-knittedness described earlier is experienced as 'one big family', with the mothering as central. This notion of the community as a family was first outlined by the German sociologist Tönnies' in the 1880s with his notion of *Gemeinschaft* in his (1955) volume *Community and Association*. He argues that communities could be considered as large families because of kinship ties. Since then a number of largely sociological studies have remarked on the reference to one big family made by the members of small communities (e.g. Dempsey's 1990 study of Smalltown, Rees's 1951 study of a rural Welsh community). However, in both these studies the reference to family is considered to be about kinship ties and also to cover over differences between people within the community (especially in Smalltown). However, I suggest that all of this work misses the central significance of the affective and emotional work that 'one big family' does to unite people in feeling bonded with each other and therefore safe and supported, whether they are related or not. The reference to the family form strikes me as a way of telling me that the residents felt looked after and close as in a family, that this large family in which all the residents worked together to support each other in a familial way was a form of containment or holding, with strong central support from quasi-mothers. Thus, the large community family, living in terraced houses and with the central structure of the works, provided a strong familial holding in which the residents could feel safe. This example of solidarity and cooperation developed within a context of shared time and space and shared hardships, a way of containing the anxieties that surrounded and always beset the small community. Yet, often I wondered why the descriptions of this family never seemed to contain any references to difficult emotions – hate, envy, jealousy – that beset families.

If the family-community produced a sense of integration, mobilised to keep at bay terrifying anxieties, this would be far more basic than any concerns with the emotions I have described because the basic sense of embodied containment is absolutely basic to survival. In Bick's account, as in others such as that of Winnicott and Bion, the dual relational containment of being held and the nipple in the mouth are fundamental to the creation of a sense of continuity of being, which is the most basic experience. Feeling held and contained by the community 'family' therefore I take to be absolutely basic to a feeling of being able to exist.

There are gendered aspects to this, which we will explore in later chapters, but it is important to note how the sense of family is produced through the differentiated rhythms and embodiments of the masculine and the feminine – the going to and from the works, the looking after family and the domestic economy at home. The rhythms of the steelworks community were strongly gendered, with the men going off to work and the women staying at home, as the example about female conversations in the back yard showed. I suggest that the embodied performances of gender were central to the sense of containment and safety – of knowing where you were – just as the sense of family was containing. In these practices, the role of women was central. Maintaining gender difference was something that became a difficult issue for many men after the closure, as we will see, and serves to remind us just how central distance from the feminine was for the development of a strong manual working masculinity that could provide the central force in defending the community through hard work and union militancy, for example. The loss of heavy manual work impacts on the kind of work available – much more work is now considered as feminine by the inhabitants – it is poorly paid and does not require strength. The women are likely to be working outside the home and the men are struggling to find new forms of work. In this sense, the strongly gendered aspects of the community matrix are ruptured and the loss of these gender relations is traumatic.

Many residents told us that the work of the steelworks was dangerous and dirty:

> It was hairy enough in the works when I first started, obviously, because I was er, um, serving my apprenticeship, when I came out of my time, I worked in the heavy end which, I mean, you have to have your wits about you, it's er, it was a place of, when you've got sort of er, 30, 40, 50 tonnes of molten metal going above your head in a weak ladle, it's, you've got to have your wits about you like.

Yet, this dangerous dirty work, in which no one knew whether men would come home in one piece, and so provoked considerable anxiety, also created a sense of well-being and pleasure. What emerged from interviews was that the dirty masculine body, tired from work, was a central affective trope for the community. We will explore this in detail in Chapter 5. Many men spoke of the traditional pride of the steelworkers – pride in a hard job well done, pride in collective struggle and pride at keeping going in difficult times, for example. This contrasts markedly with a sense of hopelessness presented by men who could not find heavy manual work for their sons. As John, 46, said:

> I didn't get back into full-time employment...As I said, I haven't done a lot since, well, I got to be honest with you, it's about 16 years, I've been unemployed. I haven't done a lot since then because, you know what I mean, well, there is not a lot out there anyway. I just think I'm 46 now, and I think to myself, um, I got no hope, you know what I mean. Like my boy, he's 16, he's out of school. He's struggling to find work. What hope have I got, you know what I mean?

We could argue then that the figure of the proud steelworker, dirty from his work, going to work and coming back tired, also presents a certain fixed and rhythmical quality that is containing not only for the men for whom this was both the past and the future, but also for others. While the men do not mourn the loss of difficult and dangerous work on one level, on another, their talk and actions are permeated with the effects of its loss. For example, men and women both scapegoat and ridicule young men if they take work that is considered 'feminine', such as supermarket work, pizza delivery or cleaning, as we will discuss in Chapter 7. It is this that produces the circulation of 'shame'. The men are at work and the work is tough; they come and go and the women must look after the home. They not only see themselves as the emotional bedrock of the community, which keeps it safe among all this danger, but they take the brunt of work problems as they affect the domestic sphere. In other words, they actually keep things working:

> Yes because I mean I don't know women take the brunt of things don't they, erm I don't think there's many women that don't handle the finances.
>   I honestly don't I [inaudible] men never ever told their wives how much they earned and give house keeping but I think the majority of the women they handle the finances.

.... it's the women that have got to make the money stretch isn't it?

It's the women that listens to the kids when they want something you know and err of course the generation that has been growing up have been used to having what they wanted.

Janet said that the men, on the other hand, just sit and moan at this situation, whereas it is the women who have to try and make it work. So it is women, according to Janet, who get on with it, keep continuity going despite the threats posed to masculinity by the closure, which we will discuss in Chapter 8.

Fear of people coming in

We could understand this as a complex relational dynamic, in which the other is understood ambivalently, both as threat and promise, while the concern about keeping the community together and alive in the face of its threatened demise brings a profound sense of anxiety about the very possibility of survival.

June, 37, made this clear:

Erm I know a lot of people say oh you'll have people coming up from Cardiff and living up here especially once the rail track is reopened because the houses are cheaper up here they you know they'll live up here they'll work down there and you won't know any of them because they won't have time you know to bother and I think there's that element to it as well and I think when a lot of people moved away they let their houses out to rent.

So there are different people in and out all the time and I think the community lost it's sense of direction a bit.

Very often I'll be sitting in my mothers and there's people past the window and your like who's that [laughing] it's strange because years ago you would know every person who lived in every house but very often now you'll find there's somebody rent a house down the road or something so yes it is erm it is weird.

She added that:

I think for the older generation they find it quite intimidating some-times because I think they don't trust people to be honest... and erm maybe they feel that they're invading their space a bit.

Um, you'd just walk in, in each other's houses, you'd leave your door open, you know, if times were hard you'd help each other out, you'd give someone a lift, you'd take em to the shops, you'd help em if they were sick, you'd cook em some dinner or, you know. But today, I don't feel like you've got that, you can walk down the street now and maybe you won't bump into anyone you know.

We could understand all these examples as aspects of an affective relational dynamic through which the relations of the community are sustained and that become visible in particular ways through the crisis that confronts them.

A central challenge for the residents is to embrace change and heterogeneity in the form of job change – often from manual to service sector – and its associated cultural practices and moral values. While most have managed to accommodate change, some have not and, at the same time, we heard many reminiscing narratives of previous times when everybody knew everybody without feeling that they were being intruded upon by newcomers or being subject to massive socioeconomic changes.

Many people reflected on the community in the past as a safe place where everyone knew each other:

Um, you'd walk in, in each others' houses, you'd leave your door open, you know, if times were hard you'd help each other out, you'd give someone a lift, you'd take them to the shops, you'd help them if they were sick, you'd cook them some dinner, or, you know. But today, I don't feel like you've got that, you can walk down the street now and maybe you won't bump in to anyone you know.

Kate, 52, reflected on how this feels for her and her mother:

So now there are different people in and out all the time coming from 'X' and 'Y' [nearby towns] and I think the community has lost it's sense of direction a bit, and, I know there's this' Communities First' and everything and so I do feel the communities are now slowly rebuilding but I think it's going to take a long time, a very long time...I like it round here it's home to me and I know a lot of people still living here. We've all been here most of our lives and you find there are clusters of families you know it's the mother of someone and her one son over there and the other son over there, so they don't now seem to move far.

And another resident said:

> I think now this is changing because my mother and myself very often will be sitting in my mothers' sofa and there's people past the window and you're like who's that? [laughing] it's strange because years ago you would know every person who lived in every house but very often now you'll find there's somebody new has rented a house down the road or something so yes it is weird.
> Yes I always feel safe down here yes, yes.
> But now, I mean I don't know, initially like, you don't know who they are; and you think who are they, why are they here? But then me personally I don't oppose to anyone basically, but, I think for the older generation they find it quite intimidating sometimes because I don't know I suppose they've got different values...I think they don't trust people to be honest. So, yes maybe some feel that they're invading their space a bit.

Emma, 47, reflected on why locals seem sceptical of the idea of relocating as a way forward:

> But it's not all good outside either is it? This is the problem, people are now afraid to go into the inner cities. I mean you've got people from the cities coming here and this is the problem and they just can't deal with it can they? They don't know how to cope with it. You know someone said to me they went up to London, 'Very ethnic', they said, 'Very, very ethnic', you know and I thought oh my goodness me you know even when I was there in the 70s and 80s you had IRA bombings and things like that, but I could walk home at 3 and 4 o'clock in the morning and not be bothered. So do people want to leave for that reason? It's all over society as a whole isn't it?

The difficulty of moving away

As well as people coming in, the difficulty of moving out was also expressed. This is exemplified by several stories of unwillingness to move for work. These cohered around the theme of a sense of other communities looking after their own, providing for us the sense that one is looked after within the community.

Janet, in her 60s, told me how she could not possibly leave Steeltown because it provides the basis of her sense of being and belonging, without which life feels impossible. She refused to move away from the town when her husband suggested moving jobs:

> I just wouldn't, I wouldn't move down there not unlike my brother and my sisters, my brothers went and two of my sisters but I mean I wasn't interested, I just wasn't interested he said he wanted to go and apply for a job and I said alright and err he went and he had the job so he come home and he said oh I got the job and I said oh have you he said yes I said well you've got to travel have you he said no I'm not going to travel everyday he said we'll go down there and live well I said if you want to go you go but I'm not going [laughing] and err I didn't go I said it's up to you what you want to do, you look into it and if you want to go you go by all means but either you travel or your down there on your own because I said I'm not coming.

Even younger people found it difficult to find a reason for them to move out and be separated from the network of affective relations that they know and value. Philip, the 17-year-old son of an ex-steelworker, described what would count as a valid reason and motive for him to relocate outside his community:

> No, I couldn't move. I'm a local boy like, I got to stay here. I couldn't go anywhere else, no way unless it was a different country where the sun is like, I couldn't move like, no way, 'cos here I know everyone here, I feel comfortable like, but I couldn't move anyway, not knowing anyone unless the weather's there its like very good and different isn't it, but I couldn't do that, I just couldn't.

As Philip said, a key reason for him not to move out was his realisation that he would not know people from other towns and that he wouldn't feel comfortable with people he didn't know.

Paul, a 44-year-old ex-steel man, explained why he needed to cope with his redundancy by staying local and close to his family and how he eventually decided he would actually be better off by looking after his father while relying on state benefits rather than moving out for work:

> I'm going to be made redundant now this time next year again...So I'm back in the same boat as what I was in 2001...There is nothing round here, there is no jobs now around here, and they want a certain age group because at the end of the day they'd pay your pension, they'd pay your sickness, everything else, your national

insurance. But the older you are the tendency to more sick you go. Well anybody will not pay for you to be off, they would rather employ a younger person.

I know one person who had to relocate to keep his job, and the stress on him was unbelievable ... I will be better off on state benefit, because my father is registered disabled and I had him transferred from a nearby town to here to look after him because he suffered a stroke while he was there in hospital, so I'll look after him and everything.

In this sense, we see how, for Paul, it was better to bring his father to the community than for him to move. A very strong sense of the commitment to look after ageing relatives within the community was paramount for many respondents.

Daniel, 17, whose parents were on benefits, reflected on why he had decided to stay in this town in case his parents might need him:

But I wouldn't like to [move] really because I need to stay around here, get a job to help my family like. So that's I guess why I want to stay round here really. If I couldn't find a job, I was just going to go in the army, but I don't want to go knowing like my mother or father were going to need me one day and I ain't here. So I'd like to stay round here and get a job. Round here, so I get married and I'm happy. If they need me then, they only got to phone.

The sense that it is better to stay put and work something out rather than move away for a job was a key factor for everyone we interviewed. Admittedly, we did not interview people who had moved away, but nevertheless, this points to the central significance of the relations that make up the community.

Indeed, there was a strong tradition of fathers and other men finding work for the next generation within the works, thus also cementing a sense of being looked after. For example, Colin, a youth and community worker, told of how a friend of his father was able to tell him where in the works there was a job going.

Through these means we form a picture of Steeltown as a community that in the past provided a set of rhythms of life, of affective relations and practices that were deeply containing and that, we might speculate, contained the inhabitants through a long history of struggle and difficult conditions.

So, both going away and others coming in are potential problems that are seen as a threat to the way things were, the sense that it was safe, you knew everyone and therefore you knew who you were. I suggest that this concern over both going and coming relates to anxieties about survival and the possibility of disintegration, which are quite terrifying. Thus, the community acts as a communal body and we can see this more clearly perhaps in the anxieties that surround the potential and actual collapse of the community envelope, and the poor toleration of outsiders mentioned by Willoughby (2004) earlier. The expelling of dissenters to save the group is here matched by the fear of leaving as well as the fear of the incoming. In Chapter 7, we will take this idea further with reference to Earl Hopper's work on groups clinging together or breaking apart after experiencing trauma.

What can and can't be said

Another aspect of the production of the protective envelope was a set of informal rules about what was and was not to be talked about and in what contexts. The issue of outsiders coming in and the difficulties of leaving are also phenomena that have been observed within sociological studies; for example, Dempsey's Smalltown (1990), Warwick and Littlejohn's (1992) study of mining communities, Harris' 1987 study of redundancy and recession in South Wales and Sennett's (1971) discussion of city communities. My aim here, however, is to understand the relation of this phenomenon to its psychosocial aspects. Bick's and Anzieu's work on second-skin phenomena tells us clearly that the poor toleration of outsiders and incomers and the difficulties in moving away, while perfectly rational, also relate to the issue of how a community survives the chronic insecurity that I have outlined, by trying various forms of protection. This suggests that sociological studies restrict themselves to documenting the issues and do not try to understand them, but this has led, as we shall see, to attempts to pathologise certain community forms in the face of the changes produced by advanced liberalism and globalisation. As one man said, there were rules at work about what you could say – you could malign your fellow male workers but never the family – this was considered out of bounds.

Similarly, tacit agreements between workers stated that certain topics were out of bounds. Tom, 46, reflected on men's own rules about what can be said and joked about and the sacred place of each other's family:

Yeah. We had an unspoken rule where we never, never spoke about families to any degree and so no one could take the mick out of anybody's family or that wasn't on.

Just never abused anyone's family, you know, verbally or you know as a joke or whatever.

Take the mick out of each other something rotten but not about the families, that was a step too far.

Similarly, families would not talk about their own problems outside the family. As the wife of a man who had been seriously depressed said:

I didn't know whether he'd be here when I come home, because he was really ill and urm I used to go to work and when your in work people don't always want to know what's going on at home, you know you go to work you've got to be pleasant you know I've still got to do my job so I didn't tell anybody in work.

One woman counselled her sons when their father died not to show long faces to others but to mourn within the privacy of the family. These practices demand that one carries on, that one keeps trouble and grief within the family and just gets on with things.

And I think when there is grieving to do they don't do it in public... My father always said to me when you got grief and you've got a problem that grief is yours. Everybody got their own problems and their own grief. Do not put your problems and your grief on anybody else when you do meet them put a smile on your face, when you go in and close your door then the smile can go. Yes I mean when my husband died it was a shock to us. Umm I was out. I came out I had things to do and I would not have let my two sons do it on their own. I didn't think it was fair, I thought, I said, no, you grieving for your father same as I am. And I'm not letting you do it on your own, I'm coming with you, so the three of us helped one another. And I came out and people were a bit taken aback because I was out but that that was the way I did cope. And I spoke to people and if anyone wanted a laugh I'd laugh with people. So did my two sons 'cos I warned them, when we go out no long faces. And that's what we done what happened behind our closed doors was our business.

The comment that 'everybody got their own problems' is telling. Certain kinds of practices around what can be said and to whom allow the issues that might rupture solidarity to be kept within the privacy of the family. It could be argued that such practices of speaking and silence

(Walkerdine, 1990) are defensive practices that help to promote community solidarity and prevent community breakdown by keeping negative aspects that could produce discord away from the public space. By this means, a historically fragile community that only has its members for support is able to continue and not face disintegration from internal conflict. It might therefore be said that negative affects, which beset all families, are kept at bay within the community family. While this does indeed serve to hold the community together, not speaking about certain problems does show a fear of breakdown and indeed the fragility of the containment. It is often said that practices such as this are negative, but I want to stress that this is a very simplistic reading. They are shown to be absolutely necessary practices for the historical survival of the community at a certain moment, but they are not without their negative consequences and they are not well adapted to a less manual kind of work. I take this as a key example of the maintenance of the ego-skin.

The notion of Welsh communities as 'close knit' is very common in the literature (Aaron, 2002; Evans, 1974; Harris, 2007), but little emphasis is placed on understanding what this might actually mean. It is our contention that the close-knittedness is a way of beingness that allows the community to survive all the insecurities that beset it. In addition, a number of other studies mention similar kinds of issue (Aaron, 2007; Balsom, 1985; Charles and Davies, 2005; Cloke and Milbourne, 1992; Pitchford, 2001; Williams, 1985). However, the concern is how a close-knit community takes on enforced heterogeneity after the closure of the works. In Chapter 4, we will explore studies of the effects of de-industrialisation and the effects of trauma on communities, thinking also about one woman's attempt to keep her community alive.

4
De-Industrialisation, Suffering, Crisis and Catastrophe

Going on being after de-industrialisation

When we think of the implications of an approach stressing containment, affect, beingness and rhythm for the Steeltown research, we can think of the rhythms of the works, described in Chapter 1, the arrangement of the houses, the games and the washing, the meetings of women and the help from neighbours. All of these things helped to cement a set of affective and rhythmical relations that are phenomenological in character. It is these relations that, we argue, help us to understand how the ways of relating actually produced a sense of continuity of being, which allowed the townspeople to feel part of one big family, to feel cared for and to go on being – something that could not be provided any other way, because of the constantly shifting position in relation to iron and steel production and consumption. It is not surprising in this context that both moving away and strangers moving in should create anxiety as it is the relations and rhythms of the place itself that create the ties that bind and support, and in moving away these would be lost and they would be threatened by people moving in who did not share the history of mutual support.

We need also to understand how a crisis was triggered by the closure in 2002. It is our contention that because the ways of providing for continuity of being were the practices and rhythms connected to the works, its closure signalled a threat to all of that. This is amply exemplified by the interview extracts we have included so far. We could say then that the closure threatened not only the possibility of work and therefore material survival but also the heart and soul of the community, through its puncturing of the social and affective relations that held the community together.

A classic study of the effects of the closure of manufacturing on a community is *Marienthal* (Jahoda et al., 1933 [1972]), which is the study of an Austrian community built around a mill, closed during the depression of the 1930s. It is a fascinating work using what the authors call sociography, which prefigures in many ways a phenomenological approach, by doing things like noting speed of walking. It combines quantitative and qualitative forms of research. For our purposes, what is hugely significant is its understanding of the relation between lack of money when out of work and psychological states. The authors develop a scale in which families were ranked from unbroken, through resignation, to despair and finally apathy. The longer the unemployment, the less the money, the worse the emotional state became. Time dragged and we begin to see the effects of the shifts in the temporal rhythms. In Steeltown, we note that the temporal rhythms changed from agricultural to industrial time, to go to a time of formlessness, of non-work. The Marienthal study makes it clear that this shift – of having no money and nothing to do – unsurprisingly gets typically worse as time goes on and money decreases. It also demonstrated that there was not a mobilisation of resistance as during times of hardship when industry was alive, but increasingly despair, apathy and inaction. When we understand this, we see how crucially important were the community support practices developed by Steeltown and how dangerous it was for those residents when work collapsed.

Zippay (1991) studied unemployment in the Shenago Valley in Western Pennsylvania in the 1980s after the closure of a steel mill. Many of the displaced workers were plagued by anger and depression. They felt frustration, loss and uncertainty, with a loss of pride and a sense of betrayal. Some 57 per cent reported worsened marital relations, 53 per cent temper and irritability, 75 per cent depression and 28 per cent problems with alcohol. Many commented that had they been the subject of a natural disaster they would have been inundated with counsellors, but in an industrial disaster they got no help. People did feel that they were not alone with their problems but tended not to talk about them, and while some felt that the disaster strengthened relationships, most did not.[1]

The continued central importance of community for providing a sense of ontological security is outlined by several studies. Crow and Maclean's (2004) survey of research on family and community argues that 'communities continue to be an important component of what provides many people's sense of security and belonging' (p. 70). Sennett (1971) argues that community members denied their differences in order to reinforce their shared sense of identity when it came under threat. Steeltown is a community that has indeed come under threat, and we have reviewed the ways in which clinging together served an absolutely central function in relation to survival. Indeed, Crow and Maclean (2004) agree with Richards (1990) that 'people respond to the forces of change by regarding community as a potential source of material and emotional security in an uncertain world, and thereby are led to pursue involvement in community rather than abandon it' (p. 75). And they cite Bulmer (1986a) who argues that 'the solidarity of community life in earlier generations had a forced quality, at least among the poorer parts of the population. Poverty necessitated the development of arrangements whereby material assistance from kin and neighbours could be drawn on in times of particular hardship' (p. 75). He argues that self-help networks were a realistic response and the neighbourhood itself was a safety net. Crow and Maclean also support the view of community as a haven or refuge for those dominated by impersonal forces (Castells, 1997, p. 64; Jankowski, 1991, p. 193). This argument is very close to the one I have put forward. However, it is important to note the ways in which the modus operandi of communities like Steeltown has been seen as backward looking. Tönnies' original 1887 study proposed two kinds of interaction: *Gemeinschaft* and *Gesellschaft*. The former related to the family-like form of communities and the latter was oriented more to individualisation. Discussion of the latter has increased ever since the 1960s when Goldthorpe et al. (1968) studied the affluent worker by looking at car workers in Luton. They argued that it was good that communal mutual support had passed away in favour of better government support. They argued that this privatised families and so people came to prefer mobility to cohesion, the latter being understood as stagnant. Indeed, Beck (1998, p. 36) has argued that the shift away from the male breadwinner model has meant the transformation of the relationship between community and locality. Beck's (1992) and Giddens' (1991) arguments about the disembedded character of local activities can be found to be based on these ideas (Crow and Maclean, 2004). Puttnam (2000, p. 23) argues that such communities produced what he called 'bonding social capital' but were not able to develop 'bridging social capital', as we discussed in Chapter 2. Beck argues that community dissolved in the 'acid-bath of competition' (1992, pp. 94, 116) but that it also created a longing for intimacy, security and closeness. Crow and Macleod think community is far more resilient than Beck suggests.

Goldthorpe, Beck and Giddens fail to engage with the centrally significant understanding that the practices of Steeltown began in hardship and cemented ways of doing things that produced bonding, which made the members of the community feel safe within 200 years of chronic uncertainty. The loss of the practices and the central steelworks around which such practices grew up has to be understood as a serious catastrophe that takes away the central plank of people's security. In this sense, Goldthorpe's argument fails to engage with the difficulties that gave rise to this way of coping, and Beck and Giddens' arguments fail to understand the complex psychosocial character of this 'disembedding'. Thus, the patterns of change within Steeltown and similar communities that have been observed, moving from relative homogeneity to heterogeneity because of the labour market change, has a profound affective quality.

Beck, Giddens and Hardt and Negri (2001) all in some way predict the decline of community or communal beingness in favour of individualisation. As we discussed in Chapter 2, there is no doubt that globalisation and advanced liberalism have intensified modes of liberal regulation. However, all of these authors seem to make the same mistake of equating the shift in governance to a simple shift in subjectivity. Beck and Beck-Gernsheim (2001) argue that people become solitary, with their individual fears – what they call 'naked, frightened aggressive ego in search of love and help'. 'In the search for self and for an affectionate sociality, it gets lost in the jungle of the self.' The solitary confinement of the self, they say, is a mass sentence, so that community has to become reciprocal individualisation. What Beck and Beck-Gernsheim do not engage with is how a group of people who helped each other through a struggle and who longed to be safe and free from exploitation developed ways of making each other feel safe over generations. Those people see the freedom to choose for the sham that it is and find other ways to stay together and in some ways to subvert it. While it is true that they can never return to a joint struggle of the kind they used to have around a central employer, nevertheless, the Becks operate with an odd concept of the subject. That is, their subject seems to have to change absolutely with the change of regime. They do not offer an understanding of complex affective cross-generational transmission. Earl Hopper (2003b) argues that groups feeling overpowering anxiety, lack of safety and ontological security cling together or break apart. It is this that is at the heart of the matter for the people of Steeltown. While the Becks assume that breaking apart is an automatic result of what they call individualisation, this is not necessarily the case. It can result in the kinds of terrified clinging that we can witness in many places. Nor is there evidence that rampant individualism is what consumes everyone. Many of those in Steeltown are avowedly against such a move, and in any case their response is more complicated. While Giddens (1991) recognises the central importance of ontological security, he argues that we can choose our life path. He opposes to this what he calls barriers to emancipation. While it is clearly the case that freedom of choice was limited in the past because of constraints in relation to sexuality, gender, morality, class mobility and so forth, again the view of the subject is one who can simply and easily take up a choice, can desire to have a biography. This is not in any simple sense what the people of Steeltown want. And in any event, the freedoms to choose that Giddens puts forward are themselves bought at the price of the exploitation of others, even if many of those others have been removed to the global south.

Bauman also has a very negative view of what he calls 'communal dependency, surveillance and enforcement' (in Beck and Beck-Gernsheim, 2001). While this may have some validity, it misses the point and it is a description and not an explanation. It can be argued that this is what allowed the communities to remain stable despite attacks from the outside and nobody would necessarily say that all defences are totally good – they can have very negative sides and effects.

While it is also correct, as I have noted, that there is a tendency towards in-house family entertainment, reliance on the family and so on, what those who engage with the loss of community in this way fail to deal with is that simply because the labour market and regulation of labour changes, with a different governance of the working subject, this does not mean that people and groups change easily or overnight or indeed that the predicted changes will happen in the way that is expected.

MacKenzie et al. (2006) use data from interviews with ex-steelworkers on redundancy, some of whom were based in Steeltown, to develop a discussion about class. In particular, they argue that the interviews displayed 'an ongoing commitment to a collective orientation' (p. 848). They further argue that a collective identity was maintained both by the experience of the redundancy as a collective and through the work of the union.

> It has been argued that the collectivism that was intrinsic to the steelworker identity, although heavily premised on the occupational community, extended to a sense of class identity and solidarity. The group identity of the steelworker was based on a sense of distinction, but rather than leading to excessive particularism based on the occupational community, it served as a basis through which class based

thinking and class based identity were articulated, and allows do for the recognition of shared structural location, and problems in common with workers elsewhere. Through further abstraction a deeper purpose can be ascribed to these developments in terms of providing a defence mechanism to afford a sense of protection against the changes affecting these communities, not just in terms of material loss but in broader social terms. Ultimately, the assertion of this collective identity can be seen as a means of resistance against submergence in the life the external labour market has to offer, one characterised by low pay, lack of security and loss of identity within an existence akin to Beck's (1992:100) vision of an 'individualised society of employees'. Indeed, the crisis of redundancy that removed the occupational basis for collective identity provided the imperative for its re-articulation. (ibid., p. 848)

MacKenzie et al. are arguing that it is the attempt to keep on calling themselves steelworkers that provides a collective resistance to individualisation for ex-steelworkers. In this sense, they understand it as an attempt to maintain class solidarity. However, I think that we can take their argument much further by relating it to the understanding we have been developing in this chapter. That is, that collectivism, as they call it, is contained within the relations and practices we have been describing and that their affective character is absolutely essential to understand in order to explain how communal beingness has been developed and maintained. Thus, in these terms, we can understand what they see as resistance as being a complex psychosocial and affective relation that itself defends against the threat of annihilation. While Mackenzie et al. discuss this in terms of the pains and losses of the changes, and this is undoubtedly true in these data, I think we have evidence that it is much more strongly built into the fabric of the community through its affective organisation. That is, it is the rhythms and patterns of everyday life, both materially and emotionally, that held the community in place and provided what is looked back on as a place of safety and security – the terraced houses, the patterns of work organisation, the rhythms of the gendered organisation of work and domestic life all provided a sense of space that allowed the community to feel emotionally contained – what the psychoanalyst Didier Anzieu calls a psychic envelope. This is a community founded on a collective organisation to engage with the exploitative and dangerous conditions, something that has endured for generations.

If we think about the arguments made in Chapter 2 (Walkerdine and Bansel, 2009), this means that class is lived specifically and in relation to the complex conditions and relations within certain locations and settings. Thus, we cannot make overarching and oversimplistic statements about the effectivity of the shifts in labour market and consumption. We have to understand the specificity of place and history as a way of reading the response. In that sense, it can be argued that governmentality approaches – for example, that of Rose – are too simplistic if they attempt to read subjectivity and experience directly from discursive organisation and mode of governance. The differences between Steeltown and Sydney (Walkerdine and Bansel, 2009) point to the differences in the way in which the same kind of shift in governance and labour market change is experienced in different locations. The specificity of location, history and so on provide the bases of complex practices of class in which there are differences in response to shifts in the labour market and forms of governance. Workers in Sydney and workers in Steeltown are both subject to the same kinds of labour market changes but these are experienced differently. The first and most obvious point to conclude from this comparison is that while globalised work practices and neoliberal modes of governance may be predominant in both countries, local conditions mean that these are not experienced in the same ways at all. These local conditions must be understood to include the relationalities and meanings through which work is understood, experienced and embodied within any particular location. This includes not only historical issues of nation and community but also class and gender, and how these enter the relations through which working lives are lived, that is, small and large histories.

This suggests that we must also be wary of reading Mackenzie et al. as evidence that class is simply the existence of forms of collective organisation when these are locationally and historically specific. What is more, the existence of collective forms of organisation is not a complete buffer against the shift from a homogenous to a heterogenous form of community.

We would argue that all workers look to find a temporal continuity and flow that allows them to feel that they can still exist – what Guattari (1989) refers to as the continuity of existential territory. We have seen in the Chapter 3 the central importance of the production of an affective territory that maps the patterns of belonging and being. When this territory is forcibly transformed, annihilation anxiety can be very strong and so ways have to be found to repair it or to be able to transform, to become something else. This, as Guattari recognised, is a difficult exercise that needs to be undertaken with a great deal of support. While the trade union and the women provided much support for the men, the changes in the organisation and type of work provided for those who had experienced something else – a rupture in the flows of time and space. This rupture has to be repaired in whatever ways are available, to allow a sense of going on being and therefore to prevent annihilation anxiety.

In understanding that the transition from the modes of beingness associated with the works are put under threat by closure, we are arguing that there is not a simple shift to individualisation but then we are also arguing that there is also not a simple resistant collectivism. The entire relations are much more complex than this. We have argued that certain effects follow from the development of long-term threats of annihilation, produced by the experience of chronic insecurity. This has produced modes of beingness that developed over two hundred years but that are severely threatened by the closure of the works because they are dependent on the social relations associated with the works for their existence.

Suffering and trauma

Given what we have begun to understand about the time leading up to the closure, and the ways in which this figures in interviews after the closure, we can be aware that the closure presented a new chapter in the attempts by residents to shore themselves up against the effects of the chronic insecurities that they have had to live with. The losses of the affective relations and practices, the modes of relating and the rhythms of life that went with the works are losses so serious that we could describe them as catastrophic. In the next four chapters, we will understand in detail how these changes impacted on men, women and young unemployed men. However, first we want to explore a number of intersecting works that deal with these issues using the concepts of suffering and trauma. In reviewing this literature, we want to draw attention to three distinct periods in the life of Steeltown. The first is the 200 years during which the works was open – a turbulent and insecure time but one when the iron- and steelworks was the centre of the town. The second is 2002, when a catastrophe occurred and the steelworks closed forever. Finally we have the period post-catastrophe until the present.

We mention these three periods because we are going to make reference to a body of work that mostly relates to the effects of a social catastrophe, such as war or genocide, whereas we are attempting to deal with the effects of long-term suffering and insecurity added to by a catastrophe event and its aftermath. Although our review of a very extensive range of literature will be far from exhaustive, what we are attempting to do is to find those works that engage with suffering and to understand how they frame the issues, and to see how far we can apply these to the situation in Steeltown.

There are a number of theoretical frameworks that deal with these issues and it is to these that we now turn. We will review some work that takes as its object trauma and suffering. The clinical literature on trauma has grown considerably in the last 20 years. As Kai Erikson (1995) tells us, the history of an understanding of trauma develops a psychological analogy with the effects of a physical trauma. That is, damage to the body that is understood as a part of a physical injury is recast in terms of the psychological effects of a social catastrophe, such as anything from a crash, through a highjacking or war to genocide. He outlines the way in which what he describes as 'traumatic memory' becomes the object of medical discourse and practice and is gradually taken over by psychiatry without any clear and unchangeable object.

Allan Young (1995) argues that trauma begins in the nineteenth century in relation to the development of concepts such as repression and dissociation. The work of Janet and Freud emphasises the way in which psychic life parallels physical trauma. The work of WHR Rivers in relation to the effects of the First World War on combatants was important but there was no clear agreement on theory or symptoms. It was post-war American psychiatry that utilised experiments, epidemiology and psychometrics to transform traumatic memory into post-traumatic stress disorder (PTSD). He argues that this relates directly to Vietnam. This is further elaborated by Ruth Leys (2000) in her historical approach to trauma, who also argues that concepts of trauma move from traumatic memory to a focus on the image itself – a repeated seeing of terrifying images. This focus on the image downplays the complex unconscious and relational aspects of trauma in favour of a disorder focused on the repetition of intrusive imagery with the downplaying of feelings of survival guilt often associated with work on genocide (Leys, 2007).

In this respect the issue of haunting and traumatic memory takes on a particular life in relation to psychoanalytic debates, but Young argues that this shifted in the 1980s by the adoption of a discourse of PTSD by the American Psychiatric Association. In particular, it is noteworthy that the discourse of trauma in a number of (contested) ways argues that there is a psychic effect of the equivalent of a blow, that is, an intrusion, with most work stemming from responses to war from combatants and later genocide. Thus, I argue, following Young and Leys, that there has been a tendency, especially in American literature, to equate trauma with suffering, and to operate as though all difficulties, all suffering, is a medicalised condition called trauma, which can be survived.

Other approaches

One of the issues that becomes clear is the attempt by some social scientists and others to move away from a psychiatric and individualising discourse, which understands all suffering as the survival of a trauma, thus individualising and medicalising it (e.g. Berlant, 2004). Thus, we find several attempts to either change the terminology from trauma to suffering or to insert the adjective 'social' or 'cultural' before the word 'trauma'. For example, Iain Wilkinson (2004) argues that suffering should be understood through sensation and experience as a social and cultural phenomenon. The ways in which people directly encounter the social meaning of their affliction is central. He emphasises the importance of narration but also of the difficulties of speaking and of feeling pressured by professionals to talk about it (Walkerdine, 1991).

Kleinman et al. (1997b) also use the notion of social suffering:

> Social suffering . . . brings into a single space an assemblage of human problems that have their origins and consequences in the devastating injuries that social force can inflict on human experience. Social suffering results from what political, institutional and economic power does to people and, reciprocally, from how these forms of power themselves influence responses to social problems. (ibid., p. ix)

Similarly, Kleinman et al. (1997b) discuss the central importance of cultural representations of suffering, noting in particular the centrality of a global political economy in which there is a market for suffering in which victimhood is commodified, medicalised and pathologised, with a mediatisation of suffering, in the sense of commodification of experiences of atrocity and abuse and pornographic uses of degradation.

What they call the interior images are made into trauma stories, which then 'become the currency, the symbolic capital, with which they enter exchanges for physical resources and achieve the status of political refugee. Increasingly those complicated stories, based on real events, yet reduced to a core cultural image of *victimization* (a postmodern hallmark), are used by health professionals to rewrite social experience in medical terms'. The person first becomes understood as passive and unable to represent the self, then as a patient suffering from

PTSD, and to receive assistance they may in fact have to display medical symptoms, thus transforming one who suffers from political terror into one who suffers from a disease. Of course, because this is often the only way to get help, the sufferers themselves often want this. So memory and resistance is lived as failure to cope, paranoia, guilt (Kleinman and Kleinman, 1997a, p. 10). The appeal of experience; the dismay of images: cultural appropriations of suffering in another approach by Alexander et al. (2004) uses the term cultural trauma. They use a cultural sociology approach and attempt to widen the study of trauma to take in social suffering and cultural processes so that it is not simply defined through a psychological discourse. However, two things need to be said here. First, as Leys points out, just because one engages with the social, this does not negate the subjective effects of traumatic experience. Secondly, this approach fails to engage with the embodied aspects of experience, by concentrating on the discursive (Walkerdine, 2010). However, Alexander et al.'s main concern is to demonstrate how trauma becomes a master narrative, a way of talking about the impact of disasters that then minimises and downplays any other way of understanding the situation. This means that everything from the nature of the pain, the victim and the presentation to a wider audience through the mass media are presented through this discourse, which has its effects in relation to the attribution of institutional responsibility and state bureaucracy. This in turn leads to a way of understanding identity as a traumatised person, memory of the disaster and its routinisation.

It is therefore important to understand that suffering, produced through social and economic events, is often only taken seriously only if it is medicalised, so that people have to experience it as trauma that can be helped. In the light of this, we might ask if the discourse of trauma has any uses to us in understanding the situation in Steeltown. Let us return to the three periods. The first, the time of the works, is a time of suffering and one in which the suffering is taken as a part of what it means to have a flexible labour force within liberal governance. I am differentiating this from the period of catastrophe in which the steelworks closes, and the time that follows it. I would argue that what we need to understand is the effectivity of the experience of these periods on the people and recognising the central importance of history as set out in the previous chapters.

While it is absolutely pertinent to argue that trauma has become a spectacle while suffering has been individualised and medicalised in order to allow sufferers to access services and assistance, nevertheless, the effect of the various kinds of suffering needs to be understood.

In particular, we need to understand the effects of the experiences on the bodies of the workers and their families. While we may be at least ambivalent to the discourse of trauma, nevertheless, as Leys points out, we need a way of understanding experience, which is not simply dis-avowed by engaging only with the way in which disasters are made to signify. In other words, how can we deal with the period in history in Steeltown, in which a disaster or catastrophe struck the town and punctured the modes of relating generated up to that point?

I want to introduce certain kinds of psychoanalytic work that attempts to present ways of engaging with traumatic experience and its relation to the social and to history, outside medicalisation. Kai Erikson (1994) makes an important argument about the community as a body, which fits well with the discussion of Anzieu (1984, 1989) in Chapter 3. Erikson argues that:

> Trauma is generally taken to mean a blow to the tissues of the body – or more frequently now, to the structures of the mind – that results in injury or some other disturbance. Something alien breaks in on you, smashing through whatever barriers your mind has set up as a line of defense. It invades you, possesses you, takes you over, becomes a dominating feature of your interior landscape, and in the process threatens to drain you and leave you empty. The classical symp-toms of trauma range form feelings of restlessness and agitation at on end of the emotional scale to feelings of numbness and bleak-ness at the other. Traumatised people often scan the surrounding world anxiously for signs of danger, breaking into explosive rages and reacting with a start to ordinary sights and sounds, but at the same time all the nervous activity takes place against a numbed gray back-ground of depression, feelings of helplessness, and a general closing off of the spirit as the mind tries to insulate itself form further harm. Above all, trauma involves a continual reliving of some wounded experience in daydreams and nightmares, flashbacks and halluci-nations, and in a compulsive seeking out of similar circumstances. (ibid., p. 228)
>
> ...one can speak of traumatised communities as something distinct from assemblages of traumatised persons. Sometimes the tissues of community can be damaged in much the same way as the tissues of the mind and body...but even if that does not happen, traumatic wounds inflicted on individuals can combine to create a mood, an ethos – a group culture almost – that is different from (and more than) the sum of the private wounds that make it up. (ibid., p. 231)

Indeed, echoing Anzieu (1984, 1989), Erikson (1994) claims trauma can create community by drawing a kind of protective envelope in which the traumatic experience has to be expunged by acts of denial and resistance. For him, people can suffer individual trauma after a collective disaster but they can also suffer collective trauma:

> By collective trauma ... I mean a blow to the basic tissues of social life that damages the bonds attaching people together and impairs the prevailing sense of communality. The collective trauma works its way slowly and even insidiously into the awareness of those who suffer form it, so it does not have the quality of suddenness normally associated with 'trauma'. But it is a form of shock all the same, a gradual realisation that the community no longer exists as an effective source of support and that an important part of the self has disappeared.... 'I' continue to exist, though damaged and maybe even permanently changed. 'You' continue to exist, though distant and hard to relate to. But 'we' no longer exist as a connected pair or as linked cells in a larger communal body. (ibid., p. 233)

People acting in the same collective rhythms are more than their constituent parts: 'it is as if the individual cells had supplied raw energy to the whole body but did not have the means to convert that energy back into a useable personal form once the body was no longer there to process it' (ibid., p. 234). One can, Erikson suggests, speak of a damaged social organism just as one can speak of a damaged body. He describes the way in which due to toxicity in a lake, a community couldn't fish, couldn't make a living and, in the end, had to move – there was drinking, violence and so on. Sometimes post-disaster utopia comes about and the community tries to regroup and dress its wounds. Communal trauma can, he suggests, take two forms: damage to the tissues that hold human groups intact and the creation of social climates, communal moods, that come to dominate a group's spirit (ibid., p. 237). He is particularly critical of the medicalisation of trauma through the use of the discourse of PTSD.

As we have seen, this bears a striking relation to Anzieu's work on the community or group envelope. Indeed, he uses the term 'protective envelope', which can create a community by drawing the envelope around the group, which aims to insulate the collective from further harm through acts of denial and resistance, in which things do not have to be explained because all carry the same pain. We have seen this through the examples of concern with whom is inside and whom outside the community, the issues of family, of the difficulty of moving away and the regulation of speaking and silence. He argues that the social body has a set of rhythms, which can be damaged just as a physical body and, in this sense, his work certainly fits with the case that I have been trying to make of the importance for the rhythmical organisation of community time. In our analysis, the collective trauma has damaged the affective relations through which the community held its members and provided a sense of going on being in a most profound way. I am arguing that this profundity reaches to the most basic levels of existence so that what is experienced is a matter of life and death, of annihilation.

The long period of suffering from the eighteenth century to 2002, which itself no doubt contains many moments of suffering – threatened closures, lay-offs, strikes, depressions, hunger, pit disasters – brings its own pattern of affective relating, defensively, as Hopper suggests. However, difficult as it is, it becomes a settled pattern that is threatened by the final closure of the works. Here, the shared history and shared affective practices no longer work and death stalks the community. Then we have a third phase in which ad hoc attempts are made to shore up the community in such ways as to defend against the threat of annihilation. In Hopper's terms, this involves coming too close or moving too far apart.

So, again, we can think of this in terms of feelings of being unable to leave, to move, to let others in versus feelings of needing to get away, of being unable to bear staying, which we explored in Chapter 3. Admittedly, we have seen less of the latter experience, but as we shall see in Chapter 8, issues are present in the interviews with the young women and of course, the research was not able to include people who had actually already left Steeltown.

History

I want to now return to the central importance of history in all of this. I have stressed all along that it is the centrality of how Steeltown had managed to engage creatively with the threat of annihilation and chronic insecurity that is at the heart of a history spanning 200 years that we need to understand. Two analysts, Francoise Davoine and Jean-Max Gaudilliere (2004), who trained as Lacanians but work at the intersection of this and relational approaches, offer what I think is the most insightful work on trauma and that which has most helped my own understanding. Their work is on psychosis and war, trying to understand what they call the severing of the 'social link', in cases where a traumatic experience, in their case usually relating to wartime experience, is not communicated but held and passed down generations, only to emerge as madness further down the line. They are strongly committed to understanding psychosis through a process of joint research with the patient, aimed at uncovering the severed social and historical link, rather than moving away from the historical experience towards a developmental account. They use the work of microhistorian Jacques Revel (1996a, b), who argues that we can understand the social through an engagement with the microsocialities through which it is constituted and that therefore constitute a social link. Microhistory is a movement that began in Italy in the 1970s (Cerrutti, 2004; Ginzburg, 1993; Levi, 1991; Magnusson, 2003; Pomata, 1999) and stresses the centrality of the small details of everyday life. What Revel points to is the relationship between these small histories and larger social history. In his terms, we can understand a microhistorical perspective as being absolutely compatible with an account that stresses the centrality of a relational view of sociality, such as we have been outlining in this book. Thus, the small sets of affective relations add up to the development of social links, and it is these that constitute the ways in which larger social histories are lived. Thus, for Davoine and Gaudilliere, it is the break in the social link, the failure to be able to keep or hold that link because of unbearable experience in wartime, that means that it is held bodily and transmitted down generations, eventually appearing as psychosis. I am trying to adapt this view to think about the historical experience of Steeltown. While what has been suffered is not war, nevertheless the period of historical suffering and the ways of building relations in response to this provide us with a picture of how the microsocialities worked in relation to the wider forces of a social history. Thus, in these terms, the closure of the works represents a potential break in the social link, that is, that which held the community together, which we can also understand as the community matrix. During the Second World War, the psychoanalyst SH Foulkes was collaborating with colleagues who had attempted to work with traumatised soldiers, such as the psychoanalyst Bion. He extended the work that they were doing with groups and started the work of group therapy. He used a notion he had taken from the German biologist Kurt Goldstein that an organism is more than the sum of its parts.

> The term 'network' was used to express the fact that our individual patient is, in essence, merely a symptom of a disturbance of equilibrium in the intimate network of which he is a part. I use the term network deliberately in analogy to my teacher in the mid-1920s, the neurobiologist Kurt Goldstein, then in Frankfurt. He was a

pioneer of the view that the nervous system can best be understood in theory and practice not as a complicated sum of individual neurons but as a system that reacts consistently as a whole. He called this a network and called the individual neuron a nodal point. For this reason, I have called the total system of people who belong together in their reaction a network, and the individuals composing it correspond to nodal points. It fits well that this network in its most intimate part should be called a plexus. Every single one (patient) had such a plexus around him, or was part of such a complexus (Foulkes, 1983, p. 12).

Foulkes adapted this idea in relation to groups. These, he suggests, are also more than the sum of their members. Something happens in the way that affect circulates within the group. His idea is that within any group, any communication has a certain resonance that is experienced by group members in different ways according to their previous affective experience, with which it resonates, creating complex patterns of defence and interaction within the group. He calls the 'common pool of meaning, the network of a communication', (p. 122) a matrix. For him, working with an adaptation of classic Freud, the resonances are about the individual psychosocial development of the group members but we can just as easily understand this within a more complex and historical notion of affective communication. What his ideas of matrix and resonance allow us to potentially understand is how a community matrix forms over historical time as we have shown but also how those patterns of communication create distinct resonances for people within the community, allowing for different kinds of reactions. Foulkes (1990) coined the term to express a sense of the way in which a group is dynamically more than the sum of its parts and can be said to be treating the community as a whole entity or network (Latour, 2005) or web (Arendt, 1958), whose dynamic can be investigated,[2] in much the same way as Erikson (1995) seems to use the notion of protective envelope. Thus, the matrix is a dynamic set of interrelations carried affectively. Mitchell (1988) has developed this as the relational matrix incorporating intrapsychic and interpersonal realms and Layton (2006) in relation to wider social experience.[3] Although Mitchell only applies the notion of matrix to a family group, when we take Foulkes's original idea together with more recent ideas about webs of relations and affective flows, we can see that the matrix as something that operates affectively and dynamically, holding the affective relations of a community together, might be a helpful way of thinking about things because the whole body or social body of the community of which Anzieu and Erikson talk can also be understood in the form of a matrix.[4] Deleuze and Guattari's concept of the assemblage can also be understood in a similar vein, incorporating the concept of existential territories. Whichever term is used, what we are describing is a break in the affective relations, the narratives, rhythms and refrains, through which the community was linked together.

My argument is that this has profound consequences for the inhabitants and for future generations, as we will see in the next four chapters. This is also graphically illustrated by the example we are going to explore next. This is an account of one woman's attempt to 'mend the great chain of being', as she called it. We could understand this in Davoine and Gaudilliere's terms as an attempt to prevent severing of the social link or to preserve relational continuity of being, the existential territory of community in the face of the threat of annihilation.

Trying to mend the link in the great chain of being

This case study is about the way in which affectively the community attempts to produce a dynamic that creates a group projection in order to keep the community alive.

The steelworks as an object and assemblage – a geographical, psychic and material centre – is now flattened and the ground laid bare. There is a hole at the centre of the community's imaginary ego-skin, which, if we follow Bick's proposals, brings a fear of annihilation through spilling, the dissolving of the containing boundaries of the skin. The death of the steelworks brings with it fears of annihilation of the community matrix or social body, which are played out in a number of ways. In other words, they signal death. We find it too in the higher fences, which embody the loss of the sharing of community. The sense that nothing works anymore and has to be remade is a profound and difficult challenge.

Martha is in her 60s. She told me that in Steeltown there was a 'great chain of being' that was first broken by the 'death' of the miners following massive mine closures and then by the steelworks:

> Well the first link to go was the mines. But that was ok after a while, it was devastating for the miners that was ok really because then some of em could get work here in the steelworks. Some people moved away but a lot of em came back as well. A lot of the miners came back and the second chain, the second link in the chain was British Steel. When it was announced it was closing.

And to me that was a death knell in the town. And everybody stood still, oh my god. And it was like, if that chain was broken and it was flung away and everybody just, they just didn't know what to do none of us really.

I take 'the great chain of being' to be the sense of going on being, as well as a sense of historical continuity of the community. In the great chain of being, death would have been understood as part of a natural cycle that led to the next generation, but what she is speaking of by way of breakages in the links I think is not natural death through old age but traumatic annihilation. She is thinking about trying to mend it, to bring it back to life. She recounts an attempt to mend the links in the chain of being. Steeltown, she says, is like a phoenix rising from the ashes, but the issue is how to make it rise. How to make it 'bounce back' or be 'down but not out'. This comes in the form of a project to bring Christmas lights to the town, the centre of which has been decimated as there is a huge reduction in money available for spending in the local shops. This is how she tells the story of a plan to bring Christmas lights to the town:

Really I mean erh the council hadn't put any Christmas lights up here for seven years. And we were the only town without lights and two of the girls that worked here put a piece in the paper and asked people to go to a meeting to raise funds for the lights. So we went along. And my husband said I hope you are going because you have moaned enough about it. I said yes I'm always on to the councillors. I said I they stopped dodging me now when they see me coming so we went along to the meeting out of the whole of Steeltown we had 13 people there. That included the Mayor and the Mayor's driver. Anyhow we formed a committee out of that and the first year we raised £27,000 and had the electrics put through the town. 'Cos the electrics was no good, and we bought the strings of lights and we bought a stainless steel Christmas tree which cost us over £6,000 and we had umm we had to purchase a lamp post to put it on we had to pay the council money for planning permission to dig a hole. Yeah to put the lamp post. Then down the bottom end, down at Peacocks and that there was nothing for us to attach the lights to so we bought six posts and put those in. And we got lights right from down the bottom end of town right up to here to the market, we got the Christmas tree outside the library. Which we were we're only the second people in Great Britain to have, and we've just added on year to year. We've got over 100 Christmas trees over the shops ... and we got three men that

go round every year and put over 100 Christmas trees up we now purchased a Welsh dragon and we put that down at the end of the town
there. So as you're coming in from the bottom end you can see the
dragon, we've purchased the greetings from. Yeah Seasons greetings
from Steeltown. And we put that over Wetherspoons. So this year last
year we put a lot of electrics in again but this year the money isn't
so forthcoming up to now whether we can speed things up and get
enough money I don't know but over the last three years we've raised
about £50,000.

 ... when we switched the lights on. From Woolworths right the way
through the town, right to the bottom you couldn't move. It was
literally jammed packed. Right the full length from into the town
all the way down Erh we had entertainment right through the day.
So I was out on the town actually from half past seven in the morning
and I finished eight o'clock on the night. I was absolutely shattered
but it was wonderful to see that. To see the people's faces when they
actually switched on those lights, because what we done, all the town
lights were switched off and we put the tree on first cos nobody had
ever seen the tree. So we put the tree on first and that was fabulous
and then once the people had got used to that then we switched the
lights on right through the town. And it was absolutely wonderful it
was the children they were wonderful. Just to watch their faces just
children, 2, 3, 4, 5, had never seen lights in (Steeltown). They had to
go elsewhere to see lights. And it was absolutely marvellous.

She tells me that they also ran carboot sales and bingo to raise more
money because it was impossible to get money out of the council.
In addition they have since run other activities, also by raising money.

 The affective practices that she presented to me suggest that there are
established ways of coping with loss and grief and that these must be
countered by aiming to bring life back, to mend the link in the chain
of being, to allow generational continuity to happen. Light in the dark-
ness of the Christmas lights is deeply symbolic of new life and therefore
triumph over the death of the town, and it is through the creativity
born out of the loss that allows the community to be brought back to
life and therefore for the chain to be mended and for life to go on.
It also places something at the centre of the town, not in the same place
as the steelworks site, but something that was also 'lit up' as if by the
flames from the blast furnaces. Thus we can understand the lights as a
projected object created to defend against the fear of annihilation represented by the break in the chain of being. Thus the act is one that
carries a libidinal charge (a vital force in Deleuze and Guattari's terms)

that aims to recreate or shore up a disintegrating matrix, to prevent its collapse and to breathe new light and life into it and to mend the skin. We can stress it as both a creative and a defensive act, and it dramatises for us the profoundly difficult, life-and-death struggle confronting the townspeople as they try to keep their community of affect alive and to ensure that it will be there for the next generation. This sense of continuity of being, as I have been at pains to stress, is central to the possibility of the going on being of this community. This is something that Martha recognised through her attempt to mend the links.[5]

Conclusion

In exploring the place of affective relations in the production and destruction of a tightly knit, de-industrialised community, I have discussed the centrality of affect for a relational approach to community. In this sense, the work develops and extends critiques of sociological concepts of community and shows the centrality of embodied affective relations. This allows us to think of the ways in which the energetic forces work to create and potentially destroy a community and allow us to understand the central importance of affect for any study of a formal or informal collective form. In this sense, engaging with the rupture to the continuity of being presented by the closure of the steelworks allows us to think about the central importance of the community as a projected object that holds and therefore presents us with central issues for an understanding of change as deterritorialisation. Instead of thinking simply of change as creative potential, perhaps we also need to understand it as a play of light and dark, life and death, as the example of Martha shows us so vividly. While Deleuze and Guattari stress the importance of understanding what can be created by the forces of desire, they perhaps underestimate the central significance of the production of an affective community as a defensive possibility of continuity in a sea of enforced change. How the community is formed, creates its own protective envelope, is threatened and dies, changes or survives is shown to be profoundly affective. While there is great debate about the usefulness or not of the concept of trauma, the consequences of the closure are profound in many ways, rupturing as they do the ways of being that went before and that themselves operated to provide security in a sea of insecurity. Martha's desperate quest to mend the great chain of being shows us that what is at stake is no less than the fears of death of the community and the struggle to keep it alive. In Chapter 5, we will explore how masculinity was formed and had to face change in relation to the closure of the works.

5
Producing Pride in Masculinity: The Hard Steelworker

Jim is sitting in a chair at the local youthwork office. He is 42, now a youth worker, but up until 2002 a steelworker. During a long discussion of his work with unemployed young people, he starts talking about his feelings, when he was a steelworker, of coming home from work covered in dirt. We remember being forcefully struck by the loving detail with which he described the pleasure of coming home after a hard day's work, so covered in dirt that it got everywhere – eyelashes, eyebrows – which he contrasts forcefully with the idea of working in a local supermarket, and wearing a white coat that never gets dirty:

> No, it's not, it's clean, do you know what I mean? You come home, there's no dirt under your nails, your hands are completely clean, it's not proper work, when you've been working in industry for maybe 30 years, and you're used to coming home with dirt under your nails, and you've got to spend hours getting the dust from around your eyes and in your eyelashes and stuff, and I suppose it's enjoyment, coming home knowing you've done a real hard day's work, you'd come home and you're knackered, real physical work, to where you're walking in the house, with a nice clean pair of trousers, shiny shoes, shirt and a tie, and a Morrison's' jacket on. It's not really proper work. It's not like coming in completely knackered and with a feeling of, can't wait to get in the bath and get this off. Come home from Morrison's' and just sit down in a chair and feel like probably you haven't done anything, nothing worthwhile anyway.

He contrasts the donkey jacket of the steelworker with the white overall of the supermarket worker – an overall that never gets dirty. The supermarket worker comes home clean and does not feel dog tired from a good day's work. And in not coming home tired and dirty, he cannot fully feel like a man. What was especially striking was the sense of sensuousness and the pleasurable embodiment of the performance of hard working masculinity. What was lost was not simply a sense of belonging or camaraderie, but a strongly embodied sense of being. Of course, it is not new to think of the losses associated with this form of masculinity (Kenway and Kraack, 2004; Kenway et al., 2006; McDowell, 2002, 2003; Willis, 1977), but I want to dwell on this in order to think of the centrality of the embodied feelings described by Jim. We all know very well how ways of dressing, moving, looking and feeling become central to our way of being, such that, were we to lose these, we might feel quite bereft, even perhaps not really a fully functioning person any more. Jim's eyebrows full of dirt and tired body are the result of the performance of bodily practices that, day in day out, helped constitute what it meant to be. Thought about in this way, I suggest that the loss of these practices and this embodiment becomes understandable as not only simply sad and painful, but even possibly terrifying.

In thinking about the crisis in masculinity (Clare, 2000; Griffin, 2000; Hall et al., 1978; Hearn, 1999; McDowell, 2000; O'Donnell and Sharpe, 2000; Whitehead, 2002), it is usual to think of this as a crisis in an outmoded traditional masculinity in which antediluvian and rather sexist, macho, working-class men refuse to give up their power and privilege. While this reading could make sense of Jim's affection for his former life, it would miss something very important in our view. It is that years, in fact centuries, of struggle have demanded this body and indeed many times have broken this body in countless industrial accidents or work-related illnesses, or demanded more of it through poor wages or collective bargains that demanded more work, more productivity, more efficiency. Indeed, although these examples do not come from this study, I am reminded of the professional woman who grew up in the industrial working class who told us of a father who died before retirement, who could not stop trembling and who was appallingly tired; or the father who felt so strongly that he took industrial action on his own once, which was, as she put it, 'very self defeating' (Walkerdine, 1991); or my stepfather, who had three conditions caused by his work in a boiler shop – industrial deafness, a finger severed in a machine and a skin condition caused by extreme heat – and who died long before retirement.

In Steeltown, we met men who had acute and chronic health conditions as well as serious breakdowns, also a well-known side-effect of redundancy (Avery et al., 1998; Ferrie et al., 2002, 2003, 2005; Gallo et al., 2000; Kalil et al., 2010), and we certainly heard plenty of stories of terribly harsh conditions and resultant poor health. Many men were not sorry that this had gone, but the body of the steelworker is a body forged through centuries of adaptation to the necessities and exigencies of earning a living. As Ken says, it was 'hairy', dangerous work, as we discussed in Chapter 3:

> It was hairy enough in the works when I first started, obviously, because I was er, um, serving my apprenticeship, when I came out of my time, I worked in the heavy end which, I mean, you have to have your wits about you, it's er, it was a place of, when you've got sort of er, 30, 40, 50 tonnes of molten metal going above your head in a weak ladle, it's, you've got to have your wits about you like.

What we are trying to say is that from the founding of Steeltown at the end of the eighteenth century, the hard labour of men, who had to develop hardness of body and spirit, who worked in harsh conditions for poor pay and who drew together to fight collectively for better pay and conditions, had out of necessity to embody and perform the kind of masculinity lamented by Jim, or they and their families would not survive. We are putting it this starkly because it is important to understand that this was a matter of life and death. So, how could it not be the case that ways of being and performing masculinity would sediment over time to be simply what one needed to do, and why would a community not in fact demand this of its men for fear that they would not survive. These are embodiments passed down through generations. In all their detailed subtlety, the tiny performances of this masculinity were what one learnt to do, to be. And more than this, the centuries of struggles for better pay and conditions produced pride. Pride is a word said to us again and again: pride in collective action, pride in a job well done, pride in the quality of steel, pride in the level of productivity, pride in the wages fought for and won. It was the hard body of the steelworker then that not only produced all this, from father to son, but that was so central to community survival that the community would have been unthinkable without it. Of course, this industrial history is well known, but what is less talked about perhaps is the sense of historically produced, intergenerational modes of being, deeply embodied and deeply affective, which this industrial history forged all over the world at a particular juncture and that, in parts of that world, it closed. Modes of being and doing are not separable from the historical conditions that formed them right down to the minutiae of how we feel we can be and go on being.

If a proud, hard and dirty masculinity that coped with and triumphed over the dirt and dangers was forged in communities like Steeltown over centuries, its eventual demise, especially if following doomed union campaigns, the sense of loss, betrayal and shame might be overwhelming. So rather than regaling the reader with stories of a species out of time – the industrial man – I want to ask how on earth masculinity shaped in this way manages to survive and adapt to a change so catastrophic that it appears to destroy a life produced through centuries of collective struggle. It seems to bring death.

The point is that this way of being was produced by the history described in Chapter 1. How it was lived involved a great deal of suffering and a very strong gendered division of labour, as we will explore in Chapter 6. However, the building of strength out of the survival of those harsh conditions and the fighting for decent conditions of work was what bound men together. Indeed, the men took pride in their efforts and pride in their work, though many recognised in interview that pride was more likely to have been expressed by their fathers and grandfathers and that, after redundancy, many men said that what they actually missed was the camaraderie of the works and the wages, rather than the hard and exploitative work itself.

> I still reflect back because another thing we found in this job was that umm, when people were working down on that site, that's all they did was moan about going to work, about people in work, about conditions and now when they come out, they all remember, we had some good times, you know, the camaraderie, that's the sort of things you miss. It's the camaraderie, the people, and we had people coming back saying, I didn't realise what we had down there then, until its gone because it was harder to get out of that place than it was to get in it. You know some of the things that happened over the years, and you think, well if they'd been in any other industry, they would have been sacked or whatever, you know, but that's, that's, I still reflect, I still think about it, we still talk about it. There's a, there's a local author, he's just brought a book out about it, about the times, you know, in the work, sort of characters within the works, you know, about some of the tricks we used to play. There was a, sometimes it was very sort of school boyish to be in there, you know but that, that was all part and parcel, the camaraderie, you know, that's it in a nutshell.

As Bob says:

> My father worked 35 years in the coal mines, then he come out, then
> he done fourteen years in the steel works. He'd had enough of the
> coal mines after 35 years and he came in the steelworks seven or
> eight years after I had started, he's dead now my dad. But no, the
> reason I went in the steelworks is the same, there was jobs going, I,
> when you're 15 you don't, I don't know about you, but you don't
> really know what you want do you, [laughs], but I went in the steel-
> works because that seemed the logical place to go at the time round
> here and there were jobs over there, that was 1965 and to be hon-
> est I enjoyed all my thirty seven years. I think I said it before, really
> the only thing that I miss about the steel works at the moment was
> the people, the actual contact with the people. You know the job,
> I liked my job, I really liked my job, but I don't particularly, I don't'
> miss it.

And as Tom says:

> I'm a valeter/driver. That came up when we were on holidays, people
> say what are you doing, obviously you mention your past because
> to be a valeter at my age is a bit strange, as I say it's a young man's
> game, but when people realise that you were employed by a . . . well
> steelworks, mines whatever, a big employer, they know what's hap-
> pened. People in the country know what's happened to the mines
> and the steelworks and most of them are aware the sort of financial
> packages that were on offer when you were made redundant so, the
> sort of work line you could take doesn't have to be as high stressed
> and as financially rewarded as the steelworks was. I don't need it as
> long as, well my point of view is that I have to work. I have to be out
> of the house doing something because of the pension, the finance,
> I know I'm going to get minimum wage whatever I did. You know
> the financial reward didn't have to be a great as what it was with
> Corus, so that's all I can say really is that Corus is past. I don't want
> to work for them again, I've no interest. I worked for them and that's
> what I tell people.

Indeed the pride of industrial working masculinity was both exploited
and celebrated in an industrial age that needed the hard labour of industrial work to fuel industrial growth. By the 1980s, when monetarism of
the Right was on the rise and industry in a spiral of decline, industrial

masculinity began to be denigrated. Indeed in the early 1980s it was common to hear the refrain that it was white working-class men who were responsible for the Conservative election victory, accompanied by a politics that moved towards gender and race over class as political categories. It is in this context that we begin to hear stories of a crisis in masculinity, but in reality the crisis was one of industrial jobs and the crisis created for men who had over two centuries learnt ways of coping only to face 'redundancy'. This is not to look back nostalgically at this nor to ignore the very real problems of gender relations but to attempt to understand their provenance rather than simply to denigrate or pathologise. In this sense, a psychosocial analysis needs to understand how modes of being are lived and the psychosocial consequences of the shifts in communities like Steeltown.

Pride and shame

Anthony Giddens (1991) argues that shame replaced guilt within the neoliberal context. This is understandable in relation to the rise of conditions of work and self-regulation that demand a flexible worker who is responsible for their own development and advance through their personality and efforts. Indeed, we could argue that shame is an obvious corollary of a mode of governance in which responsibility is placed squarely on the Ruth Leys (2009) shoulders of the workers to develop themselves. Failure in this context is failure of the self and its accompaniment is shame (see also Agamben, 2002; Leys, 2009). While most of the redundant steelworkers did not admit to feeling shame, it was very noticeable in the next generation, especially the young unemployed men who we shall meet in Chapter 6, and their fathers felt redundant through being unable to help them. However, many of the older men certainly felt 'redundant' because the chances of being employed over the age of 50 were very poor, as Tom illustrated. He had already been made redundant at the steelworks and was then threatened again with redundancy:

> Our employment will definitely cease on 31 December this year. After which means that they are going to get a firm in from outside. You know a firms looking into it now, they've whittled it down from 15 down to two. So it's going to be one of the two firms and it's either Xerox or Capita is going to take over our work from 1 January next year. which means I'm no longer a civil servant. That firm will then look at employing whoever's left, they don't want the amount there

now doing the job, they want, they've said that, they want to cut it down by a third.

So I would be 48 if I went now, or 49 as from next year when I'm made redundant from 1 January, so then you've got to look on the aspect of it then, who'd want to employ a 50-year-old person when they don't have to. You know, yourself you know that, you just have a look around anywhere and even the university wouldn't look at it I wouldn't have thought. They want a certain age group because at the end of the day they'd pay your pension, they'd pay your sickness, everything else, your national insurance. But the older you are the tendency to more sick you go. Well anybody will not pay for you to be off, they would rather a younger person. So I'm afraid it's just going back to like we said, it will be benefits and I think that is going to be the end of it ... to be honest with you. Or luck might have it I'll win the lottery like I previously said. There's the only options that are available. And it's not just me it's everybody that was made redundant, they're all the same boat, as they live in the eastern valleys district and it's just the geography of the place and the firms will not cover it. The government won't do anything, like I said with this rail link, nothing ever materialised yet and that's supposed to be running next year 2007. Nothing has materialised at all.

Now, we argue that this shame is historically specific and related to the rise of advanced liberalism. However, as Leys (2009) notes, shame has featured in a great deal of recent social and cultural theory. Leys analyses it with respect to debates about survival guilt in relation to the Holocaust. She argues that the recent interest in shame eclipses interest in the psychic effects of the survival of extreme violence, previously referred to as survival guilt. It is a very interesting and thoughtful analysis and does have implications here for understanding how men managed to cope with, survive and fight extreme exploitation. Originally work on survivor guilt, according to Leys, developed in the context of attempts by survivors of the concentration camps to claim compensation so that a lasting effect had to be proved. The issue was always not that people were guilty but that they were made to feel guilty by displacing the effects of violence done to them onto themselves (cf. Fanon, 2004), in other words, attempting to understand the effects of extreme violence in terms of imitation, mimicry and the need to displace hatred. More recent work has attempted to revise this view by pointing out the performative aspects of resistance showing compliance and imitation as a simulation performed for the purpose of resistance (p. 78). This opposition is typical of the split between activity and passivity that is often invoked within accounts of agency (Walkerdine, 2007). It denies a complex emotional life to subjectivity. Indeed, as Leys argues, just because mimicry may have been a survival strategy does not negate the psychic consequences of the master–slave dynamic.

Why recount this in relation to industrial masculinity? While employees in the iron- and steelworks were not slaves, nevertheless, conditions of exploitation existed and we can expect complex psychic consequences. While the performative aspects of compliance have been well documented in the industrial literature, perhaps less well documented are the industrial parallels of sadistic practices used by the Nazis, including making prisoners decide who should go to the gas chamber. Practices of the devolution of budgets, of productivity deals, of divide-and-conquer cuts, while not life and death, were and are commonplace in industrial and business practice. It could be argued that these induce complex affects of guilt and shame as well as the pride discussed above. All of these practices, of which there must have been many during the 200 years of iron and steel in Steeltown, make the workforce experience responsibility for the need for changes demanded by capitalism. This is a very complex industrial legacy, which the townspeople fought with collective action and pride. It is into this context that advanced liberalism brings individualised practices.

In the past, as many men have recounted, fathers, relatives or friends found work for young men in the steelworks. Dany, 39, reflected on how young men used to get apprenticeships at the age of 16 in the steelworks, often through their fathers/uncles who were already working there:

Yeah, we had like apprenticeships, going back 15, 20 years ago, when I sat my apprenticeship for five years in (Steeltown) they were taking on, I don't know, a hundred plus a year apprentices because it was a fully integrated steelworks. You had every trade under...you know, that was possible, fitters, electricians, instrument mechanics, welders, fabricators, boiler makers, you know, every trade there was an apprentice, or more than one apprentice for it.

Yeah my father was a committed worker yeah. He was the same as me he ruled with the foot, for 27 years and he'd be there all weathers and he'd work all hours and if he didn't have to go to work he'd have to have his arm hanging off. The apprenticeship I got was that type of you know, it'd been passed down from my father like because he was a committed worker, very hard working and yeah when I first started at 16 years you want to show willing to work you know.

This aspect of passing the work down generations can no longer work. It meant that young men did not have to do well at school, but always knew that work would be possible. Indeed, it was striking that several men commented on men not being able to read in a way that accompanied the sense of pride in dirty work. That is, they recounted lovingly the way that older men of their father's age would see reading as the wife's responsibility, bringing home any forms from work for her to deal with.

Now, this too is an issue as there is no work for older men to find for the younger ones and even manual trades demand qualifications from college, which need a level of literacy. As we shall see in Chapter 6, a large number of young men are leaving school with no functional literacy.

I am not saying that this form of masculinity is good, nor am I saying it is bad – what I am saying is that we need to understand its historical production and necessity (in the sense that these characteristics became necessary in certain conditions). We can understand its effects, both good and bad, but we need this historical understanding to avoid pathologisation and to appreciate how particular conditions produce their affects and defences, which can have good as well as deleterious consequences for the men and those close to them (e.g. women and children) So, looking from our vantage point in the present, a strong gendered division of labour, close surveillance of ways of doing masculinity and femininity can seem very stultifying, but they arose out of necessity.

Crisis of masculinity

More recently, the idea of a crisis in masculinity (Clare, 2000) has been put forward as a way to understand further the gendered dimension of the difficult transition into adulthood through employment experienced primarily by young working-class men reaching maturity at the start of the twenty-first century. Within debates about the social construction of masculinity, waged work has traditionally been seen as a crucial element in its construction (Willis, 1979). Similarly, masculinity has always been depicted as being deeply embedded in both the social meaning of work and in the history of institutions and economic structures (Connell, 1995). Furthermore, the difficult transitions into adulthood through employment have also been associated with the huge expansion of low-paid and insecure work, especially in the service sector; for example, the so-called rise in poor work (Bauman, 1998) that has become more endemic in the United Kingdom since the beginning of the 1990s. Therefore the rise in poor work has also been associated with a shift in the gender division of waged labour and in the gendered associations of employment and consumerism as an arena for the construction of social meaning, new forms of inequality and identities. In this sense, the type of questions that are often asked (McDowell, 2003) include: What happens to men's sense of themselves as masculine when the sort of work associated with masculinity disappears, as it has in many ex-steel communities? To what extent will young working-class men be prepared to undertake service work for low wages in common with increasing numbers of young women? And, to what extent do these young men feel that doing service work, which they often see as 'feminine', will also be experienced as an affront to their masculine dignity?

A number of possible answers to these questions have been offered, such as how working-class young men have always been portrayed as macho trouble makers behaving in 'laddish' and loutish ways and hence are often seen as a danger to the wider society. (McDowell, 2003; Pearson, 1983). Similarly it has been argued that the relative success of young women in the new labour market as well as the rise and influence of feminism have also contributed to exacerbate men's current anxieties and fear of failure, which have also increasingly manifested as suicide attempts among young men (Faludi, 2000). However, the nature and newness of the idea of a crisis in masculinity has also been questioned, on the grounds that rather than a single crisis the mere notion of masculinity has always involved a relentless need to prove oneself as manly enough. Therefore rather than a crisis, it is an ongoing process of continuous suspicion and doubt about the proper achievement and performance of masculinity (Kimmel, 2005), but this makes masculinity an ongoing, continuous object and thus denies history. Likewise, it has also been suggested that instead of a crisis of masculinity as a primarily gender issue per se, a more fundamental transformation in the relationship between waged work, gender and class is taking place (Bauman, 1998; Beck, 2000; Giddens, 1991; Sennett, 1998), mainly in terms of new forms of class-based inequalities in which working-class men feel their standards of living are threatened by service economies.

While I agree that the idea of a crisis of masculinity as a gender issue does not quite capture the complexity of the changing connections between waged work, gender and class currently taking place worldwide, still both these overall sociological arguments see the embarrassment and the fear that working-class young men experience when they imagine themselves doing 'feminine' work as a totally explicable situation.

One gets the sense that there is no subtlety and that masculinities are treated almost as things, solid and given. What is missing also in all these depictions is the crucial sense that masculinity also involves a performance and as such it requires constant psychic affective work, and that the historical dimension that we have been at pains to set out is absolutely central in understanding the production of the shifting relations of masculinity.

Gendered division of labour

Throughout the period of the steelworks, a strong gendered division of labour placed women as guardians of a home stability that was matched by the militant hard work provided by the men. This is a fantasy presented in many ways in cultural products about industrial workers and their families in Wales and beyond. For example, Richard Llewellyn's book *How Green Was My Valley* (later made into a film) gives us a clear view of a romantic fantasy of a father and mother providing the stable building blocks of the home and community, weathering storms of strike, industrial accident and migration. To present this as a fantasy is not to say that it is not true. Rather, our aim is to show the embodiment of such a fantasy – that one can embody and perform such masculinity and femininity is central to the possibility for survival that we outlined in Chapter 4. We do not want to say that this fantasy is itself ideological and therefore imposed upon the workers. However, it would not be surprising that, if Hollywood utilised the fantasy, the idea of the solid, strong, proud manual worker, salt of the earth, bedrock of the nation's wealth should not have been in use within capital from the inception of industrial work. Using a psychoanalytic approach to this fantasy, we could understand that it requires a great deal of work (Walkerdine, 2007) to embody it and should not be understood as in any sense natural. The body of the worker has to be honed and, I should add, strongly separated from the maternal, as I will go on to demonstrate. However, I should also point out that this body was necessary to withstand the rigours of the work, and the development of the system of the family wage (Whitehouse, 2004) meant the cementing of a strong gendered division of labour. Gail Bederman's (1995) study of the transformation of American manhood illustrates the centrality of late nineteenth-

and early twentieth-century discourses, including political speeches by the likes of Roosevelt, who tried to save manhood from 'the perils of over-civilisation' by issuing calls for a return to the strenuous life and a resurrection of savage qualities in order to stave off the possibility of a neurasthenia produced through the nervous middle-class white boy who repressed their masculine impulses (Grant, 2004). We might also point out that this particular image of industrial masculinity was specifically developed and presented as an ideal masculinity precisely to counter feckless, work-shy or feminine characteristics, which would culminate in loss of work, claims on the state and the failure to become 'labour' or to serve as the basis for the production of capital or indeed to counter capital. What we must understand therefore is that the embodiment of this masculinity was necessary to undertake hard and dangerous work, but it was also strongly put forward as the real masculinity – that which is vital, strong, virile and closer to nature. Embodying or living this masculinity results, as we have seen, in a sensual enjoyment of hard labour and its bodily consequences – tiredness and dirt. To have these is to be a man in the tradition of hard men. Their absence is frightening and painful. It was traditional within cultural studies to view such embodiments as ideologies therefore communicated representationally and semiotically. The investments in such fantasies have also classically been understood using a Lacanian lens, which stresses the relations of desire invested into masculinity and through which masculine as control over the maternal is experienced. While we will certainly point later to the central importance of the maternal within the power of these masculine fantasies, it is also necessary to understand them as communicated bodily, not simply discursively. The pleasures of dirt, sweat and tired muscles are physical sensations. Thus we can also understand them affectively and their experience as communicated both to the body by the labour and from one body to another in the experience of working. The conversion of painful experiences into pleasure can be understood as that which helps cement the strong feelings of loss and fear associated with the loss of hard work. The separation from the maternal is more complex, but we will argue in Chapter 7 that femininity acts as both a central container of anxiety and as an object of desire. So distance from the feminine acts as a way of defining difference, which was also cemented by practices such as the family wage or policies such as we saw in relation to early twentieth-century United States of getting men away from sissiness and into hard work.

The point is that the fantasy of masculinity is experienced as real both through the demands of work, sexual relations, and political and economic discourse. It is cemented through the many practices through which its embodiment is demanded and it is experienced as a pleasurable accomplishment. How can something that makes one feel alive be readily given up? Why would men not cling on to it to avoid feelings of death and feminisation? This is not a 'crisis in masculinity' (Griffin, 2000; O'Donnell and Sharpe, 2000; Whitehead, 2002) so much as a crisis in capitalism as represented by the shift in the labour market. That men might be slow to shift to the new required forms of masculinity says little except that the men as 'labour' were never at the centre of concern, their subjectivity always to be honed to the demands of capital not by their own needs and experiences. However, it might also be said that the men of the valleys, along with other industrial communities, used their masculinity creatively – they used the power of their bodies, the only thing made available to them, to resist, to create unions and to fight for better conditions of work.

Coping with change: Becoming entrepreneurial

In this section, we will explore how different men coped with the necessity to move from steel to other work. We must remember that the loss of work and the resulting change are involuntary. There is no simple move to something that the men want to do. Like other studies (Banks, 1995; Dorling, 1997), we found that age was a significant factor in how change was managed, as we discussed in Chapter 2. Younger workers were more able to let go and learn from their previous manual work experiences, seeing redundancy as a challenge and opportunity to further retrain, reorient and find other ways of developing careers. Older workers seemed to have less motivation and interest in mobilising their personal and social resources to face redundancy in the way the younger men did. While all the younger men (30–45) seemed to embrace change and its impact on their masculinities, however stressful, by contrast, the older ones (50 +) stressed respect and appreciation, being acknowledged and financially supported for the hard manual work they had done for many years, and to have the right to a life less stressful and more fulfilling in their own terms.

The older the worker, the more likely they were to resist change, and this was especially true in relation to men over 50. The employer allowed men of 50 and over to retire, and so this is what they did. While they counted themselves as lucky, their removal from productive labour at such an early age was very hard for most of them to bear, especially when they found themselves stuck at home and not being able to get out. Several refused to do domestic tasks formerly undertaken by women and reflected a sense that it was terrible to be trapped inside a feminine space. Mr (Z), 62, had been retired as an ex-steel worker for three years. He reflected on how he had been trying to adapt to his new life at home:

> The only thing I would say, the worst time is from October to March, the short nights, you know, it's dark at 4 o'clock and it, you know. When you've got the summer, you see I've got my huge garden, I'm out in the garden, but sometimes from October to March – that's why I took up the computer courses – it can be a long day if you're not doing things, you know, cause you're content, you know, and you think oh... Watch the blooming telly, So, the worst time is probably October to March, but err, you get by that anyway, you know... Well, it's dark at four o'clock now and, you know, the nights are, you know, you haven't got much daylight, have you, you know. It tends to be colder and miserable and everything. You can't be out in the garden. In the summer you're out in the garden, pottering and digging and err, so, if there is a worst time, it's between October and March, you know, but err... my wife drags me off shopping sometimes and I try to adapt to that but... yes, for the first two years after my retirement my wife found it very, very difficult, because she wasn't used to having me at home all day... Because I used to work shifts, she wasn't used to me around all the time, you know, I'd be in work. So my wife found it really difficult. I used to get on her nerves, right. I used to really get her down. She said, can't you get out or something? I used to really get her down because, like I said, the majority of the time I was always in work.

In addition to this, there was a physical impact with a serious amount of chronic illness, as we have documented.

As we outlined in Chapter 2, the union provided a fund that allowed men to retrain for other work. It encouraged the men to think of their hobbies and outside work interests as the possible basis for new work. This meant that possibilities that had never been considered before were now open to them and the men considered a range of options. In one case, some of these interests involved transforming a personal interest in music, and through the support of the local union, getting help to get further training and support to transform this interest into becoming later an independent guitar maker. Similarly, two had an interest in helping others and some of them became youth community workers, helping young men locally. Others exploited skills retraining opportunities and became managers providing access to further sources of training and support for those unemployed ex-steelworkers who want to retrain.

In other cases, men simply decided to become the main formal carer of their partners and or parents (especially those with partners and parents suffering from chronic and debilitating illnesses). A few others also contemplated at some point the possibility of doing more formal care work, such as work as nursing assistants and/or care workers although in the end none of them followed this work path on the grounds that the pay and work conditions were not good enough.

Overall, among most of the men who actually transformed their working lives, these job changes also involved a varying degree of re-accommodation of the domestic gendered division of labour, especially among those in their mid-30s upwards. Some actually expressed satisfaction in being able to be closer to their small children and be involved in their caring and education. Others mentioned that their partners (who also worked either full or part time) were expecting them to share their domestic chores, like washing, cooking and cleaning. Although they appeared in agreement with these arrangements, some of them found it important to stress their still being the 'breadwinner', something we will revisit in Chapter 8 from the women's perspective. For instance, some men mentioned how it seemed easier for them to emphasise the importance of making a contribution to their share of domestic chores, such as by highlighting how useful it is to have a man who can fix new electric wall sockets, fit new lightbulbs or replace electrical components in a washing machine. In doing this, these men seemed to reprioritise the value of their domestic work by making it clear how their contribution to other domestic chores (e.g. vacuum cleaning) was comparatively secondary to acknowledging how a man is needed in the home to deal with electrical repairs and other technical aspects of home maintenance that seem more manly. However, a large number of men simply took whatever work they could get that would allow them to stay close to their families.

In addition, while some men were able to move on, others were not and joined the ranks of the long-term unemployed and the chronically sick or disabled. Often these men (some of whom were the fathers of some of the young men we worked with) ended up becoming chronically disabled after experiencing a combination of previous work-related accidents and illnesses, so it often became more difficult for them to even contemplate the possibility of relying on their bodies to go back to do hard manual work. As mentioned above, some of them had partners and/or parents who were also suffering from chronic and debilitating conditions, thus making their family situation even more critical. The result was that some of them were on temporary benefits, while others became the main carers of their partners and relatives. Another less common route for those not being able or not wanting to go back to work were those already classed as chronically disabled who were relying on state benefits on a permanent basis.

Elsewhere (Walkerdine and Bansel, 2009), we have shown that the Steeltown workers made moves towards work demanding entrepreneurialism but that these were not accompanied by aspirational talk, as was the case with a group of workers in Sydney, Australia, with whom we compared them. As we will see, the move to neoliberalism was lived in a way that emphasised adaptation to local conditions and giving something back to the community, rather than getting on and getting ahead. We must remember that communalism was absolutely central to the survival of the Steeltown community. Not being better than others was taken for granted, which made the idea of aspiration and individuation an anathema to most men.

Shifting relationalities

For all of those who managed to make a move from steelworker to entrepreneur successfully, the transition involved shifting relationalities. In other words, the men were part of relational networks or matrices (see Chapter 4) that had to shift in order for change to happen and this shifting meant changing relations of time and space as well as gender relations. In Chapter 3, we explored the idea that during the steelworks era, affective practices and relations produced a way of surviving chronic insecurity. This included the ways in which men referred to the central importance of camaraderie. If we think about this in relation to change, we can see that this gave affective resources with which some men could go through the change in situation together, to imagine and share a future together. The collective second skin that was produced, while defending against annihilation, did perhaps allow them to share and contain the difficult work conditions together. However, the male worker's body was the site of considerable violence and aggression done to it in the form of dangerous work, daily harshness and humiliation. Several men reported that the camaraderie was what kept them going when the works was open, but that it required that they contain harshness, humiliation and aggression for each other through the development of the group skin. The toll on the body could be harsh. For example, John told me that he could not say 'no' to demands at work that he was finding difficult. He said that he could not cope with a difficult boss but could not say no to him. He felt that not coping was letting his workmates down and he experienced considerable shame. Because the way of containing the difficulties of the job relied on practices that did not involve talking about difficulties, he felt that he was letting his workmates down and that they would not understand because the shared way of working demanded the endurance to keep going no matter what. This was what was transmitted bodily and in the many ways in which they helped and supported each, made jokes and developed shared affective practices in the works. It was the break in this containment that we see when John has a breakdown. Similarly, we can understand the many instances of heart attacks, stress and chronic and acute illnesses reported as another example of the breakdown of male containment surfacing on and in the body. While many commentators note that de-industrialisation involves a shift from community to family and from public to private, as we saw in Chapter 3, we might actually say that this is incorrect in the cases we are exploring but the relations themselves are reworked. In two of the cases, the worker continues to be heavily involved with the community but in a changed way, though a way that seeks to echo and invoke the former relations.

As I have documented, it is the union that suggested that workers should think about their interests and hobbies as the basis for future jobs. This itself is, of course, a big shift, which blurs boundaries once made very rigid within working-class manual work. However, for those workers who took up the union's suggestion successfully, the shift was experienced less as an aspiration than as a revelation. Two men in their 40s became youth and community workers and both moved from leaving school with no qualifications to pursing a university degree while working to support the young people of their town. As one, Jim, a community worker, formerly a steel worker from the age of 17 to 38, said eloquently: 'I didn't realise there were jobs like this.' This is not an entrepreneurial or aspirational statement. Rather, it signals the opening up of a world of work previously unknown, rather than any sense of wanting or needing to work towards a new or better form of work, or for upward class mobility. This shift happened for one of them because he mentioned the fact that he enjoyed coaching children at rugby and from a first interest in social work, youth and community work was suggested to him.

Urm, there was I think up £3000 per employee, urm, to go in and use the training, basically anything you wanted to do…but people from Careers Wales came in, urm, other agencies came in to try and find out exactly what your skills were, were there transferable skills you could use from inside so as you could use outside, urm, obviously what you wanted to do, urm, through coaching rugby and things like that, urm I sort of knew I had a bit of talent with working with kids and that, so my first choice was either, was teacher or social worker…But the woman said to me, which is another girl that works here, she said have you ever thought of youth work, and I said what does that entail, and she's wrote down a lady's number, she said phone her and make an appointment to go and see her. Found out then that she was the head of the youth service in [the local authority], so I went to see her, started doing a bit of the training, urm, after completing the initial first two sections of the training I enrolled for university, because I knew the money was there and it was only one day a week, so I enrolled for that, started doing a bit of voluntary work in the youth club, urm, two, I think it was, I got accepted for university in the October and started, I managed to get a job with the Prince's Trust, urm, in January, the start of January, urm, and I haven't looked back since then…if somebody had told me like four and a half years ago that I'd be doing this now, managing people, I'd have told them they was bonkers, complete change but, urm, I'm lucky everything has worked out for me. I didn't realise, when I was still at the steel works, I didn't realise there were jobs like this, do you know what I mean?…so I'm, I'm fortunate like that, that I've fallen into something that I really enjoy. Compared to the steel works this isn't like a job.

That last phrase tells us how he understands the new world of work as a revelation in which the rigid boundaries between work and pleasure have been broken down. But what we see is that he had never sought these out. The history of steelwork in the area, often done by father and son for generations, produced class-based modes of relationality in which aspiration may have been frowned on or distanced from. We can glimpse it in terms like 'class traitor' or 'pencil pusher' – terms commonly used by working-class men to describe non-manual workers. These serve to create sets of relations in which difference is othered, keeping the community solid. In this instance, however, othering has been forced onto the ex-steelworker, and he is able to enter a world about which he knew nothing and that does not feel like work.

In terms of shifting relationalities, the youth workers have changed their relation to the wider steel community by undertaking work that supports the now disaffected youth of the community. They feel that their understanding of steelworks masculinity helps them to support these young men and to recognise their problems. But this has changed the youthworkers into 'pencil pushers' and entrepreneurs – they now commonly have to apply for funding to keep their work going, but also undertake work that does not feel like work. We might classically understand such a shift through a discourse of upward mobility, but what seems to be the case here is that the attempt is made to keep the affective relations of the community going by shifting relation to them. In addition, the gender relations at home changed to accommodate the fact that the men no longer earned a family wage and that the wife worked. In Jim's case, his wife argued that he should take his share of domestic work and that if he did not, she would give him a very hard time:

> I don't know my Mrs has always been assertive. I suppose she's better educated than you are about that things should be shared, jobs should be shared and things like that. When I grew up my mother did everything for me. Until I met my wife, who I've been with for 18 years now, I'd never papered a wall, there's loads of things I haven't done. I don't think I could even cook, I don't think... I think as much cooking I'd done was like beans on toast, never cooked anything else it was all done for me. No, my Mrs wouldn't let me get away with that. There's two things I don't do, I don't do... I don't wash clothes and I don't iron, and that's the only things I don't do, because I can't. That's something I realised because I really enjoy cooking it's not like a chore. The majority of the men I know, if they're not working then they do the housework, they do it all even the ones well, even in the steelworks shift, the boys used to clean the house, do the washing and everything before they came into work, but that's only fair see... If your Mrs is working, you've got to share the chores. My 16-year-old daughter's the one I can't get to do anything.

Thus, the relations of time and space within the family shifted as well as those of the wider relations of the town.

Another example was told to us by Jane. Her brother used to be a steelworker, was made redundant and started drinking heavily. He and his wife split up and then he managed to get a very hard job in a carpet factory. Because the work was hard on his back and because he earned half of what he earned in the steelworks, his wife went out to work.

They reorganised the family work relations in order to avoid having to move away from Steeltown for him to find better work, a move they did not want to make, not least because their daughter was about to sit her GCSEs and they did not want her to have to change schools.

> And my brother's a very stable person erm never really see him angry he's very calm and likes to go out for a social drink with his friend but he's started drinking a lot ...
>
> Erm not, not a lot to alarm you but a lot more compared to what he used but his wife was saying you know he's on a couple of cans in the night which he never did really he'd go out on a Friday and Saturday, he was going out on the weekends and getting really drunk and I know he to me he struggled with it a lot just in his self they, him and his wife split up err.
>
> Yes they're back together now but I just think it was the stress.
>
> He was I mean I think he was there when the last coil was run off so that was 2002.
>
> 2002 yes so yes he was there so he would have been.
>
> He's 40 now next month yes so he would have been 36. Erm I think it did have a very big impact he did try and look on the bright side, he didn't have a huge mortgage because erm he bought the house erm 19 years ago and it was a terraced house which needed totally regutting so he just had a loan for the house erm so he did look on it in that way because all his friends had bought these big houses and erm but I just think he, he did lose his self for a bit and he didn't really know what to do. I know that one day he went into work one night and they had to send him home because, because they could smell drink on him erm but he left erm he had his payout he didn't know whether to try and start his own business but he applied for a few jobs he got one very quickly because he could have gone to Port Talbot or erm, err but he wasn't willing to relocate because his daughter's GCSEs were that year as well and she's very bright and erm he didn't want to risk her education so he said no and the one in Port Talbot was 12 hours, 4 days on, 4 days off so he said you know [inaudible] 15 hour days, 4 days at week and he said at what cost you know I'd never see my family really especially if I'm working on a weekend so he decided not to go down there so he did take a job erm down in X Carpets International erm money's nowhere near what he's on so his wife had to get a job as well.
>
> Yes erm the first two months he was in that factory I didn't think he was going to stay because he said it's very hard work I mean I even

see him he couldn't lift his arms up to put his jumper on because his arms were that sore.

Because erm he said he tried to explain the machine is really long you've got a 105 points on this machine and you've got this big coils which you need to put on with a thread for carpets and what have you and they're like between 5 and 10 kilos.

So he couldn't lift it he lost erm he lost about a stone in six weeks and he's only about 12 stone anyway erm so yes he struggled with it for a while but he loves it now you know he's on erm a different shift pattern so he's on more money now and his wife works part time erm their daughters 19 and their other daughters 13, so yes they've come through the worst of it but it was a very big struggle for my family erm and a big change

In this example we see that in order to accommodate the changes brought about by redundancy and diminished pay, it is the relations of the family that have shifted, creating in effect a new relational matrix, with much pain and suffering on the way.

To take another example, John aged 49, the man who had the breakdown discussed earlier, was interested in music and this led him through the encouragement of the union, and by way of the union retraining fund, to train as a guitar maker. This involved weekly flights from Cardiff to Scotland for one year. He set up as a self-employed guitar maker from the living room of his family's small terraced house. This job move was clearly entrepreneurial. As we saw, before he took it, he suffered from depression, which he attributed to poor relations with his boss at work in the steelworks. In his new career, he was doing well and had become a 'minor celebrity' in the town. This shift also resulted in his working at home and thus placed the shifting relations within the family. During his time of transition, John saw a counsellor weekly and wrote a private book just for himself, detailing his life story. Something in that work enabled him to face the future and undertake a successful change, though with no workmates to count on anymore, the burden of support fell to his wife, who, like his workmates, maintained a dignified silence outside the home, telling no one of her husband's depression because it would be a burden to others. We discussed this practice of public silence that allowed troubles and divisions not to be aired, and so cemented a cohesion based on a tough second skin.

His work relations, like those of Jim, also blurred and shifted, challenging the separation of work and home. Having previously worked in a factory and to factory hours, he was working in his living room. This shifted not only his temporal relation to work: he reported working as early as 5 a.m. or as late as midnight if he wanted to:

> ...and it's more relaxed and if I want to, er, if I'm up here at five o'clock in the morning I can make a start and you just do it whenever you feel like doing it. Perhaps I might do it late in the night, perhaps it might be 12 o'clock when I'm doing something but at least I'm here.

But his spatial relation – work and home – were one. More than this, he had taken over the family living room, which meant the family – his wife and two teenage children – were displaced to other rooms. Thus, the shift in family and work relations were profound to the extent of entirely redefining what work meant in his life. If we imagine his work and his family previously as separate yet connected relational matrices or webs, they then shifted dramatically, so that the overlap was more complete but with a dramatic shift in the inhabiting of relational space and the social relations of family in the home. So the shifts were clearly articulated as shifts towards entrepreneurialism that have had dramatic effects on the relationalities through which his subjectivity was produced and performed. Like Jim, the shifts in his working life and work identity were dramatic. He described having been on incapacity benefit after the depression and recognised that he could simply have stayed on benefits: 'If the business wasn't successful, you'd just call it a day, shut the box up and stay on the sick, like. But it's not what I wanted to do. I wanted to work'. He acknowledged a painful past compared with a happy present, but the interview statements present a sense of relief that he had work he liked and a safe and secure financial future, which allowed him to go on foreign holidays to Turkey and to own an investment property with his redundancy money, rather than a sense of striving or aspiration.

> Just gone from strength to strength. So I got...I do private lessons three days a week and a Saturday morning. Erm, and I've got a few days then that I'm in the workshop, you know, I do repairing, I do building, whatever. Er, at the moment I'm doing...building like two guitars that I'm working on at the moment. So since the works have closed, my life has completely turned out, like. For when [Researcher] first came here, well I didn't have no plans or nothing I had. Started, I actually had started doing the guitar training but it was more as an hobby. I didn't think at the time that it was going to turn out into a business, you know, I didn't think it was going to go that way. But,

er, that's the way it's gone and it is, well it's really successful from my point of view and to work from home as well. I pick my own hours, you know.

Yeah, so I know, not this year maybe next year I want to take it to the next stage, I want to take it to schools and colleges and things like that, then. And, erm, maybe do some talks on it, about the construction of the guitar and just tell people how easy it is, you know, they can do it themselves, like, if they really put their mind to it ... 'Cos it's such an unusual job, people are interested in it, like. And, the kids that have come here, you know, for lessons, they tend to ... they do tend to look up to you, like. It's hard to explain in words, like, but it's ... it is like as if you're a celebrity.

John recognised that had he not been depressed and made redundant, he would have been commuting to another steelworks a great distance away, whereas he could work from home and was happy. And it was happiness, not aspiration, that motivated him:

Well (wife) will tell you like we've never been so well off like, we've never been so um not financial, well financially as well yeah, yeah even though we're not, we're not earning as much as I was down the works, it's just that we don't spend so much. You know what I mean, I used to change my car every two years well we're gonna change it this year now but we've had that car for years and years and years. I was due to change it when the works was closing and I thought I ain't and I just kept it you know. Watch what I spend it you know, Sky telly we got rid of that and just things like that you know. So really financially we're better but what it has taught us is that we wasted so much money like. Down the works like I was on £26,000 a year no problem without working any overtime and if I'd gone to Port Talbot I would have been on £30,000 a year well it's good money but I ain't motivated by money like, money doesn't motivate me. Once we've got enough to pay the bills and everything. It's happiness that motivates me in that and I am happy. I am happy.

Indeed he summed up his position clearly: the difference was that he could enjoy life, whereas the alternative faced by generations of steelworkers and their families was a hard life and then death.

But otherwise you know. What's the saying? For some people life is hard and then you die. And that's what it's like sometimes. But that's what I felt for a long time. But um now I've got things to get up for like, things to get up in the morning to do and whether I've got a lesson or play the guitar.

This hard life and then death is what people endured in Steeltown. So, like Jim, John's working life had changed dramatically. We can certainly recognise aspects of neoliberal discourse – the shift to celebrity and the sense of now being someone are all aspects well understood within governmentality theory. His work practices shifted in a clear neoliberal direction, but what we see from the extracts is a relief that the entrepreneurialism had worked, that they had enough money, that he was happy and no longer faced a hard life and then death. These are signs of relief, not aspiration. While it is true that both men displayed enjoyment of their new work, and the positive benefits of neoliberalism, we could understand this shift as formed in complex relations in which the specificity of the history, of the location, of the previous practices of work, of family, of masculinity were all significant. What we also notice is that the central shifting of the family and community relational matrices brought with it a shifted relation of time and space. The wife and children seemed to have lost their living room, the husband's work can happen at any time from 5 a.m. to midnight, according to his needs and wants, and this was a quite enormous shift – a far cry from fixed work hours in the works. In fact, he decided to use the living room of his house (which had a big window facing the street) as the perfect space to display his guitars and his work to people passing by. The living room in his house had a door that separated it physically from the rest of the house and so this arrangement seemed to work for him, in the sense that it provided him with a space with a window facing the street to display his guitars and his work (as opposed to renting an office elsewhere to set up his guitar business). However, this change in his house also meant his family would not be able to use the living room anymore as a living room and therefore John then had to build further rooms upstairs in the house in order to provide his family with additional space. The effect of accommodating these shifts of time and spatial relations on the other members of the household is significant. The relational matrix shifts to accommodate them, but there are also consequences in the ways of relating that can be experienced psychically, affectively and materially.

This presents a much more complex picture than simply saying that the public relations of community have been sacrificed for the private, family relations, but it illustrates how the shifting of relational matrices has, in Studdert's (2006) terms (mentioned in Chapter 3) shifted what he calls the web of relations and what I am calling, after relational psychoanalysis, the relational matrix (see Chapter 4). In Studdert's terms, we are creating new 'whos', but these whos are characterised by shifting material, and psychical and affective relations, as we have seen. If we understand the shifts in this way, we move away from an individualised version of the effects of advanced liberalism to a complex account of the actual energies and relations that make up the mobile and shifting community, in which we do not simply have individuals but whos constantly created and recreated in the relations themselves. This allows us to focus on the relationality itself and not on either the 'social' or the 'individual' as separable domains.

In thinking about these shifting relations, we can present a way of thinking about the transformation of masculinities within their historical context. While we can see that there was certainly a crisis for many of the ex-steelworkers, it was an extension of the kind of crisis they had lived with for many generations. That is not to say, however, as we argued in Chapter 4, that it was not absolutely catastrophic for some men or indeed for the community, while it allowed change and transformation for others. In Chapter 6, we will explore how the difficulties created by the closure were echoed right into the next generation of young men.

6
The Next Generation

Introduction

Marc, an unemployed 18-year-old who left school with no qualifications, told us that he would rather sell his car than pursue any of the
work options open to him, such as food industries or stacking shelves
in the local supermarket. Given that at this time there was no rail
connection (this was opened in 2008) and given that Steeltown is geographically isolated, we began to see how much must be at stake for
Marc. In this chapter we will review what was happening to the young
people who we interviewed and discuss our further study in which we
followed up young unemployed men and their families.[1]

When I sat at my desk, thinking about the enormity of what Marc
was prepared to give up, I began to understand that something hugely
significant was happening for him. That is, he would rather be without
work than stack shelves in the local supermarket. It was this that led us
to think about a second study in which we might try to understand how
feelings could run so high in young men like Marc. In Steeltown and the
surrounding area, there was 33 per cent youth unemployment in 2005
(ONS, 2010). So work, any work, was hard to get and what there was
was mostly in the service sector – particularly supermarket work, and
services such as cleaning and food delivery. I decided to pursue this with
Marc a little more by asking him what it was about stacking shelves in
the supermarket that was so unacceptable and embarrassing. He told me
that he didn't want to be seen by his mates and others in the community
doing this work and especially handling 'feminine' products or working
on the till. He reported that one young man had left the job because
some of his mates had come along and messed up the shelves on which
he had been working. When pressed about whether he would consider

work in a shop selling tools, 'do-it-yourself' items and so forth, he said that he would. It gradually became clear that what was embarrassing was the perceived feminine nature of the work, as we shall see later in this chapter.

At first this sounds like a case of peer pressure, but this begs the question why young men felt the need to police each other and in fact prevent their friends from working. Gradually the enormity of getting rid of the car rather than take the work begins to make more sense. It struck me immediately that this had to have a connection to the loss of heavy industry, as this was the only work that Marc found acceptable, but it was also the kind of work that no longer existed and was therefore impossible to get. I wondered if the unresolved loss of some of the fathers had affected these young men so that they felt they had to embody a hard masculinity that was no longer open to their fathers. However, the truth proved more complex than this. But, with this in mind, we applied for, and obtained, funding to undertake a small study of six unemployed young men and their parents, using three psychosocial interviews per person in which we could gently explore the kinds of issue that might emerge for the young men and their families. This dialogue develops through the use of three one-hour interviews in which the rapport between interviewer and participants is built up over time, allowing the possibility for the development of a sense of safety. This is supplemented by two interviews with the mothers and fathers of the young men, using the same format.[2]

It turned out that the youth and community workers who were ex-steelworkers knew very well that these issues existed – they had felt them themselves and particularly recognised the sense of proper masculine work that we discussed in Chapter 5.

Mike, 42, who was an ex-steelworker who had become a youth community worker specialising in work with young unemployed men locally, reflected on these issues:

> ...the self assessment and inspection done by [local council] took place then, so I've got a copy of the inspection on here which points out exactly what we have been saying about the need for more work with post-16 young men who are not re-entering education or not doing anything basically. They've identified it through the inspection but it had been identified a long time before that.
>
> It isn't really that detailed, no, which is one of the problems once young men leave school, they don't access training, any training, further education or go into employment. They go off the radar

basically. Nobody knows where they are, what they are doing. Especially because you can't claim any benefits between the ages of 16 and 18 as well. We think that's a very important age to be...to make sure they are doing something, but there is no way of tracking them because they haven't got to report, to sign on for any benefits, they're not turning up for training, they're not doing any education. So for two years nobody knows basically where they are.

He told us that these were the young men who had not done well at school, often barely managing to learn to read. In the past, reading was unnecessary and some men told us that their fathers almost had a pride in not reading – reading materials were taken home to the wife. So, these boys, a bit like Paul Willis's (1977) lads several decades earlier, were longing to be men and had followed the path of many generations of men before them who left school with no qualifications. The difference now was that they followed them to the dole queue rather than the works. We saw in Chapter 5 just how a particular kind of embodied masculinity was central to the works and therefore to the survival of the community. These young men, it seemed, longed to inhabit it but could not. No wonder then that the armed forces recruited so heavily in the area. Because they had no qualifications and because, according to the youthworkers, they would do any practical activity so long as it did not involve reading and writing (at which point they left), they could not be helped by any of the education or training initiatives currently being made available.

Of course, this trend is well recognised by initiatives such as the Extra Mile Project from the Department for Children Schools and Families (2008). However, its literature makes clear that its understanding of the problem lies in the lack of aspiration of these young people, who need to be helped to understand that they can do things that they never thought possible, hence the aim to raise their aspirations. As a product of the extension of academic education to working-class children, I would be the first to admit that the opening up of new possibilities is exciting and important for children. However, the problem of aspiration is complex. Unlike our study of workers in Australia, who were full of aspirational discourse (Walkerdine and Bansel, 2009), the Steeltown workers built their community on cooperation. Their continuity was produced through their all acting together to support each other and through industrial workers supporting each other both at the workplace and through collective action. I think it might be fair to say that to aspire might feel for some in these circumstances like a betrayal of solidarity, though, of course, many parents saw the writing on the wall and eventually wanted their children to get an education. The neoliberal discourse of aspiration had no place in the Steeltown before the closure. It is a discourse introduced by a Labour government that had to contend with the rise of finance capital and the decline of industry. To aspire, it suggested, was the only way out and indeed this was made a virtue of as we saw in the work of Giddens, cited in Chapter 2. But as is obvious, these young unemployed men had one aspiration and one only – to get the kind of work that was not available. Of course, we must remember that the available service work paid a fraction of the wages paid by the works. Overall, ex-steelworkers used to earn £22,000–26,000 p.a., but after the closure of the steelworks those who managed to get employment in other fields were earning on average £12,000–15,000 p.a., and who would want that if they had the choice? But I think something else is going on that creates this longing for what is not possible. Rather than see this as a kind of latter-day resistance in Willis's sense, I want to understand its relational complexity. How do these young men come to want so desperately, to the exclusion of everything else, the one thing that is not available?

Intergenerational transmission

In Chapters 3 and 4, we explored the way in which the experience of suffering throughout the 200 years of the works produced forms of relating and organisation, modes of beingness, through which the community survived and developed. When the works finally closed in 2002, this marked a shift, a rupture, in the modes of relating and being that had been passed down generations. Because these were built around the works with the rhythms, times and spaces associated with them, they began to founder when the works closed. Although, as we have seen, some men did indeed make a successful transition through the production of shifting relationalities to produce new whos, some did not. The figures for acute and chronic illnesses associated with the closure in our small study alone reveal that, from the age of 40 onwards, there was an increase in chronic stress and anxiety, psoriasis, arthritis, depression, alcoholism and high blood pressure. We also had one example of a massive heart attack in an ex-steelworker when he was 37. This type of symptomatology and its further psychosocial consequences has also been documented in other studies (e.g. Avery et al., 1998; Ferrie et al., 2002, 2003, 2005; Gallo et al., 2000; Kalil et al., 2010).

The unemployed young men who took part in our interviews were suggested to us by the local youth workers. It turned out that half of them had fathers who had some form of chronic illness or disability, the most common being chronic irreversible work-related physical disabilities, followed by a combination of other chronic stress-related diseases, such as cardiovascular disease and chronic diabetes. This immediately made me feel that the idea that the young men were attempting to act out a masculinity no longer available to the fathers and therefore, in some way, to keep hold of it for their fathers made sense. However, this proved to be a simplistic reading. So in this chapter we will outline how we gradually pieced together a sense of complex relations between fathers and sons and a much broader sense that the entire community was involved in the feelings experienced by the young men.

During many of the interviews in the first study, person after person told us that the people of Steeltown were coping. 'Down but not out' was a common expression. There was little overt hint of a falling-apart or breaking-up. Yet when we arrived in Steeltown to conduct the interviews with the young men and their families, the world appeared much less ordered and more chaotic. It was hard to reach people: they would not turn up for interview, or forgot, or changed their minds at the last moment. The very strong feeling we had was one of a chaotic life in which nothing was stable and all that could be done was to keep going from moment to moment on the tiny money provided by the government. Not only was it difficult sometimes to contact some of the research participants, for example, but once we managed to contact them, sometimes we would hear that they were no longer living with their families, or they told us they were not feeling well enough even to leave home to attend our interviews (because of tension and/or forms of violence at home). At other times, others commented that they were so stressed just trying to get by on a daily basis that they could not see a time when they would feel in the mood or disposition to meet up and talk with us. We had more than one cancellation, but sometimes people did not cancel but simply failed to be at home or to turn up. Similarly, while we were staying in Steeltown week after week, we would hear how some local men died recently and sometimes unconfirmed rumours relating some of these deaths to serious problems of debts and chronic stress. At night we sometimes witnessed vandalism in nearby neighbourhoods, so the whole place seemed more insecure than it had when we conducted the first study, when most people tried to be resolutely upbeat.

This told me something significant about what was happening for these families: the attempts to cope with the situation of chronic poverty and uncertainty – not accompanied by the comforting company of fellow sufferers, that is the solidarities formed in the works era, as we have outlined – were producing the very sense of falling apart (cf. Hopper, 2003b) that characterises the chronic anxiety that we argued the community strove to prevent in earlier times. These people, it seemed, were no longer part of a community that looked after its own poor to prevent them from going to the workhouse but, in true neoliberal fashion, they had become isolated and fragmented, perhaps from those working, perhaps from other families in the same situation. It is difficult to tell. But there is no doubt that these new poor and workless were manifesting the symptoms of extreme annihilation anxiety. In this situation it would not be strange for young men to dream that they might be the strong ones who with their industrial muscle would make everything all right again or indeed for their fathers to imagine that their sons might avenge them. So a reader might wonder why a person would not take any work to avoid the situation, but human beings do not work in this way. The feelings of conflict, of demand to work, of the need for food, of the shame of feminisation, of the embarrassment, the longing and the dreams conflict with each other and conspire to keep people stuck inside a chronic and terrible anxiety. The experience of this is to be unable to act no matter how much one wants to because one's skin, one's boundaries do not feel strong enough and all one can do is to stop oneself from dissolving. This, we suggest, begins to capture the world of the new poor today.

When I arrived at the doors of our participants, I was usually told that the father would not see me and that he didn't want to, or have time to, be involved. At first we thought this a terrible failure on the part of the project, but we gradually began to realise that the refusal was itself data that we needed to read and understand. The mothers and sons told us a great deal about the fathers, but, apart from one, no father could communicate to us the immensity of his feelings. In order to explore the impact of the relations between fathers and sons, we will explore what emerged in some of the interviews.

Let's begin with Marc. If we follow my interview with him closely, we can begin to see more clearly how I try to understand the issues about the refusal of available work. Marc was 17 and lived with his parents (both were unemployed and on benefits). We do not have the parents' point of view because both refused to be interviewed. He was the eldest of two brothers (15 and 10 years old) and two sisters (13 and 1 year old). Marc had one year's experience of work in a paint factory, after which he was made redundant because the company went bankrupt. Ever since he had tried every day to find similar manual work but had been unsuccessful given the limited number of manual jobs available in his community. In the meantime, he had done voluntary community work in a local group aimed at helping young unemployed men feel more confident about themselves and learning to seek help and find jobs. Marc also did basic training (National Vocational Qualification (NVQ) in bricklaying) and would have liked, if only his parents had the means to support him, to try some training in plastering as a way to improve his chances of becoming self-employed.

Interviewer: So what type of work are you interested in finding now?

Marc: Plastering or something. I want to get a job so I have the money to keep my car on the road and like to do some training on the side as well, like go to college and do plastering.

Interviewer: For instance, have you tried like, in McDonalds or Tesco?

Marc: No, I wouldn't want to, I wouldn't like to work in something like that.

Interviewer: Why?

Marc: I don't know it just ain't my thing like. All your friends would come in, it's embarrassing I think. I'd rather go in a factory out the way, they can't see you then can they? I don't mind work and that, I just don't like, somewhere like that. I just ... I just ain't into things like that. My mum was saying why don't you try and get in Tescos and that or Morrisons, I don't know why, I just don't want to work in somewhere like that. It just ain't my thing. I don't like the thought of them seeing me working and that.

Interviewer: Why would you not want them to see you working there, when they are shopping?

Marc: Embarrassing isn't it?

Interviewer: Why?

Marc: I don't know, I just don't like that. I get embarrassed. I ain't into things like that.

Interviewer: So, would you rather prefer to work where you become like more anonymous, more private or what is it?

Marc: Ahh, that's what I mean about being in a public place, and people come in and I just, I don't know, I'd just get embarrassed ... I wouldn't mind going in, like if I worked with my friends in a factory, but I just wouldn't want to work in somewhere open,

like where you just come in, like Morrisons, people go in everyday don't they, or Tescos, like if I worked in Tescos and my friends
would go in, I just don't know I would be embarrassed, wouldn't
want to do something like that. Embarrass me that would... You
know, like seeing my mother's friends walking down the aisle and
I was stacking shelves or something, I'd probably go and hide, I'd
just feel so embarrassed, people see me working and that, I couldn't
do that.

What was salient for me initially was Marc's sudden slight change in
attitude. Instead of looking straight at me, as he had previously, he
now started looking a bit down, and the tone of his voice became
less confident as he was trying to convey and explain to me what he
would feel and do when he imagined himself being recognised in public shelf stacking by local people who knew him, especially his male
peers. His admission that he would probably hide from them also gives
an idea of the intensity of the embarrassment he imagines experiencing
if found doing a job that he felt was not appropriate to his gendered
sense of worth and dignity. I also wondered whether this embarrassment also involved him having a conflicted sense of his masculinity
when he referred worryingly about being constantly policed by his male
peers and him his needing to be prepared to face possible accusations
of having been seen doing a type of work that they might regard as
inappropriate to his sense of masculinity. I then tried to explore to
what extent this embarrassment actually also had to do with an explicit
avoidance of being seen doing 'feminine' work and whether this form
of embarrassment could be experienced differently in different work
contexts:

> *Interviewer:* Ok, so I take it perhaps a job in McDonald's may not
> seem appealing or even appropriate for you but, imagine, if you
> were offered a job to stack DIY stuff and tools, etc., would that be
> embarrassing as well?
> *Marc:* Well no, 'cos if you are in a shop you stack anything don't you.
> All girls' stuff and I don't know, food. Everything, I just wouldn't do
> that but if it was like you said DIY stuff, that's like man's stuff isn't
> it? For men, it wouldn't bother me then.
> *Interviewer:* Oh right. So it has to be like a, like a manly thing for you
> to take it, otherwise it's not interesting? Or is it also because you
> reckon your male friends would start making comments or jokes
> on you?

Marc: Probably, making rumours then don't they. I don't know, saying, they seen me doing this, seen me doing something.

Interviewer: So, do you think it is only you who feels like this or do you reckon perhaps other guys and your male friends would also feel embarrassed?

Marc: Yeah.

Interviewer: So, would you say that this happens more between the boys than the girls?

Marc: Girls don't bother do they, girls don't care do they?

Interviewer: They don't care?

Marc: They're not embarrassed, they'll do anything for money won't they? More like, on a till more for a girl than it is for a boy like, so I don't think a girl would be bothered. A couple of my friends work in Tescos, working on the till who I went to school with. They're not bothered, I talk to them all the time, they're not bothered. I know if it was me I'd get embarrassed couldn't talk and just go out feeling embarrassed.

Interviewer: Aha, so is it mostly a boys' thing?.

Marc: Yep, my friend used to work in Morrisons stacking shelves and like if I went in with my mother or somebody would go and talk to him, but he was only up there two months. He left, he said it was just embarrassing. So he said I ain't looking for a job in a shop anymore.

Interviewer: So you reckon that job for him felt as if he was doing a girls' job?

Marc: Yeah.

Interviewer: All right. For instance, what happens if a boy err, takes a job stacking shelves in a shop, like Tesco what would your friends do to him?

Marc: They'd all tease him then don't they? Say he was stacking, I don't know, stupid stuff, like with my friend, they reckon he was stacking all girls' stuff and that, all bits, all tampons and stuff like that. I couldn't do something like that.

Interviewer: Did your friends make fun of him?

Marc: Yeah, but then he left, he went to a factory. He said it was just doing his head in. So I know if I went in something like that they'd be the same with me like. One day one of my mates he was also working in a shop sorting all the food out, all the crisps and the chocolate and that. All the boys were going round mucking them all up, chucking them all in different ways. He had to go back then and sort them all out. He'd just done all that like. I know I go up there just to tease him. That's what it's I like.

Marc seems to have a strong gendered sense of appropriateness and exclusivity when assessing the type of work that feels more appropriate for himself. While his need to conform to the expectations of his gendered self as a man in the public realm of work may give him some sense of reassurance in his maleness, at the same time, it shows the associated costs of doing this by simply conforming to these expectations. For instance, his relationship to it involves not only insecurity and fear but also submission to the policing of his peer group. Like some teenagers, he seems to be resigned to conform to the pressure of his male peer group in order to avoid being ridiculed in his sense of male self-worth and dignity. In this sense, his refusal to do 'feminine' work seems to be merely a tactical response in order to conform to the expectations of his male peers. However, we were not clear whether the emotions of fear and avoidance being seen also involved a sense of conflictive gendered experience. For instance, if the assumption of being a proper man includes a sense of positive identification with the values of his masculinity, such as the idea that he is supposed to be willing to conform and to sustain a type of public persona that rejects everything that is associated with feminine attributes, then the feelings of fear of being constantly policed by his peer group suggest that this form of gendered identity may not be just assumed unproblematically. While this is expressed in general terms as plain embarrassment, it also shows how his sense of manliness is thoroughly implicated. This is also reflected in his reservations and his fears when he remembers how some of his friends have been ridiculed and bullied in the past by their local male peers when found doing service work. His reflections also contrast in part with previous research on the avoidance of 'Mac jobs' and service work (Lloyd, 1999; Mac Dowell, 2003) by young men where the main reason given is that they refuse such work primarily because it is low paid, short term and with no career prospects. This does not mean these considerations are not equally relevant to Marc but rather that the key motivations and reasons he gives for his refusal to engage in service work primarily involve his performing a proper gendered sense of self and dignity, while pay and career prospects seem to be less central in his reasoning and in his decisions.

We also wondered to what extent what seemed to us to involve a rather rigid observance of clear male gendered boundaries and cultural male gendered conformity in his relation to both jobseeking, and his male peers could perhaps be experienced quite differently from his own perspective. For us, his gendered conformity suggested that it also involved a sort of limiting conflict gendered experience of his sense of maleness, in that he felt it was not possible to think or act differently from his peers, but he was expected to conform and submit to these expectations in order to avoid being ridiculed and bullied, facing accusations of not being manly enough. This fits the issues of staying close together and the development of affective containment that we outlined in earlier chapters. However, we can understand only too well the central place of that conformity in maintaining the community matrix and therefore in a sense of survival. I also wondered not only whether the embarrassment Marc felt and his refusal to do 'feminine' work were also the result of a personal conviction but to what extent he would be able to think in a different way if he were apart from the influence of his male peer group?

> *Interviewer:* If you were asked to deal with customers in public, for example, when they ask you about something in the shop that they want to buy, etc., would that be embarrassing?
> *Marc:* No I wouldn't mind that. Like if I went like say to Cardiff to work in a shop that wouldn't bother me then 'cos I know there's people down there who don't even know me and it wouldn't even bother me at all. But if I'm working in a shop like round here or somewhere nearby, I know there would be people coming in there that I know, I know nearly everyone, I just wouldn't like that. It would just embarrass me I think. I couldn't work in a shop, having like friends and that walking in and shopping and whatever seeing me stacking shelves or something or on the till, I just couldn't do something like that. I'd just be embarrassed. I don't know, I'd go and hide probably if I see them coming. I'd get so embarrassed. I just don't like working like somewhere where all your friends are going to come in or your friends parents or family or anything, its just embarrassing.

Marc's anxious refusal to do shop work now seemed to be less problematic, at a conscious level at least, provided his male peer group were not aware of him doing this type of job locally. Interestingly, he seemed to have internalised the expectations of his peer group in a way that did not suggest he was inherently personally convinced and emotionally invested in the systematic need to refuse anything 'feminine' for the sake of it. Instead he seemed to manage to stand up to his male peers by making sure they would never see him doing shop work and hence saving his male dignity in front of them. Likewise, the fact that he shared with us (in the private space of the interview) that he would also be prepared to hide from his local male peers in embarrassment or even to eventually accept working in a shop shelf-stacking outside his community also suggests that perhaps a part of him could see that shop work might not be so problematic in itself, and that he could even try doing that type of job should economic need become even more critical by imagining himself safely doing that type of job outside his community. His further reflections on this also suggested that perhaps his own relationship with the 'feminine' might not be that fixed or stem from a particularly oppositional personal conviction but rather the result of him conforming to the expectations of his peer group and his local male culture. However, I still wondered why while a part of him seemed to be aware of the limiting effects of his conformist relationship with his male peer group, at the same time he had not found a way to secure a job outside his community and what prevented him from trying this.

Marc clearly explained to us that he would not have any problems stacking shelves in a 'DIY' shop and how, by contrast, he would be completely not just embarrassed but also very afraid of being seen by other males stacking shelves in a supermarket, especially handling feminine products, and that his strongest fears revolved around the idea of being bullied by his mates if he was seen doing this kind of work. It therefore became clear to us that his fears and embarrassment were directly connected with the perceived feminine nature of doing particular jobs (e.g. stacking shelves in a supermarket or working on the till), which were locally seen as done mostly by women.

> *Interviewer:* What, are you planning to do if you don't find work here? Have you thought of some other option; for example, doing shop work n Cardiff? Are your parents able to support you while you manage to find a suitable job?
>
> *Marc:* I don't know. I haven't got a clue. Just keep looking for a job. Factory work or something like that. Just keep looking and hoping for the best. I don't know if I'll find one like, whether one is going to pop up one day like. Just keep looking 'til I find something . . . I was also tempted to go in the army. But I wouldn't like to really because I need to stay around here, get a job to help my family like. So that's I guess why I want to stay round here really. If I couldn't find a job, I was just going to go in the army, but I don't want to go knowing like my mother or father were going to need me one day and I ain't here. So I'd like to stay round here and get a job. Round here, so

I get married and I'm happy. If they need me then, they only got to phone me then haven't they, at least I can go home then if I need to.

Interviewer: What do your mum and father do?

Marc: They're unemployed.

Interviewer: Both?

Marc: My father's disabled, he fell out of a lorry and hurt his back. He had to have two discs out of his back so he's disabled and my mum had to look after the kids, 'cos my little sister, she's only two and he can't do much like to look after a baby. So my mum has to look after the kids and my father's well, like a cripple basically, yeah. He can do a bit, move about and that but, yeah, capable of playing with the baby like. So she's watching the kids while I try to look for a job.

Interviewer: Has your mum worked before your father's *accident*?

Marc: Yeah, yeah.

Interviewer: Doing what?

Marc: Hairdressing.

Interviewer: So if it's not the army, in the longer term, what else would you like to be doing when you become an adult person?

Marc: I don't know. Like if I get a job now, hopefully just do that job as long as I can like. Like 'til I get laid off and look for another job like, but when I do get a job, I'd like to try and go self-employed doing something.

Interviewer: Try to do something like what?

Marc: Go self-employed. Go to college and do a trade, while I'm working, so I'm earning money, so I can keep my car on the road and do that at the same time. That's what I'm hoping to do. If I get certificates for plastering, I can go self-employed then can't I? Become a labourer and do it that way like.

Interviewer: So in the future, you would be already prepared to switch from one job to the other?

Marc: Yeah, yeah. I wouldn't mind that as long as I get another job. Yes, get laid off and go to another one.

Interviewer: Do you come here often to help [community youthworkers] and the community work with boys?

Marc: I do, they call it, youth club volunteer work. If [community youthworker] needs help and that he just phones me and if I ain't doing anything like, if I'm around, I'll go and help him. I also look after kids. I just play pool with them all. Have a game of football and that, table tennis and like if someone's naughty then I just say you either behave or you're going to have to go and if they're naughty again them I chuck them out.

Interviewer: How long have you been doing this?

Marc: About a year. Been with [community youthworker] back and forth. When I had that job, I could only see him on my four days off.

Marc's assessment of his potential study and job options also showed his gradual awareness that even if he would still prefer salaried manual work, this might be difficult, and hence he also contemplated going back to college and getting his plastering credentials in order to become a self-employed plasterer. Thus from the point of view of his changing masculinity, this also suggested that he was not resorting to simply becoming an unemployed young man depending on benefits, like both his parents, but that he would still be able to explore other ways of earning a satisfactory living for himself. However, he did not quite answer my question about why he had not tried doing shop work outside his community. Similarly, when he spoke about not trying the army because his parents might need him, it suggested that looking after his parents might also prevent him from trying to do shop work outside his community and that he had to take a great deal of responsibility towards his parents, who were themselves struggling and had nothing left to help him. His desire to stay around the area, look after them and get married and settle down was to be a man, to take the masculine bread-winning role as the provider – exactly what his own father could not do for him. He was the one who fantasised looking after them because they were terribly stretched, and so he was left alone with his conflicted feelings about how to be a man. The way the family dynamic worked might have given him a sense of duty and a commitment to remain locally bound and available to help his parents within the relative safety of his community. Similarly, I wondered to what extent seeing his father coping with permanent disability also influenced his relationship with him. For instance, he did not need to idealise his father as a breadwinner because he was not able to fulfil that role. Instead, being the oldest son, he might have felt that perhaps he had to become like his own father for himself while also being a more solid or reliable presence at home in order to support both his parents and his younger brothers and sisters. Thus, I wondered to what extent a form of intergenerational repetition and transmission was at work in relation to the complex feelings expressed. Likewise, it is also important to consider the relative impact on Marc of doing voluntary community work to help young unemployed men as well as the male influence of his male community worker. The local youthworkers set up this scheme precisely to provide support and indeed a sense that because they had shifted from being steelworkers, the young men too could face the possibility of change.

On a second interview, I was also interested in sharing with Marc my impressions of his own views about 'feminine' work as well as seeing if he would agree or not with mine, and whether his views on 'feminine' work remained as firm as in our initial interview. I also tried to explore the extent to which he would allow himself to consider other wider context situations I was asking him to reflect on, such as how young women seemed to be finding some jobs more easily than men and whether he was aware of the magnitude of the changes in the labour market and what these might mean for him as a man.

> *Interviewer:* Last time you were saying that if needed, you would also consider getting a job stacking shelves in a shop but only if the job was outside your community so that you could avoid being seen doing this, but have you actually tried this?
>
> *Marc:* No, I just ain't going to do something like stacking shelves.
>
> *Interviewer:* But is it still because you think that it's a women's job.
>
> *Marc:* Yep, it's embarrassing innit.
>
> *Interviewer:* Uuh.
>
> *Marc:* It's embarrassing doing stuff like that.
>
> *Interviewer:* Is it?
>
> *Marc:* So let the people who wanna do it innit do it.
>
> *Interviewer:* Yeah.
>
> *Marc:* Laugh...Someone who wanna go stack shelves can go and apply for the job innit. I ain't stacking shelves I ain't doing stuff like that and that's the end of it.
>
> *Interviewer:* Yeah, it seems as if women now are finding a bit more options to get jobs even many of these are short-time contracts or part-time posts compared to men, so I was just trying to understand why some young men, for instance, wouldn't bother trying these jobs.
>
> *Marc:* Well fat chance innit. Would you stack shelves?
>
> *Interviewer:* Yeah.
>
> *Marc:* Would you?
>
> *Interviewer:* Yeah, I mean if I needed the money, of course.
>
> *Marc:* Well I wouldn't, even if I have to sell my car. I mean if that's what you wanna do it innit, something like that, one day man.
>
> *Interviewer:* I was wondering if you are aware that the manufacturing industries are almost disappearing, and that will mean that people will need to rethink the type of work they want to do their and

their priorities, so um umm things are changing, the way of making business is changing also so it seems as if people need to be more flexible more open to different job options. So how does that feel, are you aware of that?

Marc: I'll think about that later after I've done this health and safety thing.

It was interesting to see how Marc was clear in confirming his refusal and embarrassment at the possibility of doing shop work because it is a 'feminine' job and not appropriate for him. However, while he still remained firm about his decision to avoid doing 'feminine' work, he was, at least for the moment, able to also consider that there could be other ways of thinking about what is at stake when considering job prospects. In this sense, when he told me that he would think later about what we mentioned in relation to the changes in the labour market, it also leaves open the question of whether either Marc found my comments too abstract and hence he could not elaborate further on this, or he would perhaps be able to imagine that his sense of proper manliness and dignity would not be so threatened should he allow himself to try doing 'feminine work' (either temporarily or for a longer period) outside his community because in this way he would avoid being seen and ridiculed by his male peers. Similarly, Marc's interest in engaging in a training scheme (health and safety in the forest), which incorporates drawing on a rather gender-neutral side of the training (health and safety), suggests that his reflections do not primarily involve his resorting to a melancholic response as Kenway et al. (2006) suggest (Jimenez and Walkerdine, 2011). In any case, his reflections and work-training plans did not completely exclude the possibility that Marc might still be sensing a form of compromise formation or conflict between the paternal values on work and maleness and his own growing sense of who he was as a young man and what he was prepared to reconsider after his own work and growing-up experiences as a young man. However, Marc's reflections also suggested that while he was able to contemplate doing 'feminine' work, he also needed to sustain a sense of proper maleness appropriate in the context of his local male culture and one that could not be easily threatened through exposure to women and the world of 'feminised' work. In this sense, his way of approaching jobseeking and his unemployment situation did not simply involve melancholia, and while he still seemed to prioritise almost defensively the preservation of his sense of manliness by avoiding doing work that might suggest he was not manly enough, this did not mean that he was irresolutely stuck in the past and/or that he could not mobilise his thinking in relation to work and maleness in order to imagine other viable work scenarios that he could try. In this sense, Marc's reflections were consistent with previous research on men doing service work (Henson and Krasas, 2001). This situation would then suggest that on the one hand Marc was also very able to think on his own terms and realise that he could actually do 'feminine' work outside his community, provided he was not seen by his local young peers. In this sense his reservations in relation to his male peers (avoiding being seen by them doing 'feminised' work) suggested that while there certainly might be forms of melancholic masculinity in the ex-steel community we studied, I do not think this means that melancholic masculinity had become the only cultural norm for all the men in this community. While I did not interview Marc's father or mother, it did not seem to me that Marc's partial refusal to engage in 'feminine' work already reflected an intergenerational repetition of a process whereby Marc might be refusing to rewound his already wounded and humiliated incapacitated father by adopting a rigid and immobile masculinity. In that case, what made Marc so embarrassed? The literature on embarrassment links it to shame (Agamben, 2002; Leys, 2009). He was embarrassed, it would seem, because he was ashamed of being seen performing femininity in the town. To understand this, we have to think about the history of masculinity in the town as we have explored in Chapter 5. How is shame circulating in the community? Does it have its counterpoint in the pride of hard masculinity which so characterised the works era? How is shame carried in the relationalities of the town? And does this pride defend and protect the workers against anxieties about annihilation, about not being able to support their families and therefore for the community to survive? Would it be far-fetched to imagine that the terror of not being strong enough in a context in which harsh working and living conditions were the norm, in which the workhouse was an ever-present threat, was passed down through the generations?

Using the matrix

If we refer back to Foulkes's work on the matrix, which we introduced in Chapter 4, we can understand the matrix as the place in which affective communication and practices that attempt to shore up 'the great chain of being' (see Chapter 4) and contain anxieties about annihilation, exist. The matrix operates according to a complex dynamic, producing patterns and resonances (small histories) and different responses to catastrophe (large histories).

Taking this example further, we can look at the classic study of anxiety in a hospital by Isabel Menzies Lythe (1960), who explored the ways in which nursing staff in a hospital were engaging in patient management practices that, although working at one level, were also causing rapid turnover in the nursing staff. What she began to understand was that the very routinised practices minimised friendly contact with patients, and she proposed that these practices were ways of defending against anxiety about patient suffering and death. The staff had to face this suffering every day and this produced a feeling of overload that touched their own anxieties about death. Thus, she argued, the very predictable routine of the practices contained a defence against very basic anxieties about death. Here the matrix is the pattern of communication and practices among the nursing staff, and the group defences they built unconsciously into their practices defended against unspoken and possibly unthought anxieties about death. She checked this out with the staff in a series of meetings, and this understanding was formulated. If we think about the steelworks in this way, we can see the way in which it is feasible to argue that embodied practices of hard masculinity could be formed as a defence against annihilation anxiety. When I use the word 'defence', in no way do I wish to imply that there is something pathological or wrong about what the workers did. Rather, I want to suggest that because the threats were very real for these workers, they had to find ways to cope and to survive. We could call them coping strategies, but to my mind this is a very rational way of thinking. By calling them defensive, I am signalling that they contain embodied affective processes that do not necessarily work in conscious rational ways. While the nurses in Menzies Lythe's study could see that their routines and practices contained this anxiety, they had not been aware of it, precisely because the practices had helped to keep the feelings of anxiety away. That was their function and so while, of course, the routines and practices of the steelworkers helped them to cope, I am proposing that at the same time they helped keep at bay the ever-present anxiety inherent in the precarious existence that the steelworkers led. As we saw in Chapter 1, this precariousness lasted the entire time during which the steelworks was open: 200 years. If we think about it in this way, it is the relations of time and space, the routines, practices and ways of relating, the ways of holding the body, of experiencing the body covered in dirt or the tired muscles, which we have discussed in previous chapters, which contain and transmit the affect. It is these that provide the ways of being a man across generations and therefore forever pass on the same defences against the terrible anxieties of annihilation. Indeed, Deleuze (1994) argues that all organisms are made of repetition and division and that every combination makes a partial self. This means that every moment is experienced as what he calls a multitude of small perceptions, which are experienced at the same time in a sensorimotor bodily way and as a recollection of that moment, so that each moment is at the same time perception and recollection. We could think of the experience of bodily dirt in this way. It is experienced as a bodily sensation in the moment but it recalls other moments, and in recalling them it enters a realm of fantasy and mythology, as we might think of dirt-covered workers going to the pub after work and enjoying a pint together after their tiring dirty work, in a way that recollects the dirt but also transforms it, ritualises it, celebrates it, but is itself a universe of its own small perceptions. So, every encounter is thousands of small perceptions, intensities, dreams, hallucinations and projections. That is why I am suggesting that hard masculinity is not so much to be conceived as an ideology, if that means the imposition of a discourse that obscures the reality of things, but as a sensual experience, both actual embodied and virtual, in fantasy, which creates and joins in a matrix-like form or what Arendt (Studdert, 2006) calls a web of relations. I am further suggesting that these sensory and fantasy aspects are transported across generations by their inclusion in those very experiences and that these experiences contain within them ways of warding off, or defending against, the threat of annihilation because of the constant historical living with fear in the era of the works.

While it is therefore relatively easy to understand how this is passed down through generations and indeed how the sense of pride in the ability to withstand this, to be tough enough, develops into what analysts would call a reaction formation, we now have to think about how the absence of the practices through which pride can be experienced and remembered leads to Marc's shame. We reach again the question of how shame circulates within the town in the way that pride had once done and how this shows up and relates to Marc's shame at his inability to find work he considers masculine. If the embodied experience of masculinity contains within it the anxiety of annihilation, then not being able to 'join the men' must contain a very high level of anxiety indeed. In fact, if my thinking is correct, it contains the very anxiety that the hard workers could not express but that was nevertheless conveyed in the multitude of small perceptions, that is, the threat of dissolving, disappearing, of spilling out and not existing (Bick, 1968). So, we can begin to see that this is very frightening. Nevertheless, the exigencies of the need to find work are also very demanding and while we no longer have the workhouse, the regime for the unemployed is extremely harsh. So, in Avery Gordon's (2008) terms, a ghostly presence of steelwork is still perceptible for Marc and others.[3] It is important to state that the process I am describing is not about roles. The idea of a role comes from the sense of imitation and identification in socialisation. It is understood as a normative process. What I am trying to describe here is different in that conformity arises from a shared attempt to engage with real material threats and dangers that produce catastrophic anxiety and therefore must be defended against. The resulting norm is an attempt to cope with this and patterns of relating are built around it. That it becomes normative is a testament to the anxiety that provokes it – we must remain like this or disaster will strike again. I am not saying that this is a consciously expressed sentiment, but I am proposing that it is affectively passed around the community and down the generations. The strong men then provide a comfort for all that they can be protected, are safe and secure. In this sense, the strong masculine body of the steelworker was absolutely central to the fantasies and practices through which the safety of the community was sustained. The loss of the works therefore is experienced not only as a loss of work and income but as a loss of the men, of real men, of a strong masculinity. This double blow makes the whole situation feel doubly catastrophic. Indeed, it is the closure that allows us to see, because it brings to the surface the central role played by the male body of the steelworker, so obvious in its absence. This is why so many men and women, young and old, as we shall see, presented this loss as a loss of real men, as a shift to femininity and homosexuality. It is this absence that allows them to express as a gendered issue how the new forms of work are so hard for them and present an overwhelming and almost unbearable loss.

In Chapter 7, by reference to the second study of unemployed young men, I want to show how the young men lived with the contradictions of shame and the need to find work, and how these are experienced not only by the young men themselves but also in relation to their fathers and others in the community.

7
Women, Gays and Mammy's Boys

Fathers and sons

In the next phase of our work, we interviewed a further small group of six young unemployed men and their families. Our first idea, as we started earlier, was that because some older men had understandably great difficulty in accepting that manufacturing work had really gone, some young men, who had themselves not experienced this work, might feel conflicted about the lost industrial masculinity of their fathers and in some ways might be trying to protect that masculinity or embody what their fathers could no longer do. Issues around this work did turn out to be at the heart of conflicts between fathers and sons, as we will show, but they did not end there, so we will also discuss how others in the community were just as important in keeping this sense of masculinity alive for the young men.

What we gradually learned from our interviews was that fathers and sons were experiencing considerable conflict and distress over the sons' taking up of service work. As we have already noted, although we found it relatively easy to interview the young men and their mothers, only one out of the six fathers was willing to talk. The mothers and sons told us clearly what the issues were for the dads who did not feel able to talk, and this caused distress for the sons, who, of course, cared deeply about their fathers', mothers', brothers' and sisters' opinions of them. It is in this complex mixture of the relational matrix of the family that we find how the losses of the fathers get tangled up with the hopes and sense of future of the sons. Tony, 24, was already a father of three children and had neither school nor work credentials. He told me about his difficult experiences with his stepfather when he took on a pizza delivery and a cleaning job:

> I was once a delivery driver for Dominos Pizza. I don't know whether you seen the uniform you got to wear cream trousers, a red t-shirt, a baseball cap, a bum bag and things like that and he [his stepfather] found that, well embarrassing. Urm you have to wear the full outfit you had a Dominos Pizza belt, and everything . . . If I was out doing a delivery, and he spotted me, he would purposely make out he didn't see me like, not be seen talking to me basically because of what I was wearing and what I was doing like . . . I then offered my brothers a lift home in the car and they all refused to get in the car with me and said, you look like an idiot basically, you know, what the hell are you wearing? You look a fool looking like that, and that was the attitude they had, they wouldn't get a lift home with me like, because of what I had to wear . . . They used to laugh all the time and they never once went to the shop as long as I worked there. I don't know whether it was embarrassment or what they never showed their face at the shop, never once. Everybody, not just my father and my brothers but my mother too, they all used to laugh when I would go up in what I had to wear, that uniform, and my friends also used to laugh at me . . . My mother did say to me once, you know they are all taking the mickey out of your stepfather because of what you are doing, so basically get a proper job, my mother was basically saying . . . If I went to his house, like he'd go, you know, he'd go to the pub or something, you know he would go out to the pub every time I went there for a couple of weeks, as if he was physically embarrassed about, you know, too embarrassed to talk to his own son like or to be seen with me, and then I had to quit that job, and once I did that then he was back to normal, you know he'd stay and he would talk to me again and he'd say like come to the pub with us.

This painful story struck me forcibly. In Tony's way of telling the story, all of his family ganged up on him to ridicule and embarrass him about the work and the uniform. So what he felt that he experienced was their shame at his work and his appearance, so much so that they would go out of their way not to be seen with him. Shunned, it seems by the whole family, he gave up the work. However, the kinds of job that the family appears to want him to get are no longer available, so we are left to wonder if they would actually have preferred him to be unemployed, a situation that he was trying to avoid in order to support his own young family. It seems as though he was caught in a pincer movement, but the pressure must have felt intense to give up the job rather than have the work, poorly paid as it doubtless was.

But in the next extract we see that Tony fared no better in another job he tried, working as a contract cleaner.

> Yeah, once I was working as a cleaner on the factory floor and you know I had to walk past with a bin or perhaps a mop and bucket and you know they [female colleagues] would start talking to each other and laughing at me and things like that like, you know. Yeah, it was quite embarrassing for a boy; you know to be laughed at by a bunch of girls.
>
> *Interviewer:* So can you remember, what did you say to those girls? How did you handle that?
>
> *Tony:* Well you know, I asked them what was so funny like and they were saying Mrs Mop and things like that and calling me names and you know, so well like I say basically round here it is classed as a woman's job being a cleaner and things like that, they class it strictly as a woman's job. There is lot of boys as myself that wouldn't apply for that kind of job again, and I know a lot of friends who wouldn't even think about applying for that kind of job, but at the end of the day it was all that was going on, and I had to bring in money for my family and I took it, but you know, three weeks I stuck it out for and I couldn't take no more. I was going home and feeling depressed you know because people were laughing at me and aggravating me all day for eight hours.

We begin to see how Tony felt that there was nowhere to turn because he was not only shunned by his family but also by women cleaners to whom he was not related. We can begin to understand that the feelings of shame projected onto the young men were not simply confined to the family but were circulating around the community. Nor were they confined to men – Tony's mother and female workmates also joined in the ridicule. It is important to understand what was happening in the town that this shame was projected onto young men who had to bear the brunt of it and thus were placed in a kind of catch-22, where they needed work but were ridiculed for taking the work that they could get. We can understand the women's reactions as the result of the resonance that the young man doing cleaning had for them and therefore their own reaction to it, as we discussed in Chapter 6. Later on in the interview, Tony recalled other similar incidents that some of his male friends had to face while working on the checkout in their local supermarket:

> I've got friends and if they see a boy working on the checkout in the local supermarket they kind of like call him all the sort of things, call him names and bully him. Like call him a woman and things like that and say you are doing a woman's job, you know. It is not a mans work it is a woman's job like, that is the way they see that kind of job, a woman's job like. They bully them and aggravate them. I know people who have and they tend to call them like gay and things like that you know and to some people it hurts being called that like. You know they call them a gay and mammy's boy working on the till and you know, there are a lot of things that they do say and a lot of it is using bad language like and not so polite words.

We begin to understand the ferocity with which the shaming emerged. If it was so ferocious, psychoanalysis tells us, there was a very large affective and energetic charge. In other words, there was a great deal going on, circulating toxically around the town. In order to understand this circulation within what we could call the community matrix, we will explore further the issues raised by Tony, including issues of femininity and heterosexuality, as well as thinking about the intergenerational transmission of trauma. However, first of all, let us try to understand what Tony's struggles with his stepfather tell us about the difficulty faced by young men like Tony in breaking free from the shame and bringing about a change for themselves and others.

I was struggling in the interview to understand why Tony didn't stand up to his father, family and others, given that he had his own family. So, I asked why he still needed the approval of his stepfather when deciding what job to take. He replied:

> I think it's because like I've always been his, like his closest son, really to be honest. I'm closer to him than the rest of my brothers and that's why he's sort of like picking on me to then follow him in his footsteps sort of thing and learn a trade like he has, and become a businessman in that kind of way but, like I said yesterday, I'm not sure if that's what I want to do at the moment. I would rather make my own decisions, do what I want to do, not what others and my parents want me to do. I think instead of being against what I want to do, they should support me really in what I want to do.

So it seems that the ridicule may have been designed to force Tony to follow a path that his stepfather felt was not only more manly but with better prospects, but, perhaps it was because I asked a question that implied that he needed to stand up to his stepdad that he told me that he wants wanted to find his own way, but he also tries tried to understand his particular treatment of him as a sign of specialness, closeness and love, rather than rejection. Thus, what seemed to be troubling Tony was the realisation that, although he could be critical of his stepfather, at the same time, he could not, at this moment, avoid being isolated from his parental family and by implication being isolated and ridiculed as an improper man or a loser by his local peers. Therefore he still felt frustrated and resigned to conforming to his stepfather's views in order to avoid feeling rejected by him and his family. In this way, Tony's conflicted situation seemed to be reinforced by the realisation that, on the one hand, he needed his stepfather emotionally but at the same time he was slowly realising that his stepfather made his emotional support conditional on Tony's conformity to his expectations. So, Tony was caught in a pincer movement, one typical for young people, in which he wished to follow his own path but was pushed and pulled by different parental expectations. This in itself marks a shift for young men like Tony in Steeltown, who would previously have gone to the works and where there may have been no question of their trying to do something different. But clearly here the conflict was extremely hard for Tony to bear, perhaps not least because it was not only his stepfather shaming him but his entire family and other members of the community. This is an experience, so we hear, that is very familiar for young men, who indeed reinforce it by ganging up on anyone who dares to do service work.

We cannot hear about Tony's situation from either his mother or stepfather, so let us turn to another father: Andy, the only one who allowed us to interview him, to hear about his own dilemmas with respect to his children. Andy was 46 years old, married with two teenage children and had been chronically unemployed (for 16 years). He left school at 15 with no qualifications, worked for a couple of years as a car valet/driver in a garage but left this job and took temporary work in the local council doing various jobs like fencing, bricklaying and roadwork for four years until he was laid off. Soon afterwards he met the woman who was to become his wife. She was later diagnosed with diabetes and arthritis and, unable to work, she registered as chronically disabled. Since Andy could no longer get work, he became her main carer. This meant that both he and his wife had been on benefits for nine years. He had a 17-year-old son, Peter, who left school at 16 with no qualifications, who was looking for work locally but was unable to get a job because he had no work experience other than a two-month training placement in a local supermarket.

He told me about his last job 16 years ago and how he thought he got to where he was at that point in his life and the implications of his chronic unemployment on his children:

> My father was in the steelworks and he was made redundant in '77, just after my mother died. He had to finish then because we was little, and there was no one else to look after us. So, they made him redundant because he had to look after us because we was all children at the time... And he always said to us the steelworks, was a job for life.
>
> I started off with a government training scheme and they took me on full time. And then the council wanted the youngsters again below us, they took them on and paid them less. They was paying them £19.50 a week, and rather than pay me a tidy wage, they'd rather take youngsters on... That's how it was and as I said, I haven't done a lot since. I've had one or two factory jobs, which I didn't like, well, they was twelve-hour shifts, you know, the night shifts and god knows what, and it just weren't for me like. I didn't like the council policy and I just came out and, in a way, I did regret it, because I didn't get back into full-time employment... I got to be honest with you, it's about 16 years I've been unemployed and I haven't done a lot since because, well, there is not a lot out here anyway. I just think I'm 46 now, and I think to myself, um, I got no hope, you know what I mean. Like my boy, he's 16, he's out of school already. He's also struggling to find work. What hope have I got, you know what I mean?... My partner, she's claiming disability allowance. She's diabetic and she suffers with arthritis. So, I'm down as a carer for her.

This difficult story tells us that Andy found it hard to stick to the only work he was offered, hard factory work on the night shift, and indeed resigned himself to long-term unemployment and caring for his wife, who was a diabetic and on benefits. This kind of story of chronic unemployment and ill-health is, of course, not atypical of people living in communities such as these, but we can begin to see a pattern of inter-generational link, with his own father having been made redundant at a previously difficult time for the works and when there were already poor prospects for young men. It is possible then that Andy's own father's experiences and losses may have impacted badly on him. It is difficult to take up opportunities that are offered if, fundamentally, you do not feel safe, as we have explored previously. Perhaps his feelings of hopelessness for his own working future, combined with his wary good wishes for his son, showed some of the ways in which he has coped with unemployment and the associated shame and his family. In this context, I started to wonder to what extent the shame and despair over not being able to return to full employment and provide enough for his family could get unconsciously projected into his own son, so I asked him to reflect on this.

> I wouldn't say that it has had an effect on the children, like my son Peter and my daughter have had no problems, because they grew up with it [his unemployment], but I know in the past I have provided for them... I hope I can continue, you know what I mean, in the future, but as I said, my son now he is doing his best to try and find tidy employment, and we stand by him in anything that he wants to do, anything whatever he decides we stand by him, and I will provide for him as long as my eyes are open, I will continue to do it.

As we have seen, both in the case of Tony and his stepfather and also in the case of Andy and his son Peter, the ways in which fathers transmit to their sons their own difficult feelings of loss, pain and shame about the lack of manly manufacturing work get enmeshed in a complex context of disappointment, lack of hope, despair and grief. This then gets rationalised and projected onto their sons as the need of fathers to make sure their sons will not be subject to the same difficult experiences that their own fathers have were subjected to after the succession of redundancies over many decades in the community. Furthermore, the ways in which their sons assimilate and think about their fathers' projected feelings of despair are also connected in complex affective ways with their own needs to see in their fathers some kind of idealised strong supportive image that would also serve to consolidate their own masculinity and would make them feel safe. In this context, it can be difficult for sons to disentangle the extent to which their own difficult struggles in trying to find jobs and their avoidance of service work belongs to them or is a combined effect of the relationship with their fathers' own difficult past and the associated expectations and values in relation to massive unemployment in their community. For example, would Peter feel bad if he had got work where his father failed? In this sense, the reflections of Peter, 17, further illustrate these complex father–son dynamics:

I wouldn't do women's jobs, and I don't think they'd [his parents] like me to do that either. Some men don't mind being on the till, but me, in particular, didn't like doing that because I felt it was for women... although I'd manage to do that sort of work for short periods, just so I can get some cash to help with my daily expenses.

So, we see that, like many other young men in his situation, Peter refuses the available work. Other young men also thought that obtaining jobs that are socially considered manly (e.g. the armed forces, manufacturing work) was important to their sense of self-worth when seeking work (Lindsay and McQuaid, 2004). We might wonder what aspects of service work the young men see specifically as feminine and why. When I asked Alan, 17, about this, he replied:

That's a good question. I don't know. But, you wouldn't see, well, you mostly see women doing that job in [a local supermarket], now, in't it? It's just like, oh, I can't think of the word now... uhm, o yeah like a stereotype... So, when someone says, like look at that shelf stacker, you stereotype someone and you think, oh, yeah, he's going to be like a gay person, kind of thing... Until you see them and, it's totally different if you talk to them. They might be really, really tough or hard and it's how people think at the end of the day.

Alan's reflections show he has some implicit grasp of the notion that what people consider feminine or masculine is, to a considerable extent, the product of social conventions and that the process of stereotyping allows the incorporation of aspects deemed as ideal for men (often a sense of assertive confident, stoic non-vulnerability, combined with unconscious normative splitting of any other aspects of male identity that culture deems as inappropriate for men); for example, a temporal straightforward repudiation of and distancing from aspects that are associated with femininity (Layton, 2002). This is also illustrated in Peter's reflections that he would not mind doing service work as it would give him some income that he urgently needed. Although, as we have seen, these feelings and experiences were common not only for young men but across generations, and not only in the family but across the community, one or two families did reveal other aspects that are worth considering.

Mx, 17, was prevented from attending interviews for possible jobs because he had to look after his younger sister, while his mother took his disabled father to a hospital appointment. They were too poor to find a sitter. Max gave account of one day in his life and how sometimes he could not quite do all he would have wanted/planned to try to find a job:

> There was jobs going in (a factory in a nearby town). A friend got a job there, and there were still some vacancies, so that day he got his job but I could not go cause my mother had to make an appointment to take my father to the hospital. She'd book it on one of those days and I'd just get up and look after the baby for them to go to the hospital or whatever until she comes back. Then the next day I'd go out myself straight over there but there was no jobs anymore, which was gutting like ... and we just stayed in the house then, I just play with her [his little sister], just keep her happy. I'd look after her, I don't look after her all the time, but if she needs me to I will. I don't, that don't bother me. Like if families go to hospitals for like tests or anything, I will always help out.

In a previous generation, as we have seen, a neighbour would have been on hand to help, but this situation has clearly broken down. In addition, of course, hospital appointments can be moved, but people with no sense of their own entitlement and power do not necessarily know this, or perhaps they have no phone to change the appointment. In any event, it all gets too complicated and confused, and it breaks down. Everyone is so stressed that no one is able to help. This entanglement itself deserves to be understood.

Of course, we also need to consider that what we are depicting here as a rather chaotic situation between this young man and his parents from our perspective might be for them the most obvious and logical way to sort out the priorities of the day (e.g. to take the disabled father to his hospital appointment) and, in this sense, a possible job for Max might not be one of the top priorities in this particular scenario, though this way of understanding and arranging their priorities had an unfortunate outcome for Max, as he lost an opportunity to try to find work.

The only family that appeared to offer a different view is that of Aylwin. His mother was studying for her GCSEs and so was very encouraging of her son to do the same.

Anna, 36, had just recently separated from her partner and was also working and studying for her GCSEs. She reflected on how she had managed to cope with these changes and challenges in her life and how she had also encouraged her son to do his best at school and in his involvement with local community projects:

...there were times then I got to the stage that I was feeling down, and obviously I did think, yes, I thought, oh, there's no end to this. And then when I did move away from everything, and I sat and I thought about it, obviously I went and spoke then, I did go and see a doctor, my own consultant doctor, just to explain how I was feeling. And like it was good to talk to somebody else, but then obviously I had help off the doctor, because I wasn't sleeping, because obviously there was a lot of stress thinking, oh, how am I going to manage, which everyone does, you know, if you lose one step of life. And then, of course, I confided in my parents then, and I explained everything to them, and I just got on with it. I did what I had to because of my children, there was nobody else was going to help my children, it was my responsibility, I'm the one who brought them into this world, so I thought, well, they need me to be strong enough to support them on what they've done, and this is how I think I've got on in my life like I have, and also how my children have got on. And obviously I hope that it carries on with my youngest one, you know, like I said to you yesterday, there's a lot of families out there who are not so fortunate, you know, I've had good parents, I've got a lot of good friends, you know, I haven't been left on my own, so I've had to learn to support myself and my children, but you do it just to, the way of life, you've got to, you know, you couldn't be closer, didn't dwell on it, didn't dwell, but it don't go away, and if you sort, you face the problems.

And obviously when I spoke to my own family, obviously I had a lot of their support, because they realised that, yes, I had gone into a, as we call it, as a rut, they knew my circumstances had changed, and they said, well we'll help you as long as you need us to help you. But I thought, no, I've got to do it for myself. Yes, it's great to know that they're there, and I need something I can pick up the phone, but I thought if I don't stand on my own two feet, I'll never be able to survive, because I'd be always relying on somebody. And I thought, no, you've got to learn for yourself, you've got to provide for yourself, sit down and think, write everything down. And that's what I done, I wrote things down, what outgoings did I have, what did I need to have, and that's how I worked everything out with my circumstances.

He was happy [her son Alex] because he knew I was happier, and Alex is very mature for a young boy, he had to be then I think, because he seen things that went on through the relationship, and yes, it did have an impact on my children, because every child sees it, you know, they hear things, and I did think how it would affect them, but as it was, it turned out Alex to be a stronger person as he is today for being like what he's seen and he's had to, well he helped me along then, you know, because we are the type of family that we can sit and talk. I've never hid anything from them, I've always been open with them...And I made that decision, which made me stronger, and it made the children stronger, because they supported me then through it all, you know, if you understand what I'm saying. It was, yes mum, we agree with you, we will support you, and they have, they've stood by me through all we've gone through, they've been right by the side of me. And Alex has grown up to be a very, very mature young boy, well a young man as I should say.

Anna had managed to set an example for her son, which was important for him. She told us that he had just been given an award for garden work of which she and he were justly proud.

Women, gays and mammy's boys

To explore the circulation of the intergenerational aspects of the transmission of hard masculinity, we want to turn to the point made by Tony about the way young men who undertook feminine and embarrassing work could be understood as women, gays or mammy's boys. In order to understand this, we will explore the production of masculinity as distance from the feminine as well as Judith Butler's heterosexual matrix.

What are these terms doing, and how do we understand their circulation in this context? All the terms are other to heterosexual masculinity and all demonstrate an anxiety with proximity to the feminine or feminised. This suggests that what has been hailed as a 'crisis in masculinity' (Edley and Wetherell, 1999; Hearn, 1999; Kimmel, 1987; MacInness, 1998; McDowell, 2000; Payne, 1985) possibly presents this crisis in too realist a way. That is, it presents masculinity as a possession of an anatomical male, whose masculine identity has been threatened by changes in work, as we argued in Chapter 6. However, what we begin to see here is that the problem is not a problem with the masculine per se but a problem with the feminine. Or, indeed, we could argue that all problems of the masculine are indeed problems associated with proximity to the feminine (Walkerdine, 2007). These three terms appear to articulate the problem as concerning too much proximity to, or not enough distance from, the feminine. This suggests to us that the problem is not the work per se but the proximity to the feminine that it represents, which must be repudiated at all costs. In the days of the steelworks, the feminine was kept in a domestic space, from which men were distanced by their working lives, but to which they could always come home. We might suggest then that for boys, the problems of separation from the mother[1] are paramount and in the steelworks the young man was wrenched from the feminine space in order to develop a hard-edged masculinity that was protected enough to withstand the rigours of hard, heavy, manual work. In other words, in order to withstand the rigours of heavy and dangerous work, it was necessary to become 'hard'. This hardness meant an attempt to keep at bay all aspects of softness and dependency, which might impede their withstanding of the harsh conditions. 'Mammy's boys' are, of course, boys who are close to their mothers. If repudiation of the feminine was necessary and the pushing away of all that might be considered close to it, in order to survive, then all signs of weakness had to be kept at bay. What we are proposing therefore is that alongside the material conditions there were sets of bodily dispositions, manly practices, ways of organising, modes of affective relations and unconscious defence, all designed, as we explored with Menzies Lythe's nurses, to maintain a situation that was extremely difficult, but that had to be maintained in order to bear the work. As we have explored before, at the heart of this matrix is anxiety – anxiety about the feminine mixed with anxiety about survival. Since mothers are central to the raising of children and to the nurturing of dependent beings within our culture, these two anxieties come together. As we saw in Chapter 3, Bick and Anzieu's ideas about survival and annihilation anxiety can be related to early experience. In this instance, we are attempting to understand a set of historically produced practices and defences that become normative in a historical context in which their appearance is necessary to the feeling of the possibility of survival and that can ultimately lead to the production of pride in the hardness sustained, which we can find in demands for increased productivity as well as successful union, political militancy and resistance. We do not wish to undermine these very important victories or resistances, nor to pathologies or to psychologise them. However, we feel that it is necessary to understand the difficulties and anxieties that relate to the coping with difficult (or perhaps we should say almost impossible) work conditions for 200 years, that is the experience of exploitation, in order to understand just what the young men were telling us.

The young men graphically showed us enormous anxiety circulating within the community about breaching the defences of distance from the feminine. The new work context available to them demanded much greater proximity to the feminine, with its notions of service (and indeed low pay) in a historical context in which the shift away from a macho masculinity was presented as normative. Of course, this form of masculinity had indeed oppressed women for many centuries, but it is our view that nothing is helped by its pathologisation or dehistoricisation. What is needed is to understand it. It is a form of masculinity that is itself historically specific. If this hypothesis makes sense, the problem for these young men was not only that they could not find work, in any simple sense, but also that they were caught in an emotional turmoil, in which they were literally caught between the projections of others and their own anxieties. The projections of others are plain to see in the examples we have given of the forceful attempt to stop young men taking this embarrassing and shaming work. To explore this, we suggest, we have to understand it having an enormous energetic charge. We have explained this by use of the idea of the place of the feminine in producing anxiety about dependency, built so strongly into practices that even when the reason for the practices in the form of the works are gone, it is the affective charge, the 'unthought known' (Bollas, 1987), that has become the community's holding pattern, its matrix, which, like Menzies Lythe's study of hospital wards, remains and circulates. If this is a projection onto the young men, it hits home. They were a vulnerable target, at the cusp of adulthood – struggling to break free of the family. What we need to understand therefore is about the transmission of these anxieties to the next generation. This has been described in clinical terms as the intergenerational transmission of trauma (Chapter 4).

We suggest then that it is not the young men who were ashamed but that they were made to keep the place of shame, a place passed down through the attempts of the previous generation to hang onto work and masculinity, through various setbacks, redundancies, closures and its effect on their sons.

It is clear from the history that we have recounted that the closure represented the latest in a long line of work and family-related suffering, which had its own complex affective impact. As we mentioned earlier, women were seen as the emotional bedrock of the community. We have argued elsewhere (Walkerdine, 2010) that the place of women provided for many a sense of ontological security and safety, assuring the sense of the possibility of continuity of being and a defence against fears of annihilation that may have been endemic in a community beset with dangerous work in poor conditions.

We have also noted that Tony brought together women and mammy's boys with gays. Thus, the issue of homosexuality as too close to the feminine or insufficiently heterosexually masculine was raised. This was also seen when Tony mentioned that it hurts to be called gay and that he was well aware that many men dread and avoid becoming the target of such hurtful, shaming name-calling, because the content of the bullying reflected an apparent unmanliness that further disqualified them in relation to other men. In other words, in order for those epithets to be effective in their ridiculing function, those who received them, gender had to resonate and to circulate within the matrix and to provide particular resonances for these young men. Dynamically, this was achieved through relational repetition compulsive responses, enacted as name-calling and bullying, all of which carried the unconscious traces of the gendered conflicts they shared as heterosexual men. In this sense, the fear of 'feminisation' in the workplace also appeared to centre on the idea that by working in physical proximity to female colleagues there would be a point at which they would become demasculinised and stop being men and therefore become something else (i.e. a woman or a gay man). This fear of feminisation because of working in female-concentrated occupations might also seem unlikely and disproportionate, given the current research evidence showing how most men entering into feminine occupations very often resignify in masculine terms the work they do in order to further preserve their privileges as men and to maintain a hierarchical position vis-à-vis female work colleagues (Cross and Bagilhole, 2002; Hall et al., 2007; Lupton, 2006; Nordberg, 2002). However, this demonstrates a very real fear for these young men of being swamped by the feminine to such an extent as to be terrified that they will no longer be men.

This issue is further taken up by Judith Butler, who also uses the concept of the matrix to define what she terms the heterosexual matrix (Butler, 1990). Freud's (1917) paper 'Mourning and Melancholia' was an attempt to understand ways of dealing with and understanding the effects of loss and war neurosis. Within it he proposed the idea that unresolved grief was caused by the survivor's internalised image of the deceased becoming fused with that of the survivor, and then the survivor shifting unacceptable anger towards the deceased onto a new complex self-image. Butler (1997) re-reads Freud's paper in order to produce an understanding of heterosexual gender development as melancholy. She has argued that gender identification is founded on, and is the expression of, forsaking the same-sex object choice (e.g. parents of the same sex as the first love object). Some of the implications of this mean that such a closing-off interrupts our inherent bisexuality such that identification with heterosexuality expresses but one aspect of our sexuality. What is lost or repressed through the early formation of a heterosexual identification is the loss of possibilities, the loss of what could have been. To Butler, this process represents a loss of possibilities that is generally unacknowledged in culture. She also suggests that heterosexual culture creates a dichotomy between male and female, and between masculinity and femininity, dictating that what one can 'be' and what one can 'have' are different (Jay, 2007). Thus, a boy ought to desire the feminine and be the masculine; for him, gender identity rests on the foreclosure of desiring men. Because early childhood homosexual attachments in heterosexual boys are never quite realised, they are never quite lost. Thus, Butler's rereading of Freud's notion of melancholia as heterosexual gender also resonated with our data, although in a different way. It could be argued that for the young men, these fears, reservations and the shaming and bullying that they produced also constantly indirectly highlighted the presence of conscious gendered conflicts that, in turn, created an unconscious tie with homosexuality because the increased proximity to the feminine compromised and questioned their whole sexual orientation. As we have outlined, collectively shared but unavailable to be acknowledged, gendered conflicts cannot easily be mourned or resolved, thus creating an unconscious tie between heterosexuality and melancholy. It is in this context that Butler (1997) has reckoned that heterosexuality is a melancholic compromise and gender is a symptom of this melancholy.

But what are the implications of all these revisions for our understanding of melancholic, shaming and other gendered elements in men's responses to the loss of heavy manufacturing work, unemployment and the ways in which they shape gendered attitudes to other forms of work?

The loss of manufacturing work is by definition always a very conscious and often shared event that leads to a sense of traumatic collective loss. This type of loss then can be relatively more easily mourned and dealt with (hence reducing the likelihood of developing melancholic responses) because it is collective and the collective remembering and rituals associated with the sharing of this type of loss (e.g. public rituals, collective mourning and the work of trade unions) alongside the sharing of experiences of massive collective unemployment allows for other ways of coping with this type of loss that does not directly conflict the sense of being in a gendered way. Some of the associated effects of collectively sharing the loss of their main employer meant that these men had to think and respond in very pragmatic and immediate ways, by first prioritising their economic survival and hence focusing their coping efforts on dealing with the aftermath of the redundancies. This need to survive in an economic sense means that these men could not even afford to remain melancholic for as long a time as others (Jimenez and Walkerdine, 2011 Kenway et al., 2006) have suggested, because this would also have entailed having further material losses (e.g. their means of survival and their homes). This meant that their usual gendered conflicts, although still dynamically present, had to be put to one side in order to first deal with the most pressing issues resulting from the redundancies. Indeed, our interviews show how while some men went initially for melancholic longings as an initial desperate attempt to preserve some sense of continuity with their working past, eventually, through the process of remembering and retelling their experiences as steelworkers, they started seeing opportunities to evoke other moments of contradiction, unease, disappointment, lack of solidarity and hope, alongside depictions of the ruthless and exploitive managerial practices that used to keep them subservient and not sufficiently valued as steelworkers. This is one example from our first study, involving Huw, 54:

> The thing was while I was still working non stop I did not realise I was getting ill and the big problem I had is that I couldn't say no to my colleagues demanding my attention and help all the time...Then when I wasn't working because of the depression, I stopped everything...I felt that I wasn't entitled to go out and enjoy myself. That was a big factor to me being ill because I was losing my mother as well...and I nursed her for ten hours a day until she died. And then on top of that the steelworks were closing it just, it just finished me off you know it just finished me off...It was very difficult also thinking that people would not understand or respect what was happening with me because I did not have a broken arm or leg and yet I was completely unable to work.

Thus it was in the process of trying to retell those memories that some of these men became more aware of the various meanings and effects that being a steelworker had had on their former identities. Later on, some of these men also started articulating in their narrative a sense of frustration but also relief that those difficult times had gone and that now they were in a position to reconsider and move on, and start facing the realities and challenges of the emerging ascendance of other forms of work. However, those reflective moments also signalled that these men were no longer in a melancholic state, since they were able to retrace and resignify the content and meanings of their memories of their past work with a more critical sense of the inner experiences that their identities as steelworkers were supposed to characterise. This is another example from our first study, involving Lloyd, 49.

> I went through difficult times, self-inflicting ... I don't even have any pity, you know, the works closing wasn't my fault but, I'm not stupid, if things are not earning a profit, or if it's not based in a suitable place, I understand that these things happen. It upset a lot of families initially, and many had to go out of the area, but overall most of them, the steelworkers, have actually got jobs. Those who want jobs have actually got jobs, and me personally, this [youth community worker] is the job which I've always dreamed of. Since I was ill, if ever there was a job for me ... if ever there was something that I was good at, it would be interacting with people, communication skills, helping people, that sort of thing. I would say that I was good at it in my life. I always had respect for old people and young people, and ... so for me personally, even though I went through three years of dark times, times which if you had a crystal ball you could say would be worthwhile in the end, but obviously you can't see that. But to me personally, everything what happened to me has made my life a lot better.

As we have seen, the sharing of traumatic loss allowed Huw and Lloyd to eventually mourn their loss and move on, and reorganise themselves and re-train and find other ways of making a living while also revisiting their ways of being male. However, as we also mentioned, other men found it very difficult to deal with their losses and hence were more prone to resort to other related forms of coping; for example, projecting their frustrations and gendered conflicts onto others – often their own sons and others in their communities. Thus we can see shame, embarrassment and such as a way of maintaining what had gone, a kind of melancholic remembering, which involved a strong repudiation of homosexuality. However, as we have also seen, Huw and Lloyd were able to move on to other forms of relating.

The silence of fathers

During this research, only one father was willing to speak to us. We heard a great deal about fathers from mothers and sons, but virtually nothing from fathers themselves. So not only did fathers appear to feel terrible shame and distress in relation to their sons, but they were unwilling or unable to talk about it. Rather than seeing this as a problem for the study, we decided to take it as data, to attempt to understand what the silence might be saying. Half of the fathers were either disabled or long-term unemployed. These were men themselves unable to embody the hard masculinity they sought for their sons. Let us speculate about their feelings about their inability to embody the masculinity that ensures the continuity of the community, its survival. While the mother at home typified the emotional bedrock, the father at work in the steelworks supplied the other aspect of the possibility of continuity, as we explored in Chapter 6. The men brought pride, surviving and taking pride in dangerous work in harsh conditions. Coping with exploitation, with strong union collective action for better conditions, they fought hard for many generations. This is the source of the pride – good hard work, collective struggle, fight. This kept the community alive. We can suggest that the shame experienced by these men and projected onto the younger ones was the other and opposite to the pride. Could it be that allowing in the 'feminine man' would be to admit a final and painful defeat – the defeat of the fathers who could finally not keep the juggernaut of globalisation at bay, the fathers for whom collective action and resistance finally failed and was impotent. This brings back the reality of power, poverty and servility: silly uniforms that have to be kept clean rather than the proud clothes of a steelworker. If pride has collapsed, is shame like a cancer eating at the community, tearing at its heart? If this is right, the gender and sexual fantasies that were there at the inception of the steelworks were no less present at its demise.

Social catastrophe and trauma

We saw earlier that when we began the second study we were confronted by a feeling of a completely other community. Here in the world of the unemployed, things were haphazard, people didn't keep appointments, they were understandably obsessed by getting from day to day on hardly any money and, lacking the routines of a working life, they had found other more haphazard rhythms (Henriques, 2010 to sustain them, such as getting up late, hanging around with no fixed return times, turning off phones or not topping them up and so forth. So, while one half of the town, it seemed, had found ways of coping with the changes, the other had not. In order to understand this, we want to explore the literature on the intergenerational transmission of social suffering and trauma. In Chapter 4, we reviewed the large literature on social trauma. I want to draw attention to Earl Hopper's work on the effects of trauma on groups, which we introduced in that chapter. Hopper argues that trauma activates and provokes the fear of annihilation, which can be experienced as a psychic paralysis. This can be experienced in a group as attempting to keep this terrifying anxiety at bay by either clinging together or breaking apart.

We can perhaps see this in the scapegoating of the young unemployed men. There was an attempt to cast them out – the father's friends who would not talk to Tony, the father who refused to go to the pub with his son, the cleaners who called the young man Mrs Mop. It is as though all will be safe if this intruding element is not allowed in. The circle will not be broken. But, in addition to this principle that Hopper draws from experience in group processes (Hopper, 2003b), we also need to understand how the organisation of gender and sexuality are played out. Problems of proximity to and distance from the feminine are painful in these examples: the women cleaners who suggest that the young man is a woman (Mrs Mop) and thus cannot be the object of female desire, the father and his friends who refuse to let the young man into the homosocial space of the pub, the father who implies that his son has let him down.

'Get on with it and don't show your emotions in public' is the advice of one woman in her 60s to her sons. Grief should be contained privately within the family. This affective practice no doubt served to aid community cohesion and to stop difficult and dangerous emotions from circulating. However, this strategy, well adapted to survival of crises and difficulties during the time of the steelworks, may not work so well now. Then, just coping and getting on with things allowed the community to continue, for the safety to be maintained even in the most difficult circumstances, and it produced a community of 'survivors' who would not be defeated but would battle on. This demonstrates how a classic humanist attempt to get townspeople to talk about things may not work at all, indeed may be resisted at all costs, as threatening annihilation. This issue poses a serious concern for work with young people and traumatised communities.

So, using Hopper's concept of trauma, we can see how this might apply in Steeltown, but we have not yet explored the intergenerational transmission sufficiently. We have argued that patterns of defence are built into everyday practices, that keep at bay an anxiety that then comes to the fore, supplemented by attempts to push out that which threatens the collective space. But much of the clinical literature focuses on the historical transmission of trauma across generations. Research on intergenerational transmission of trauma began with work on children of holocaust survivors and continued in relation to difficulties and pain suffered by children and grandchildren of those who have been caught up in war or genocide (Danieli, 1998). Trauma in these analyses is usually considered to be the result of defensive responses to the original event passed down through generations by means of attachments, family systems, modes of socialisation and so on. They are understood as affecting physiological responses, such as anxiety, through increased cortisol production (Yehuda et al., 1998), patterns of individual development, producing vulnerability to stress (Bar-On et al., 1998; Denham, 2008; Kellerman, 2001; Luthar et al., 2000). There is also literature on resilience and rituals employed to commemorate (Hollan, 2004; Kidron, 2004) and move on from historical trauma or unresolved historical grief (Yellow Horse Brave Heart, 2003; Yellow Horse Brave Heart and DeBruyn, 1998). In this sense, resilience is understood as the achievement of positive adaptation despite major assaults on the developmental process after exposure to severe adversity or significant threat (Luthar et al., 2000). Although there is some reference to patterns of family relating using Bateson's concept of social ecology (Bateson, 1972), there is little attention to complex historical antecedents to a traumatic incident, nor to how previous ways of relating and practices have to shift after the event, nor indeed to community and family processes in general. A rather medical model is used to chart individual patterns of development, except in those cases looking at the development of ritualised practices (Kidron, 2004).

What I want to think about here is the ways in which, as we have seen, modes of relating and affective practices already coped with historical contingency before the closure of the works. We might conceptualise some relational shifts outlined in Chapter 5 as adaptive or resilient in that the shifts in the relational matrix allow other possibilities to emerge. However, in other circumstances, what we might call adaptive mechanisms adapt around the site of pain, like scar tissue grows around the site of a wound, healing but leaving a weakness. We could argue that so-called resilient practices can be like this. They can allow the silenced event, the unspeakable or incommunicable experience, to be communicated as 'unthought knowns', that which is experienced in the body and is known but is not consciously known in a way that can be talked about. Thus modes of relating in families may mean that a father who has not worked, who follows his own father in not working and sees his own son not work, swallows feelings of rage, shame, humiliation, unmanliness, which at the same time he tries to avoid passing on to his children, but which all the time is present in fits of rage, depression,

drinking, which then become part of the affective relations and practices of the family. I was struck by the fact that half of the six families
had a parent or parents who were themselves chronically ill or chronically unemployed. In the instance of Andy, he was unemployed and
became the carer for his diabetic wife. Thus, with little money coming
in, the father's effort was focused on the wife, whose diabetes may itself
have become worse in response to the stress of the husband's redundancy and lack of work. The son may have felt unable to call on parents
who were ill or barely coping, and struggled alone with difficulties and
decisions about growing up. I think that this is why the town appeared
so divided to us, with some residents presenting a town that was 'like
a phoenix rising from the ashes' and others a town so weighed down
by chaos as to be falling apart. This corresponds exactly with Hopper's
designation cited earlier as two different ways that groups can deal with
catastrophic anxiety.

I want to turn now to a body of work that, while psychoanalytic, is
quite different from most studies of the intergenerational transmission
of trauma. *History Beyond Trauma* (2004) is the work of two Lacanian-
trained analysts, Davoine and Gaudilliere, who also work as social
scientists in Paris. What sets their study apart is their absolute insistence
that they are interested not in developmental processes but in history.

> *History Beyond Trauma* is not a book about the individual's develop-
> mental or psychodynamic history prior to trauma or breakdown. It is
> about the history of families on the other side of – lying beyond –
> the societal trauma that has devastated them and about forces within
> their social structure invested in cutting that history out of the sanc-
> tioned social narrative. It is about the actual social history, crucial to
> the patient's emergence from madness, to be discovered, perhaps to
> be formed for the first time as something one can truly think, from
> the encounter with the remnants of trauma carried forward by the
> patient. (p. xii)

What characterises most clinical work on trauma is the typical psychoanalytic gaze that wanders no further than individual development and
parental relations, but what they are interested in is the way in which
psychosis can operate as 'a frantic effort to bring a foreclosed social connection into existence' (p. xi). We have discussed this earlier in terms of
the way in which they think of the social link as the central aspect of a
microhistory that conveys and connects, forming the social. If the social
link is broken, a fear that we heard eloquently articulated by Martha in

Chapter 4, then a connection cannot be maintained and the link across generations is lost. Davoine and Gaudilliere's interest is in war and how psychosis might be understood as the silenced and unspeakable aspect of a historical experience transmitted across generations that is recognisable in the symptoms presented by the psychotic, who is acting a part in a historical drama that they do not know. They use the term 'cut-out unconscious' to describe a process of something split off, cut off or cut out that has to be brought back into history:

> Regaining a foothold in history, obviously, is not reducible to adaptation to social conformity. It involves the inscription of a dissociate truth, an 'unthought known' (Bollas, 1987), known through impressions that have been split off (retranchees, literally, 'cut-off'), and the awakening of a subject of history (having nothing to with his desubjectivized homonym of historical materialism). This is even the condition of the emergence of the subject of desire. (p. 47)

They describe the work with this cut-out unconscious as (as their reference to Bollas suggests) work that does not operate with repressed experience of war so much as embodied, known by the body but unable to be brought to thought. Just because it cannot be thought does not mean that it is not transmitted. It can be enacted, just as we have described above. Obviously, they are talking about an extreme case: psychosis, at its cutting out of history. But the lesson we want to show here is the centrality of history for understanding that which might be transmitted down generations even if it cannot be spoken. We suggest that the young men and their families and fellow townspeople were trying to communicate something of great importance to each other and to us. Davoine and Gaudilliere turn to theatrical practices to help them and their patients understand the drama enacted through the microsocialities in which the historical trauma is conveyed, such as that in which the women cleaners designate the young man 'Mrs Mop'. I want to mention two forms of theatre that form part of their very rich practice. Japanese 'Noh' theatre is an archaic and highly ritualised form in which characters cross bridges peopled by humble servants who are there to mark a historical event that has been suppressed or forgotten. The traveller meets them in crossing the bridge, a bridge between life and death, and in his dreams he sees characters or ghosts returning from that history. It is not so much that the analysts enact the theatre but that they use this as a way of thinking with patients about dramatic revelations that occur when something forgotten is remembered, and that this forgotten thing enables the subject to be placed in the history that was cut off from them. Similarly, they draw inspiration from the theatre of cruelty of Antonin Artaud. Artaud was able to propose a model of theatre that engaged with experience beyond language – using, cries, grunts and bodily experiences to convey affective experience directly and understanding visions as the horrifying double that appears in what we might now call hallucinations. This experience is what Davoine and Gaudilliere call, following Lacan, the Real, and what can be understood as described by many object relations analysts such as Bick (see Chapter 3) as a prelinguistic experience – the experience of a body that cannot represent what it experiences; thus, the unthought known. For Artaud, this form of theatre is truer to basic affective experience, and it forms the basis of much of Deleuze's work on death as a creative force (De Bolle, 2010). Davoine (2007) uses Artaud's work in a brilliant and graphical way in describing work with a patient in which an aspect of herself becomes the double and the foil that reveals the historical nature of the trauma that could never be let go of or spoken about. The young woman in question comes to see Davoine for analysis, describing herself as living among the living dead. She did not know who the ghosts were with whom she was surrounded. It transpired that her mother had been deported for her part in the French Resistance and she learnt as a child that her mother 'would not be coming back'. Thus, in effect, she had never been informed of her death. Yet Davoine had a dream that she barely noticed at the time, but which in the fullness of time she interpreted as referring to the time in which her mother, while heavily pregnant with her, had been captured by the Nazis while attempting to deliver letters across the demarcation line for the Resistance. This is Davoine's resonance with the patient's story. It is this that she takes to be Artaud's double. A double, he says, has a long memory. For Davoine, this allowed her to get closer to the experience that could not be reached by the young woman.

Later in the analysis, the atmosphere became torpid and no words seemed to be able to come. Davoine took this as a sign of working at a level at which the 'unthought known' cannot convey an experience held in the bodily memory and cannot be symbolised. The young woman is hospitalised after another psychotic episode but leaves the hospital to attend a session with Davoine at which she unleashes her fury. She describes the scene as one of pure cruelty in Artaud's sense: very violent in which the character (or event in Artaud's terms) was a very old Jewish woman full of rage and inspiring terror. She says:

> This character was in fact more like a puppet than a character seen in all its complexity. It was performing on the utmost limits of the human and the inhuman to bring to light not a character, whom I immediately identified as her mother who had returned from Auschwitz, but (and Artaud insists on this) an 'event' (p. 151). An event beyond the boundaries of that which is human, grasped in the cruelty that those who escape never wish to evoke again. (p. 635)

In this scenario, the analyst became Hitler, Mengele, who had tortured and experimented on her and made her experience suffering that should never have been aroused. She managed to tell her 'that I was there, beneath the carnival masks of Hitler and Mengele, so that she, or rather her mother through her, could emerge from her unsullied role of heroine and express her hatred at having been betrayed' (p. 636). It indeed transpired that her mother had been transported because she was Jewish and not because she was a member of the Resistance. Thus, suggests Davoine, theatre can be understood in the analytic context as, in Artaud's words, 'a therapy of the soul, a crisis, resulting either in death or cure' (p. 637).

Thus the historical experience that exists beyond the trauma is revealed, which allows it to be recognised and made visible in order that time may be restarted and the patient can become part of a family and wider social history that can be known, recognised and passed on, so that what follows can be understood as having its place within, and result from, that history. This insistence on the centrality of history is very important to me because it refuses to separate 'psychopathology' or 'development' or 'relationships' from the material circumstances – large histories – in which their complex small histories are produced and have meaning. It removes from the stage notions that large and small historical events produce pathology because it refuses to operate with a concept of a norm. In my view, historical events and processes are what we all live in and through, and that to count only some experience as normal and the rest pathological denies the fact that all experience is part of history – it is merely that some has come to stand for normativity, pathologising the rest. If we understand how we are produced in and by history, the issue is not whether the result is normal or pathological but on what the effectivities of particular contingencies may be, and this is not at all to deny that they may be painful, produce suffering, be harmful, be hurtful, be destructive, be life-threatening and so forth. But it is not to separate any of those processes from the complex histories that gave birth to them.

Thus, we have been at pains to argue that the suffering of the young unemployed men is a drama played out in the annals of history, in which steelworkers, housewives, cleaners, fathers, mothers, Mrs Mops, Dominos Pizza uniforms, supermarket white coats, worker donkey jackets, tired bodies and dirty faces, mammy's boys, gays and women all have their part to play in the historical drama that the community unfolds as all these players at one time or other enter the stage. It is what these players are communicating to us, are trying make us hear about the history of which they are a part, that we need to pay attention to. To understand the specific suffering of these young men, we have to understand what they are being asked to carry for history, what they are being asked to present, to hand to us so that we can no longer ignore it, as they cannot, to stop it passing unnoticed to the next generation. We have to understand what they are trying to hold onto, to make us remember, so that it can never be forgotten.

8
What about the Women?

In 1984 the journalist Bea Campbell, in her book, *Wigan Pier Revisited*, returned to the area made famous decades earlier by George Orwell. In revisiting working-class life and communities in the 1980s, she laid bare a history of women in the area that had not been told. She argues on the basis of many conversations with women, recorded in the book, that 'much of the good old values rested on the weary labours of women whose economic, social, sexual, cultural and political interests (we) re yet to be given any political primacy' (p. 225). What she uncovered was a male domain in which women were largely excluded from work and industrial politics, which was understood as the men's preserve, and that men spent little time in the house and did no domestic work. Thus, what provided a central sense of continuity for the communities was the unpaid domestic work of women. Moreover, Campbell accuses men of being heavy handed and dictatorial at home – the only place they could be masters, making the women their virtual servants.

What Campbell calls the politics of smash and grab lambasted the sexism of the industrial workers and laid bare the shoddy treatment of women, hidden by images of women's heroic attempts to support their men and communities through the long and bitter industrial struggles of the early 1980s. In this volume so far we have heard a great deal about men. As has often been the case in work I have undertaken over the years, the story of women and girls is often more obscure and harder to prise apart than that of men (Walkerdine, 1981, 1991, 1997, 2007). But, as we have seen, at the centre of the struggles of young and old men alike, as they strive to be and to retain a hardness that defends against vulnerability and annihilation, is femininity. In this sense, we could say that it is femininity, not masculinity, that is at the heart of the struggles in Steeltown. So, in relation to this, what happened to the women? And what part do they play in the drama of the history beyond the trauma? As Campbell argues, there was no redundancy for the women. The women's domestic work continued throughout the entire period of the works and into the post-works period. If anything, what changed for the women was that after the closure, they had even more to do, by going out to work, doing domestic work at home and supporting distraught men. Thus, as Campbell notes, it is their domestic servitude that provides a continuity of support for the men and for the whole community throughout the long history.

So, in telling the story of the women, we have to understand how their experience relates to and cuts across that of the role of femininity in all of this. We have seen how femininity and the distance from it has such a central role to play, so what does it mean when women inhabit the feminine and what does it mean when they might have ambitions to cross over onto the other side and get out of the house, so to speak? In this chapter, I want to explore the women's experience and then go on to think more about femininity as it also begins to inhabit the lives of some of the men. To end, I will discuss the work played by femininity in holding, carrying and transmitting traumatic experience. After all, if the distance from femininity required enormous work to keep masculinity going to avoid the catastrophic anxieties about annihilation and because there was no alternative to keeping on working, it follows that as much as it is terrifying to let that distance go, bringing up the anxiety as it does, in some senses there might also be a relief and with that relief a change can happen.

Having said that the women's experience was difficult to see at first, it is clear that what takes the eye and the emotions immediately is the story of the men. It is as though, at first glance, there is no problem with, or for, the women. But when I began to look more carefully at the interview transcripts, their place became crystal clear. Their work and emotional support were the central labour that kept a sense of continuity after the closure, at great cost to themselves. While I say at great cost, most of the women interviewed would not count this as a cost. Most said that they wanted to be in this community, giving this support to their families. What seems to be the case is that this support – domestic, financial and emotional – is what allows the men to continue to inhabit a masculinity that women support. It is in many ways the way in which they perform the duties of wife and mother, despite huge calls on their time, that allows this masculinity to continue.

In this section, I want to set out some of the issues and conflicts raised by the women and then to explore what the continued inhabiting of wife and mother might mean for them, for the men and for change. While there is absolutely no doubt that the women's efforts to support their men and families were little short of heroic, it did allow the men to stay comfortable with, to still continue to inhabit, if only in fantasy, a redundant form of masculinity.

Many women retold ambitions of moving away and adventures, particularly overseas in America or Australia, and one or two recounted tales of working away, such as being an au pair in France. But these absences were not sustained and they came back to Steeltown for relationship and family: ageing parents, husband's work and children's schools.

Although I interviewed only a small number of young, single women, they all pointed out that Steeltown was boring, that there was absolutely nothing to do except to go to the pub and get drunk or hang around, and that there were no decent shops and that there was an increasing drug problem. Yet, the feeling I got from these young women was one of resignation, almost because actually, despite all of this, they did not want to move away. I got a distinct feeling of aimlessness and hopelessness, as though the thing to do was what everyone else does, which was to find a boyfriend, get married and have a family, thus cementing the relationship to the town. Bethan was a hairdresser in her mum's salon. She had an idea of going into the police like her dad. Because police were not thought highly of within the community and she knew from her father that the police can be decent, helpful people, she thought she might be able to make a difference. Bethan imagined doing police work as something exciting, so she felt she could contribute to her community and do a job that was not boring. She imagined herself as becoming a policewoman on her own terms – working in a kind of 'funky' environment surrounded perhaps by young policemen – and she also imagined having lots of entertaining moments chasing local young vandals. While Bethan was telling me about her wishful thinking about these work scenarios, her face lit up. Here, it seemed, was a way of remaining feminine and having fun, while keeping order, particularly keeping young men in line, while contributing to the community. This scenario would bring excitement and a changed gender order into Steeltown, while at the same time preventing it from falling apart.

By contrast, her brother was in the army and didn't like being away from home:

> when he comes out he's going to have to retrain, doing something else and then, and then go looking for a job, then, then it's just that cycle again then.

This sentiment seems to convey the feeling of aimlessness and futility in the sense that all there is to do is to recognise that nothing is permanent, that change is always needed, that retraining is an issue. The cycle Bethan talked about is a cycle of chronic insecurity, but, unlike the steelworks era, there was nothing to bolster her, to make her feel a sense of belonging or containment. In this way, getting married and having a family makes sense, because it provides a semblance of security and continuity in a very uncertain world. Equally, Melanie got drunk at weekends because there was nothing else to do. She had some ideas of what work she could do but all are ideas that she hadn't followed up. This sense of inertia was very strong and was very reminiscent of work I have done before where young working-class girls might fantasise about things happening but had no sense of being able to change things themselves – they literally lacked any idea of concretely what to do, whereas middle-class girls got masses of support to help them follow their chosen path (extra tuition, a sense of possibility and money (Walkerdine et al., 2001)).

Emily passed her A levels and got two offers to do a design degree at the most local universities: Pontypridd and Cardiff. However, in the end, she turned both places down because they would have entailed either long travel and money or accommodation (and therefore money). She did not feel that her parents could afford to support her and so she gave up the ambition. She kept saying that actually she really lacked the interest, but there are many reasons why it might feel terrifying or impossible. Instead she got a job working in administration. A sense of being caught, unable to move and disliking the present situation but having no choice but to put up with it, accompanied by a sense of aimlessness, pervaded the interviews with these young women. While government discourse suggests that such young people lack aspiration (DCSF, 2008), the problem seems far more complex than this. The young women felt caught inside something that they could not change.

If we turn to the older women, this sense pervaded the interviews even more strongly.

As part of the interviews with young unemployed men, we also interviewed their mothers. These interviews convey a profound sense of having to cope with the impossible, little money, men on poorly paid and unstable work, often working away and somehow having to manage, having to balance the books and to raise children. Over and over again, like Nerys, they said:

> I've always been very independent. It was hard at the beginning when he wasn't having any money at all when he was in hospital but you just get round it, don't you?
> But you adapt and just shop a bit cheaper!

If there is one story all these women tell, whether young mothers or older women, it is this: you get round it, you cope, you manage, you get by. Generations have told these women that this is what must be done to survive and they constantly describe themselves as managing, as flexible. In this sense, their coping, managing, getting by, flexibility is the bedrock of continuity in the community. They did not face closure, or if they faced redundancy they got on and found another job. Their job, it seems, is to keep things going by constantly adapting to the changing circumstances. All of them have worked, and like work and like being independent, but managing is what they do.

While Nerys had become the only one in the family in paid employment after her husband's leg injury, she didn't see herself as the main breadwinner:

> I've always done it [work] it's not an effort, because it's normal, I've always worked.
> He did have depression [after the leg injury] but we just rode through it.

'Riding through it' for her meant never being off sick, and working through lunch hours to be home with the children. There was no secure employment, no insurance, no safety net, except the one that the women made by their own labour.

Nerys presented herself as the role model for her son, who was not allowed to do anything, but she said both son and husband saw her work as 'just sat behind a desk pushing the paper...he don't think it's hard work. He don't realise we do all that much, its hard work.' So the husband and son disavowed how hard the mum is working and wanted masculine work for themselves, which they were depressed without. Her son wanted to go in the army. If he got home and there was nothing to eat and his mum was at work, he didn't do the dishes, but went to his nan's or other family members, who would feed him. She was trying to get him to do more but was struggling. She called it 'a very lazy approach. I was never like that.' She agreed that she did the washing and so on, and didn't get her son to wash or iron for himself. She still wanted to be local and her son to be local – to know people, to feel secure. Her husband trained for things but then couldn't find work, so had to take factory work and hated it.

Tracey was a single mother who left her husband because he wouldn't work and was lazy. She managed to bring up three children by herself and had very little money. She did hairdressing from home so as to be with her children and provide stability. Other money came from the council and social welfare. While she saw her new partner as not lazy, he still could not find work, despite looking everywhere. He was working away but came back to Steeltown because he was so fed up with being away and having no stability or security. She liked the idea of more independence but just had to get from day to day on her money just to keep food on the table.

> You've got to adjust to it, you have got to learn to adjust to that kind of life, I think. Alright, there could be some people out there who are worse off than what I am, I think, because I've had to learn to survive, you live by everyday means then, and you think, well, I can't afford, I could do with going out this weekend, oh can't do that this week because I've got to pay this, you know, you work everything by itself, and I think you do adjust to it. Yes, there's a lot of crime in Steeltown, you've got some unfortunates who've turned to, they've gone on the drugs, and like I've never done anything like that, as far as I'm concerned I don't agree with it. But sometimes you've got to sit back and think, oh, because what have they got to look forward to, perhaps they come from families that have nothing, and they haven't realised how to get out of that themselves, you know. I got myself out of my little rut, as I used to call it, and yes, I had my days, I'd just sit some days and I could cry, you think, oh god, if I could just have that couple of pound more, you know, and then you think, oh, I'll be all right next week, I'll manage. And obviously my children, as long as I said, as long as my bills are paid, and I've got food in my cupboards, I don't care about anything else.

She would tell her son not to ask for anything because she didn't have it. If she had a tiny bit more one week, she would buy a Chinese meal as a treat on a Saturday. Her father noted down in a book if she borrowed even 5p, but she said that it had made her 'learn to fend for myself'.

Like Tracey, it appeared to be the mothers who were pushing their sons to find work and get by like they were, not their dads, who were swamped by grief, resentment and despair.

Sue left her violent husband to bring up her children alone. She wanted to be a nurse, travel everywhere and never get married or have children, but she married a soldier and ended up in Steeltown with a violent marriage and then five offspring. She did housework and raised the children. Her second partner was a long distance lorry driver who was often away: 'Some weeks you can see him and other weeks you don't see him.' She didn't go out to work so that she could look after the children, and while the older sons could look after the younger ones, she would say: 'He's got his own life to lead.' In fact, her eldest son was run over by a bus. I was struck in fact by the numbers of accidents, and chronic illnesses and disabilities in these families.

So, we begin to get a picture of the fact that these women were living with chronic instability with which they coped heroically by constantly shifting the ways in which they managed work and the budget. To do this, they sacrificed a great deal – certainly their own ambitions and dreams – placing an enormous burden on themselves. I was forcibly struck by the sense, which was common across all of the women, that there was no alternative but to cope, muddle through and get by, and it was they who shouldered the burden of responsibility. It was they who prevented everything from collapsing. As Mandy said, men were more affected by redundancy because they felt they had to be the breadwinner, the provider:

> If it happened to a woman then I think they'd just as you say, they're more flexible, they can look at a wider range of opportunities than perhaps a man would look at ... I was doing this job where I was made redundant from but I don't have to go back to something like that, I can look for something else. But a man I think would feel more the need that he's was made redundant, he's got to get out and he's got to get a job.

Indeed, Mandy's husband was a steelworker made redundant, and she fretted for him, but

> at the end of the day then you just think, well, you've got to get on with it. Can't dwell on things or be depressed – it's a knock-back, but all you can do is adapt and get on with it.

When he was made redundant, she was the one who rang around to see if there was any training or other support available. This, I think, made her feel less anxious about the loss of work/money. Her husband eventually took up long-distance lorry driving and then gave it up to take a pay cut and be closer to home. She said he did housework but admitted that he did 30 per cent to her 70 per cent. She put up with him not ironing because his mum did it and she liked things tidier than him, and he and their son were much too messy for her but she tolerated it. Again, the attempt to get men to participate in household duties was for some women successful and others less so. Some men cooked, others cleaned and some did half of the work, but the women often felt both guilty and resentful.

Annie counted herself as lucky to have a husband who did his fair share:

> So I'm very lucky that I have a husband who does know how to use an iron, who does know how to use a vacuum cleaner and fill the washing machine and wash up and cook.

Janie looked after her ageing mum while her husband had a breakdown and she worked full time, as well as looking after the children. In addition, she refused to tell anyone about her husband's illness because 'they all have their own problems'. Crying through two interviews, she tearfully recounted her tale – the first time she had talked about it. I got a sense of the terrible burden she was carrying by trying to keep everything going. As with the other women, she just felt she had to keep going despite everything – there couldn't be two breakdowns in the house. Everything must go on and only she could do it. This terrible burden and responsibility seemed to have gone largely unrecognised.

What is important is to understand just what these women were doing in keeping everything going at great cost to themselves. What did they get out of it? What anxieties were being defended against? We have argued that in the past, the community managed by a set of affective relations and practices through which mutual support was established and circulated. This dealt with the chronic insecurity at the heart of the industrial community. At that time, women provided support for each other by acting as quasi-families – one big family. But more recently, apart from relatives who might themselves be struggling, the women had only themselves. The men could not be relied on because they seemed slow to adapt and they found adaptation painful, but also the women had already learnt to be more flexible and so they were used to constant change and managing to find ways to bend with it rather than be defined by work. But, I suggest that the same chronic insecurity and therefore the same annihilation anxiety were present, and it was the women, like Menzies Lythe's nurses who we saw in Chapter 6, who were the ones preventing it from breaking through the surface. It was they who shouldered this burden alone. What I am concerned about here is that shouldering such a burden takes its toll. By keeping everything going, the women were keeping the anxiety at bay. The consequences of this can be a terrifying sense of panic that, if it cannot be expressed, may appear in the body.

Indeed, Connie, in her 50s, had worked all her life with insecurity and tried to put by money for hard times ahead because of uncertainty. Never knowing what was going to happen, she felt she had to plan for it, to make it work even when things are falling apart. She worked in a shoe shop but it was stressful because she had to make sales and she knew people didn't have money. She catalogued illness and death in her family and I got the sense of her always caring for others – the nextdoor neighbours and so on. Then she became ill with multiple sclerosis.

The men did not fare any better – they were also dealing with chronic insecurity while the women were holding this for them. They too suffered from industrial accidents and a range of illnesses: lead poisoning, breakdowns, depression, high blood pressure, heart attacks, dermatitis. Yet their anxiety was to some extent contained, while no one was containing the anxiety of the women. However, perhaps the women's saving grace was their work, which they refused to give up. It is this, they said, that gave them independence and companionship. Anna could not imagine giving up working: 'I wouldn't like to be without a job. I wouldn't know what to do with myself all day.'

How should I understand this situation? I was really struck by some difficult emotions when thinking about these women. The first was the troubling feeling of listlessness, boredom and resignation that came from the young women. I found that I wanted them to be angry and I wanted them to leave Steeltown and not just accept what was happening to them as inevitable. This made me irritated and somehow unsympathetic, so I tried to think about what this was telling me, what the young women were communicating to me. The overall feeling that I came up with was a kind of depressing flatness, going along, coping, getting by, without any spark, fire, passion or enthusiasm. From my own experience of such feelings, I knew that this made something unbearable

able to be coped with and related to an unsafe feeling. This feeling might well be manifest in the desire to stay put, because boring as Steeltown was, it was known and therefore relatively safe. Yet, Steeltown is not safe because its borders cannot produce the education, jobs and possibilities that these young women need. This suggests also then that while home may feel safer than outside, it is not in fact safe. We have argued throughout this book that the inhabitants of Steeltown had to find ways of coping with chronic insecurity, but that those relations and practices have broken down. The chronic insecurity has not gone away. Indeed, in many ways it has become amplified. Were these young women then experiencing the effects of a place in which nothing was certain, nothing was safe and the only way to cope with it was to stay as still as possible, to settle down, to find a partner, to have a family and to find local work, as patterns of relationship that made the women feel safe were enacted?

This kind of stuckness is perhaps also a way of thinking about what the older women told us. Engaging with the women's interviews was very hard. I found what was being said at once familiar and terrifying. All the talk of muddling on and getting by was desperately familiar from my own childhood. The overall feeling of having to manage and to adjust no matter what the conditions, to go on and not give up, to keep going. This feeling is strongly associated with my mother and on one level it is a heroic determination and refusal to go down, to be beaten. But the managing carries such tremendous anxiety. No chink can be allowed and nothing must enter, because otherwise everything would break down. For me, when I explore this feeling, underlying it is terror, terror that things might actually fall apart. This is the sense that I detected in the interviews: we must carry on, we have no choice but to carry on despite all the odds stacked against us, and somehow we must make the family work, we must put food on the table. As we have explored, centuries of insecurity would make this a way of living for generations in which money was so tight that a tiny loan had to be noted to teach the woman to manage with what she had. We could say then that these very domestic management practices, precarious as they were, were attempts to keep things going, to not go to the workhouse, to not end up on the streets, to not have the children taken away; to keep the wolf from the door – the wolf of terror, the wolf that devours and destroys and shows the flimsy line between survival and death, annihilation. This is the reality of poverty and the practices of poverty carried on through generations in the bodies of women, who come to embody thrift, frugality and sacrifice even when poverty has not actually come knocking at the door. And never ever be in debt, and this has to be managed. This, it seems, is the woman's task. And manage it these women did. Their control of the domestic economy through flexible adaptability was staggering. No wonder the women cleaners in the last chapter wanted their steelmen back.

The stories told by the women of going to work, helping their men or managing on their own, sorting the finances, looking after children and sick relatives, keeping the house clean, food cooked, washing done speak also of self-sacrifice and independence. I want to explore this a little further by thinking about how femininity and masculinity play off each other. I have seen that in the past the hard steelworker honed his body and worked it hard in the works, while the woman took care of the domestic economy and work, sometimes taking the pay packet from the man and also reading documents from the works for him. I have argued that this is a very strong division in which masculinity must be forcibly split from femininity for fear of weakness, or as the young men put it, of 'becoming a woman'. That way, just as in the woman's failure to adapt, lay the workhouse or its equivalent. So both ways of being, in their fashion, guarded against annihilation. The strong separation was necessary in order for the family unit to work. In this sense, masculinity embodied a fantasy of the breadwinner, the provider, the strong one, while the fantasy of femininity embodied nurturance, self-sacrifice, the maternal. So woman could not be anything other than maternal and man could not be anything other than strong and unfeminine: there can be no soft men and no sexual women.

But here we see a scenario in which this began to break down. The men could not always provide and the women had to let them think that they were the breadwinner or that their work was more important, or they had to help them find work. They also worked in paid employment themselves, which they approached with the same flexibility and adaptability that they had learned to use in the domestic sphere. They refused to give up the work, which made them feel independent. So, can we detect in this some disappointment in and anger towards the men, who were too rigid, would often not do their fair share of household chores, could be violent and that the women could do without? Yet at the same time, they were forced to enter into a quasi-motherly relationship with these men (e.g. finding training for them), who themselves might feel reduced to the mammy's boys they so dreaded being. Were the women and men clinging to fantasies of otherness that could no longer be sustained? Were the women (and men) actually sustaining these fantasies in order to attempt to keep the old order going while at the same time feeling a strong desire for their own lives and independence? I wonder whether we could understand the women as at some level attacking their men by their complaints but then covering it over by their taking responsibility for everything. Were the women and men then in some way colluding to keep the masculine in place to guard against their own anger and omnipotence, which was too much, and they feared they might lose their men? So the men still had to be the breadwinners, even though the women desperately wanted them to change.

How then do they begin to adjust to a new order in which jobs for hard men are few and far between, in which women are independent and work and in which the domestic sphere therefore needs to be shared by a masculinity and a femininity which can both exhibit both sides – both masculinity and femininity?

Some families reported some success in this. For example, Annie told me that her husband had a long experience of caring for elderly relatives, of cooking for himself and of domestic work, so they shared the domestic work. Jean told me that her husband was a better cook than her and so had taken to doing most of the cooking. Some men opened up a side that they could never express in the works by entering caring professions, such as social and youthwork. But some men, as we have seen, found such a move very painful.

Some older men in particular found the loss of sociality with men extremely difficult. In particular, they spoke of needing to get out of the house, as we explored in Chapter 5. What is interesting about these examples is the way in which the men took on what was previously classically a feminine position – being stuck all day in the home. Not having the opportunities of younger men to find another way to be, they missed the affective connections that had become central to their identity. In some cases, this was manifested in serious health problems, such as heart conditions, depression and alcoholism. While these are often cited as well-known effects of redundancy, our aim here is to show that what was missed was not only the work but the whole history of connectedness that had contained the male workers and that subsequently left them bereft and adrift. They had crossed over into a traditional feminine space, trapped in the home, and did not adapt by doing the housework as some of the women suggest, but felt marooned and frightened by this loss of a masculine space, which surfaced as a kind of claustrophobia in which they desperately needed to find some way of getting out of the house.

Embodying masculinity, femininity and intergenerational transmission

Masculinity and femininity provided the basis for community containment, and the ways in which a separation between masculinity and femininity served to support an industrial community with men earning a family wage.

If the role of masculinity was to provide bodily strength to withstand and to enjoy the hard punishing work of the works, and a solidarity that took that strength to union militancy, which fought heroically for higher wages and better conditions, while delivering productivity and pride in strength and a job well done, the role of femininity was to maintain continuity in a different way, that is, to provide domestic continuity and emotional stability. Of course, these gender divisions are understood as deeply traditional and reactionary in many circles, but our aim here is to show how they worked and how they made sense within the historical situation in which they were produced, rather than resort to a normative reading.

If the man went out to work, with the woman responsible for the domestic economy and literacy, we can conjecture that masculinity was produced out of a certain distance from femininity. In other words, the male manual worker through bodily strength and the withstanding of harsh conditions upheld a masculinity that was at a safe distance from femininity. It was not soft, because this would produce too little distance from femininity, which itself would make for a masculinity unable to cope with the rigours of work. This meant a very strong and defensive separation from maternal femininity, a separation to be upheld at all costs, not because there was anything reactionary or essential about it but because it was necessary. I am reminded of the work of masculinity cited in quite another context; that is, small boys playing video games (Walkerdine, 2007). This showed that the work of masculinity was to become proficient in these games but that, just like the work of the hero in classic Hollywood Westerns, the hero is beaten down again and again before the final triumph. This narrative is not unlike that of the heroic worker, who is defeated again and again in the struggle for better conditions but comes back again and again to fight another day – until, that is, the final dawn comes and there is no further opportunity for collective action. The final whistle blows and the works is forever silent. This means that the opportunities for being that kind of man are dramatically lessened and softer forms of masculinity are understood as desired to meet new forms of work (Griffin, 2000; Law and

Mooney, 2006; Lupton, 2006; McDowell, 2003; Nixon, 2006, O'Donnell and Sharpe, 2000; Seidler, 2007; Van Hoven and Horschelmann, 2005). These softer forms stress a greater proximity to femininity. Our aim is to show here how that represents a hugely anxiety-provoking experience. This is not a nostalgic look back to a lost heroic masculinity so much as the frightening lessening of a distance that might have been painfully produced in the first place. To get distance from the mother requires the suppression of feelings of dependency or their projection onto the other, the mother. In other words, while it classically has its benefits, it also has its costs. But then to reverse the process risks the opening up of separations honed through generations of practices of masculinity.

The matrixial

In Chapter 6, we used the concept of the matrix, first developed by Foulkes, to think about the dynamics in a group. The French/Israeli feminist analyst Bracha Ettinger works with the concept of the matrix in a rather different way, which extends our understanding of it. She reminds us that the concept of the matrix comes from the Latin for womb, so the matrixial space is womb-like – a feminine space in which something is gestated. She extends this concept of gestation into what she calls 'the matrixial borderspace' (2006):

> ... joint corporeal resistance, shared affective experiences, exchanges of phantasy that relate to non-Oedipal sexual difference and inter-connectivity.

She understands this as a space in which transmission happens. Ettinger's view that woman is a subject and not simply a container is crucially important for how we think 'woman'. In so many approaches, she is understood as the universal container, the connection that makes separation possible. This is common to all object relations approaches but is also common to most Western philosophy (Walkerdine, 2005). Ettinger is at pains to show how the matrixial is an active position in which affective connections are made rather than simply being a place of containment. This adds an important dimension to our discussion. We have discussed in previous chapters the ways in which certain affective relations and practices serve to defend against annihilation anxiety and in that sense serve to contain it. We have stressed these as active affective connections and this is what Ettinger stresses with her concept of the matrixial. This helps us to move away from a position in which femininity is seen as the universal way of containing anxiety and promoting separation and individuation. We saw how women were responsible for family finances and often literacy. We saw how women met and talked together over the low fences and we have seen how one woman tried to bring the community back to life with Christmas lights. In addition to all of this, which surely meets Ettinger's criteria for the matrixial, there is a way in which the women carried the burden of the men's failure to establish continuity of being by silently carrying the pain and depression experienced by the men. When we say failure, we do not mean that the responsibility for the closure rested with the men. Of course not. But in the history of the community, their struggle was part of the continuity of being. They could not keep the juggernaut of globalisation at bay. This was a force absolutely beyond their control, but this inability was a loss, a defeat for resistance and in that sense it lived as a failure. Thus the burden that falls on the women is enormous.

This is the mantle and the burden that some of the women take on – to suffer, to support, to maintain so that masculinity might in fact come back to its place and things might carry on as before. This places enormous stress on the women and can only be addressed by a shifting of the responsibility for maintaining the matrix onto men and women together, with a shifting of the distance between femininity and masculinity. As we have seen, some men (and women) found this very threatening. The successful change does involve these shifts but the community matrix cannot survive it and things have to be put in place to make continuity possible.

Bracha Ettinger (2006) understands the matrix as a space of connection through the womb. In this sense then, she relates affectivity not simply to the early mother–infant relationship, as we have seen with the accounts discussed in Chapter 3, but goes further than Anzieu and Tustin in placing the inter-uterine connections between foetus and mother centre stage. So the matrix is not the organ womb but a psychical apparatus modelled on the site of the feminine prenatal encounter (not fusion). Woman as a figure is not confined to one body but is understood as a hybrid webbing of links between several subjectivities. So, the matrixial is an active system of connections across subjects, modelled on the notion of the active feminine prenatal encounter in which connections are made but rather than through words, through fluids, feelings and physiological responses.

In addition, she uses this idea of the matrixial borderspace as a space in which just as the womb provides a permeable membrane linking the mother to the foetus, in which it is now understood foetuses experience sensations via the mother, so the matrixial borderspace is also a space of affective connection between people and particularly between women.

We are particularly interested in this because Ettinger develops her work in relation to the transmission of trauma across generations. She does this by trying to understand how memories and feelings are passed down generations who have experienced trauma (in her case the Shoa), so that there is an embodied connection for people who are several generations on from the trauma but who nevertheless feel its effects. Of course, this relates directly to what we have witnessed and understood in relation to the intergenerational transmission both of ways of coping across more than 200 years with chronic insecurity and of the effects of the closure itself, as in the case of the young unemployed men.

If we pursue Ettinger's notion of the womb as a dynamic border-space as

> a transforming borderspace of encounter of the co-emerging I and the neither fused nor rejected uncognized non-I. . . . This gives us a notion of a broader Symbolic which includes subsymbolic processes of interconnectivity. It serves as a model for a shareable dimension of subjectivity in which elements that discern one-another as non-I without knowing each other, co-emerge and co-inhabit a joint space, without fusion or rejection. (ibid, pp. 64–65)

In other words, she is adding to Lacan's notion of symbolic processes, the idea of subsymbolic connections in which emerging 'I's are connected and through which permeable connections are made. We could compare this idea to Arendt's notion of a 'who' constituted through webs of relations, discussed in Chapter 3, as well as the discussion of partial connections in Deleuze, noted in Chapter 6.

> The matrixial co-emerging partial subjects can simultaneously be seen from the phallic angle as 'whole subjects' or as each other's object. A matrixial encounter engenders shared traces, trauma, pictograms and fantasies in several partners conjointly but differently, accompanied and partially created by diffuse matrixial affects; it engenders nonconsious readjustments of their connectivity and reattunements of transubjectivity. (ibid., p. 65)

For Ettinger, the matrixial works as an inter-intra-subjective transhistoric space of connection. Is this a way of explaining how shared connections are made in many ways: the solidarity in the steelworks, the shared practices of men and women, the transmission of ways of being across generations, the transmission of experiences of masculinity and femininity and its loss that we explored in Chapter 7?

Ettinger adds the concept of 'metramorphosis'. This is a process of multidirectional change so that through the borderlinks things get transformed and become threshholds through which elements known and unknown pass. Its function is a passage to the symbolic. Metramorphosis is a creative principle – relations without relating, distances in proximity, difference in co-creation, rather than fusion or repulsion. Ettinger associates it with particular affects: awe, alertness, astonishment, compassion. She includes even something like telepathy (Campbell and Pile, 2010), which shows a passage has taken place. It induces instances of the co-emergence of meaning. Multiple and plural matrixial subjectivity is also singular and partial: it emerges from joint corporeal resistance, shared affective experiences, from exchanges of phantasy that relate to non-Oedipal sexual difference and interconnectivity to inscriptions of traumas and fantasies (ibid., p. 69). The matrixial awareness of the links with intimate strangers is the feminine dimension but it is not simply the province of women because we have all experienced it, therefore it exists as archaic traces. This is not about the rhythmical experience of presence and absence. The matrixial woman is also subject and not just an object that allows culture to take place:

> The borderspace is a psychic zone of misery (misericord). Subjectivisation in the matrixial is subjectivity as encounter. The desire is not for a lost object but for linking with the Other. (ibid., p. 124)

This has some affinities with the work of Bion (1959):

> The matrixial gaze conducts imprints from 'events without witnesses' and passes them on to witnesses who were not there, whom I term wit(h)nesses with-out events. (ibid., p. 150)
>
> A crypt, when transmissible in the matrixial borderspace, is a lacuna that corresponds to an unsymbolised event that belongs to someone else. Alone, we cannot reach it, because it was created as

joint. Its traces were, from their first appearance, already dispersed. (ibid., p. 166)

This seems to fit all of the issues we have raised throughout this book. It provides a way of understanding the intergenerational transmission that we discussed in relation to the work of Davoine and Gaudilliere in Chapter 7. Ettinger's work suggests that experiences can be shared affectively in the ways that we have described and that they can pass down through generations (encrypted unsymbolised events belonging to someone else) via a process that could be described as an affective history. Indeed, it is women analysts in general of a variety of theoretical persuasions who have been central in developing an understanding of the central importance of the maternal and of affective experience (Antonis, 2008). Although Melanie Klein saw containment as central (a concept that Ettinger criticises for its passivity), it is women who have been particularly attuned to these processes and have understood implicitly that experiences of others can be transmitted affectively and through their own bodies, which they can use to tune into and therefore to engage with what is being communicated (Antonis, 2008). I will give one example of this, which comes from the work of Judith Mitrani, an American object relations analyst who pays attention to what the analyst experiences and feels in relation to the patient in order to find a way of accessing material that is not repressed so much as unable to be thought (Bollas, 1987). Mitrani (2001) gives an example of work with a woman who was suffering from various anxiety conditions that were concerned with her current life situation. She was the daughter of Shoa survivors but her parents had never spoken to her about their experiences of the war. The silent impact of the experiences, says Mitrani, had been unconsciously passed on to the daughter. The analyst used her counter-transference feelings and material gained from the transference to intuit that certain things had happened to the parents. In other words, she was able to feel a sense of certain embodied affects and anxieties exhibited by the patient, by how she interacted with the analyst and by how this made the analyst feel to understand what she might be feeling. But, more particularly, what feelings had been silently passed to the patient by the unmentioned experiences of the parents? She said:

> It seemed clear that Miriam had been attempting to communicate to me her experience of the parental projections of those unbearable happenings occurring during the war, as well as acting out – in her body, behaviour and the transference – those happenings which

had been left unexperienced, foreclosed from articulate awareness and denied communicative language, first by the parents and later by Miriam herself in identification with them. (p. 4)

Mitrani suggests that perhaps these affects were communicated in utero – a clear link with Ettinger's work. However, she also suggests that an infantile sense of helplessness and terror that infants display may have revived for the parents, feelings of their own terror and helplessness from their Holocaust experiences in various ways, and that this was affectively communicated as a failure to contain, which would have brought its own terrifying anxieties for Miriam, anxieties perhaps that she could have no way of knowing that they were not hers, but communicated in ways to her that bypassed thought.

Indeed, at this juncture, we might also note that Davoine too understands that her own mother's terrifying experiences during the Second World War while pregnant with her may have been transmitted to her in utero and that it is precisely the mobilisation of this experience in a dream that allows her to connect with her patient's history and trauma. Thus, what becomes salient in these accounts is that Ettinger shows us how trauma is communicated in the matrix of the community, through the relations of the community in joint corporeal resistance, shared affective experiences, exchanges of phantasy that relate to non-Oedipal sexual difference and interconnectivity. These are communicated not through thought but through feelings, just as Mitrani says of the feelings of the counter-transference. They are not necessarily thought or known. Yet these experiences can be passed down through generations. Steeltown experienced traumatic historical events and suffering for many generations, and it cemented its ways of being in response to those experiences, to create a shared affect, an affect in which the role of the feminine was crucial.

Returning to the particular place of femininity, then, I have argued that the fantasy of a strong masculinity was key for the women to maintain. They had to keep operating, as many of them said, by maintaining the shared fantasy that the men were still the breadwinners, and they had to prop this up by means of constant work, to keep going desperately because the men could not. They were operating in a way that showed desperation to maintain that this protective masculinity had not died. When we cannot bear the possibility of loss or to acknowledge its reality, we often operate as though nothing has been lost, because the loss is unbearable, and we thus try to protect ourselves from experiencing it because, as we have seen throughout the book, what is at stake is the very possibility of the continuity of existence. The women showed us graphically the central importance of masculinity to the maintenance of community. By attempting to keep it going at all costs, the women make it clear that the crisis for the men was also a crisis for them. Indeed, we could say that the crisis for them both was so intertwined that we cannot think of one without the other. However, in this scenario, the women were keeping the men and themselves locked into a strangulating embrace in which the women were terrified for anything to change, to lose their men, and thus they helped prevent the possibility that gender and domestic relations might change. This was not because there was anything wrong or pathological about either the men or the women but because the particular historical relation between masculinity and femininity was so woven into the fabric of the ways of containing and surviving the anxiety about annihilation, that in our view is at the heart of the foundation of this community, that attempting at all costs to preserve masculinity as it was while also resenting it, was an attempt to prevent in fantasy the catastrophe that had already happened in reality. Davoine and Gaudilliere (2004) say that 'the imminent catastrophe, the announced doomsday, has already happened but it could not be inscribed in the past as past, since, in this respect, the subject of speech was not there' (p. 28). While they are speaking of the intergenerational transmission of a historical catastrophe, nevertheless, in this case, the catastrophe had also already happened – the steelworks had closed, but the women were operating as though they could stop it closing in the sense that they were attempting to shore up the masculinity associated with it so that the dreaded event that signalled the loss of this way of gender relating could not be allowed to happen. This was a response to trauma. How then were gender relations to change? How were the women to shoulder less of the burden on their own? It is useless in this context to argue that the men were macho, sexist and reactionary – working-class dinosaurs – who were blocking the change of the women, as I have heard said in academic circles many times, because such an explanation is completely ahistorical and fails to understand the central role of affective dynamics in the possibility of chance and transformation. Only the acknowledgement of the death of this form of masculinity can allow this change to take place, and, as we have seen, this is a terrifying prospect, yet ways need to be found to help both women and men to grieve and to be able to face the possibility of change together.

9
To the Future?

In this volume, we have told a story of what happened to the inhabitants of Steeltown after the closure of the steelworks in 2002. In order to do this, we set the closure in the context of the 200 years of iron and steel production that preceded it. In Chapter 2, we explored what life was like for the inhabitants and the impact of the introduction of political economy and the Poor Law Amendment Act. What we focused on is the way in which the production of working people as 'labour' made them moveable objects that could be shunted around according to the demands of capitalist production, which, as we saw in that chapter, varied according to national and international demands for iron and steel. Labour was then further controlled by the introduction of political economy, which attempted to discipline labour by focusing on the production of wealth and the drains on wealth produced by the poor. The introduction of the workhouse meant that the poor were in great fear of entering the workhouse, thus making workers and their families accept any conditions in order to have work. It is in this way, that we introduce the idea that far from this being a 200-year period of stability, it was one of great anxiety and chronic instability. The works closed three times, and there were strikes, lay-offs, death, depression, war, disease and poverty. All of these made for conditions that had to be borne, and we thus argue that this was what made way for the development of modes of being and belonging that were affective in character and served to develop strong ties, practices and relations, aiming to produce safety and a sense of ontological security, the idea of going on being, when all of the conditions militated against these aims.

This theme was further developed in Chapter 3, where we introduced the central importance of the concept of affective relations and practices through which this safety was produced. In particular, we paid attention to the work of Esther Bick on the second skin and developed by Didier Anzieu in relation to the development of a group skin.

In Chapter 4, we took this discussion further by thinking about the rupture in the group skin produced when the works closed for the final time in 2002. To understand this, we introduced concepts of suffering, crisis and catastrophe. It is here that we explored the central importance of thinking about the catastrophic closure in relation to the history both of steel production and of what Davoine and Gaudilliere (2004) call the small histories of the lives lived within Steeltown through this period. What happened in Steeltown in 2002 did not simply resonate for the workers and their families but impacted on everybody in different ways, as we went on to show.

In Chapter 5, we took this up by thinking about masculinity and, in particular, the kind of masculinity needed to survive steelwork and how this produced a masculine body that had to become hard, with its distance from softness and femininity. We explored how some men managed to change with the end of steelwork and how others found this much more difficult. In Chapters 6 and 7, we discussed what this meant for some young unemployed men who found the idea of going forward and abandoning heavy industrial masculinity unbearable, as did many in the community. We use these examples to think through the ways in which many in the community could not cope with the loss of masculinity associated with steelwork and how this impacted on the young men who were caught between the past and the future. Using the work of Davoine and Gaudilliere, we investigated how a number of players are acting in a drama that seeks to tell us of the history of what has happened in Steeltown and that makes the young men the unwitting bearers of that history.

In Chapter 8 we saw that the women in the town had attempted to keep everything going and to be themselves flexible in such a way that they could make continuity possible at a time when everything had broken down. The terrible burden on the women was one that they carried in order for masculinity and femininity to appear to be in their right places, that is, a fantasy of the man as breadwinner even though it was increasingly impossible for many of the men to 'win the bread'. Through a mixture of anger and stoicism, they kept everything going, often at great cost to themselves. To understand this, we turned to the work of Bracha Ettinger on the role of femininity in the intergenerational transmission of trauma.

The way forward?

As we have seen, the situation in Steeltown is tough. The women are holding the situation together in many ways, but this is terrifying for them and means that while they are heroically attempting to contain it, nothing can change. This situation is repeated in many de-industrialised communities the world over and so it is particularly important to think about how this situation might change. We have shown that, in many ways, the process of change and adaptation has happened throughout the history of Steeltown, which has attempted creatively to engage with the conditions in which the people have found themselves. As we saw in Chapter 5, some men and families do manage to adapt and change the relational matrix in which they exist. However, not all do and the transmission of historical trauma down the generations was significant for the whole community, especially those who were struggling to cope on benefits and finding employment difficult to come by, and finding that when it came it was very poorly paid.

Thus, we saw a situation in which people were struggling to get from day to day. What is striking about this is that this was then, and now we have the prospect of the draconian removal of benefits so we are left wondering how anyone will find the resources to carry on. It is in this context that we want to introduce the work of Felix Guattari and to return to Bracha Ettinger.

Ettinger (2001) argues that the matrixial is a place where affect is shared so that events that we did not witness can still be communicated to us and from us to others. Things are passed on to witnesses who were not there (cf. also Marianne Hirsch on postmemory (Hirsch, 2008)). Matrixial awareness, she says, channels the subject's desire towards the beauty and the pain, the trauma of others, the impossibility of not sharing. So, for her, trauma is passed on through the ways in which matrixial experience works – by our desire to connect, which is, we believe, what we also connect with using the concept of resonance.

> Metramorphosis is a process of intra-psychic and inter-psychic or trans-individual exchange, of transformation, and affective communication between/with-in several matrixial entities. It is a passage – lane through which affected events, materials and modes of becoming infiltrate and diversify onto non-conscious margins of the Symbolic through/by subsymbolic webs. In a joint and multiple – several marginal trans-subjective awareness, perceived borderlines

dissolve to become new boundaries; forms are transgressed; border-
lines are surpassed to become thresholds ... Relations without relating
transform uncognised other and me, and turn both of us into partial
subjects – still uncognised but unthoughtly known to each other and
matrixially knowing each other. (pp. 104–105)

Unthoughtly known to each other. This is the key. The 'unthought
known' is a term from Bollas (1987), who claims that we can know
something without being able to think it. She is talking about a subsymbolic experience. Bion (1962) also claimed thoughts can be without
a thinker or be waiting for people to think them. Thus, what cannot
be consciously known to us can also circulate between us because it is
still sending energy and this energy is what is picked up. What cannot
be said is shown, often in a weird way. I think Ettinger is talking about
this. That is, she is saying that the matrixial space is a space in which
these unthought knowns are circulating through bodies so that we pick
up, we feel what is coming from the other and we pass it on even though
we don't know what it is.

Davoine and Gaudilliere's (2004) concept of resonance allows this to
be symbolised by being able to articulate a link. Ettinger does it through
art. So, we can see how something can be passed along and passed
around through the sensitivities of women: a subsymbolic field where
things are communicated but cannot necessarily be known. This is the
place of the women in Steeltown. How can this then be known? It is all
very well for Ettinger to say that this can work through art, but what
is passed between women in Steeltown is the subsemiotics of survival
while subtly incorporating and embodying past traumas and recirculat-
ing them to the next generation. We can see this in the ways in which
young women feel stuck but cannot move. So, we have to make this
conscious – we have to enable the trauma to be reached, to be spoken, able to be borne and therefore to be transformed. Davoine and
Gaudilliere say that to do this we need other methods. What methods?
How do we name something that is not yet known but is felt, but is too
frightening to be known? They use dramatic methods, using Artaud, as
discussed in Chapter 6. In Chapter 4, we also saw that Menzies Lythe
reached this in hospitals by observation and discussion. What Davoine
and Gaudilliere do with psychotic patients is to develop a process of
research, of co-research with their patients to uncover the historical link,
the betrayals that are operating historically. Can a community of women
come together to research this? How might this be possible? Can it be
dramatised? Can it be painted? Can it be researched to find out and

bring to signification what it is? We would say that this is central to be being able to move on, to change and not to get stuck within the site of trauma.

To explore this further, we need to understand the possibility of change. To think about this we would like to turn to the work of Felix Guattari. He was a radical analyst who worked his entire life in the La Borde clinic outside Paris, with psychotic patients. Out of his experience and his radical politics, he developed a way of thinking about the future and the possibility of change that has direct resonances for the situation in Steeltown. His work begins as we began the book, with existential territories. In the introduction, we thought about the way in which the song Myfanwy linked into a longing for home, for a land to be free, to be safe. In Chapter 3, we saw how the people of Steeltown created modes of relationality, affective relations and practices, which kept them safe against huge anxieties about annihilation, formed by coping with the chronic insecurities of the iron and steel industry, but that these were then challenged by a catastrophic closure. While some people coped with that and were able to move on, we have seen that the remnants of it are still with the people; we have seen how the women and men transmit to each other complex affective ways of embodying and transmitting the lingering effects of the history that they still experience.

Guattari understood such experiences and began by thinking about the safety using what he called 'existential territories'. How does one move forward to the future? How does one leave one's safe space and resonances? How does one move out of a rut created by the places capitalism has put us in and not simply move to another territory that feels safe but stifling? In this context, the stiflingness can be understood in terms of the government's insistence on becoming entrepreneurial, on moving, on reinventing oneself. While this did indeed work for some, for others it pushed them further down and for many women they just tried to keep things going as they had before. How, asks Guattari, can one move forward into an unknown? How can one create the new paths that need to be created without slipping back into territories that lock us further in? This was his radical hope, and he described how he felt that an analysis that looks forwards not backwards, what he called a schizo-analysis, might be possible. In order to understand this, we have to think about an existential territory as not being simply the place where one is, the place that makes one feel safe, as we have seen in Steeltown, but also what we have explored in relation to the skin, the sense of being contained within one's body or within a community body against the fear of annihilation. To understand this further, Guattari turns to Freud's idea of primary process. This is what Bick described (see Chapter 3), but when Freud first came up with the concept, he imagined that a newborn baby had difficulty with its separate existence and must cope with this by producing primitive fantasies, which he called hallucinations, of that which provided the sense of safety, that is, the mother's body, particularly her breast. It is this idea – the affects associated with a basic sense of existence and safety and the fantasies associated with this, not fantasies in an adult sense, but inchoate feelings, sensations, perceptions – which he called primary process. Melanie Klein developed this further when she referred to the breast as a part object, that which stands in for the mother, in the sense that it is a fantasised object that makes the infant feel safe, or that can be clung to. When Esther Bick talks of babies trying to focus on any object – a light, a sound, a shape – she is talking about the experience of trying to find something to cling to against catastrophic anxieties about not existing. Guattari understands these issues very well because he worked all of his life with psychotic patients for whom that sense of basic safety was lacking and who found it easier to retreat into fantasies than confront the terrifying anxieties that assailed them. So, when he talks of existential territories he is talking about the place where one exists – its familiar routines, its resonances, its smells, its tastes, its bodily sensations and movements – all of which serve to keep one sensing that one is safe and that one exists. We can see in the relentless work of the Steeltown women a sense of trying to keep things going so that they will continue to feel safe, because they have become so unsafe. In this situation, Guattari might ask, how is it possible to imagine the possibility of change in which people might still feel safe but manage to create something new? We have seen examples of successful change, but we have also seen that not everyone manages this. Guattari broke with Freud and Lacan's stress on Oedipal relations to focus much more on early experience, the schizo, and how people manage to move forward, to deterritorialise, without finding a new place to feel safe that keeps them caught and without autonomy and freedom. To understand the trajectory that one passes through in life, he introduced the concept of cartography, that is, mapping the attempts to shift one's territory (see Guattari, 1989; Holmes, n. d.). But for our purposes here, we need to understand how Guattari conceives of the risky business of change in a way that does not leave us vulnerable to terrifying anxieties about the loss of our existential territories. What he does is to reference Winnicott's (1971) idea of a transitional object, that is, an object kept by a child that allows that child to play and to create by keeping an object, often a teddy or a comfort blanket, that stands in for the presence of the mother. For Winnicott, this ability to take an object and then be able to play and create is a key issue in the move to autonomy. It is this idea that Guattari uses to be able to think more broadly about the possibility of creativity, a creativity that can help move people gently, to create while allowing them to continue to feel safe. What he does with this idea is to take it outside the realm of the family alone to the whole social field, or socius, as he calls it, to the field of economic, material and ecological relations (Guattari, 1989). In brief, Guattari is interested in how such processes of creativity might work for ordinary people to create autonomous lives, in which they have some possibility of creativity and self-determination, outside the neoliberal fantasies that are set up for them to enter and outside the confines of global capitalism. He worked with the Italian Autonomia movement in the 1970s and 1980s (Berardi, 2009; Lotringer and Marazzi, 2007) and later with the ecology movement (Guattari, 1989). More recently, they have been taken up by a new generation of scholars and activists interested in changing the nature of trade-union activity to take account of the fact that activity needs to encompass those working and not working, and the lack of a central workplace, and to engage non-homogenous forms of organisation within work groups and communities. This work tends to go by the label of biosyndicalism described as follows (Ingrassia, 2006):

> Intermittence, mobility, discontinuity of incomes and laboral instablity have changed the social existence of the precariat into an experience very distinct from the pre-existing forms of the workforce. Since 30 years ago, against the permanent and unconsulted structuration of laboral activity brought forward by the boss. This structuration extended to the disciplining of the rest of social life, from the time of nonwork. This industrial worker struggled against domination understood as fixation of the body to one place and to one task. For its part, the precarious worker struggles against a very distinct form of domination: instability. This laboral instability has an extralaboral correlate: social dispersion. In conditions of stable structuration the militant tasks are to break, negate, subvert the rules. In conditions of social dispersion, the militant tasks are to invent autonomous modes of cohesion and recombination of resources and of human bonds that always threaten to escape, to disperse. In a certain sense, the present militant task of those that concentrate in intervening inside the precariat could be considered as the slow and intricate process of subjective reconstruction of the working class, taking the objective conditions of generalised dispersion as point of departure.

Contemporary capitalism produces fragmentation and introduces heterogeneity (in assigned tasks, forms of contractual relations, incomes, continuity/discontinuity in the job, etc.) and the individualization of the precariat. It is necessary to produce new forms of action that take advantage of this multiplicity. If the mass union constituted its power (potencia) on the basis of the growing homogeneity of the life of workers, biopolitical sindicalism should find its force in the wealth of differences, in the capacity to politically articulate the contemporary heterogeneity, in the will to carry this process of hetereogenization beyond the logic and the projects of capital.

While Ingrassia presents this as a new situation, in fact we have seen throughout this book that the workers of Steeltown lived insecurity all through the history of the works. However, the heterogeneity of the present situation makes the new ways of thinking about bringing together disparate groups (stable work, precarious work, long-term unemployment, within and outside work) important. Thus, using Guattari's idea of creativity (Berardi, 2009), one way of thinking about this is for communities to be able to imagine and create forms of what Ingrassia calls a non-state public sphere as a collective project. In this way, people with different kinds of precarious lives can begin to recognise each other and to recombine their efforts in order to produce a new vision, a new autonomy (not delimited by what is or is not given by the state). For this, Ingrassia argues that the network is the best organisational form:

If the structure was a system of fixed relations, proper to contexts of stability, the organizational form that will be most effective in situations of instability is the network. Without predetermined relations, open to the permanent incorporation of new elements, without a centralised command structure, the network permits a collective to be able to reconfigure itself successively following the changes of its environment, in order to always be able to act with the greatest transformative capacity. Unions up until now adopted structural organizational forms, in consonance with the structural organization of production proper to the industrial era. Presently the productive spaces, in agreement with the postfordist and toyotist theories, have initiated processes of transformation of structures into productive networks. A union that has the capacity to act taking into account the new forms of labor would be a network-union, an organization with the capacity to transform the characteristics that constitute the precariat (mobility, intermittence, heterogeneity, etc.) and change them into tools for struggle, into mechanisms of political aggregation.

However, Hamilton and Holdren (2008) use the term 'solidarity union-ism' and argue that some of these ideas developed in the 1930s also in response to precarious conditions. In particular, they argue for the central significance of mapping what people offer and what they bring together, and against fixed forms of organisation. Their model of the network has affinities with the concept of a web of relations (Studdert, 2006) used in this volume:

> Being an organiser means encountering someone else where they're at, using an idiom and appealing to values as close as possible to the ones they already have. The goal is to get close to them in order to move them (and be moved ourselves perhaps). But organising in the workplace also uses capacities everyone has. It presupposes, implicit or explicitly, a universal capacity to do and be more, that the actual does not exhaust the potential. This underlines an important part of what we see as the role of an organiser. If everyone is capable of organising then the organiser is only a temporary role, and one that is not monopolisable. Indeed, anyone who occupies that role should aim at the opposite of monopoly, at collectivisation.

It is significant that communities like Steeltown and other similar towns during the 200 years of iron and steel built a well-developed non-state public sphere with working-men's clubs, institutes, libraries and many support organisations. But their history has tended to be lost and the buildings used for other purposes or knocked down. How can a commu-nity link back with its own creative history and with it reach forward into a new future? Such issues are all the more important in a political moment when the government is going to withdraw public funding. The possibility of people feeling safe enough to make changes by them-selves for themselves and to create a new vision of a possible future has never been more urgent. Yet we can all imagine; indeed we do this all the time. We saw in Chapter 8 how Bethan imagined being a policewoman both to follow her father and to keep the men in order, while having adventures. Deleuze and Guattari (1987) would call this her 'line of flight'. That is, it is her imagined way out of the situation in which she finds herself – caught, stuck. Of course, choice, 'being who you want to be', has been much pushed by neoliberal modes of governance. Moreover, we can point to endless television series, like the

X Factor, that appear to foster ambition, imagination, aspiration and talent through forms of competition. But Guattari's vision is about how we support each other to develop a plan, a vision together to move forward not some imagination about leaving. We all imagine, everyone of us, but in our experience of research, many working-class children and adults get their imaginations squashed – they do not know how to actualise them, they do not have the means, the support or the confidence (see, for example, Walkerdine and Lucey, 1989). It is not the aesthetics or the creativity that is lacking but the possibility of support in the wider world. The means to say 'Let's try this' and then to keep being able to move and change it as it grows, to learn from it, to move the idea when it gets stuck or defeated, requires considerable communing and social support.

Franco Berardi tells us of the autonomia movement in the 1970s in Italy, involving workers movements and the centrality of autonomy from the state. Now, he says, things are different and we are required to work in a precarious state but at great speed, to be on call all the time, to be constantly in contact through mobile devices. Speed, he suggests, is a killer: it creates depression at one's being unable to keep up to speed or reliance on forms of consumption of drugs or alcohol to self-medicalise in order to cope with the speed. How can we get out of this speed? How can we find contentment outside consumption? The inhabitants of Steeltown don't have many resources for consumption and so what state support they have will disappear with the cuts in public spending, so how can they begin to harness the creativity that they undoubtedly have to create the support for each other that they need?

Steeltown has created a rock school. Watching their performances moved me to tears. It draws on the centrality of making music in Welsh and especially South Wales musical tradition, with generations making music alongside each other. The inhabitants have found a way to work together to create something that has the potential to bring them together and that binds them in a new way. Yes, they got funding for it, but people who can create this music and who have a rich heritage of mutuality are capable of mobilising their creativity and producing something that the architects of the 'big society' could never imagine. I am not saying that it is easy, nor indeed that the regeneration of the area by bringing new jobs, a hospital and a university campus are unimportant – all these things are sorely needed – but it is the spirit and creativity of the people that it seems to me offer most hope in times in which it is all too easy to sink into despair.

Notes

1 Two Hundred Years of Iron and Steel

1. An update (in 2006) of the reclamation programme of the former steelworks noted how work was under way, with contractors about to move onto the site to remediate the remaining 150 acres. Part of the ambitious regeneration plans included 75 new jobs, as well as up to 25 trainee posts for local people who would gain skills in the sector. The £200 million reclamation and redevelopment of the site was, and is being, driven forward by the local council in partnership with the government, and it was estimated to provide circa 0.5 million square feet of office space, 500 new homes, a learning campus, a local general hospital, 70 acres of parkland and open spaces including a wetland area, a primary school, a new railway station, a leisure centre and sports facilities, and a theatre (Welsh Assembly Government, 2006).
2. In order to preserve the anonymity of the town and its inhabitants, I have not included the author and title of reference works about the town.
3. Ibid.
4. Ibid.
5. We have not mentioned the important work of E P Thompson in his classic work *The Making of the English Working Class*. This is because while his argument that modes of working-class formation and resistance did not spring simply from the experience of industrial exploitation but built on centuries of radical organising within communities of the poor and working people is very well taken, it is tangential to the argument that we are making here, and it is not about Wales. He says: 'I have tried to distinguish between the experiences of different groups – artisans, outworkers, and labourers – and to show how they were coming to act, think, and feel, not in the old modes of deference and parochial seclusion, but in class ways' (p. 937). This helps people to agitate and build on the many movements that have already taken place to gain a sense of acting with others in the same situation and outside the community. Thompson argues that the period from 1790 to 1830 was that of the formation of the working class (212), and one that corresponds to the opening of the iron- and steelworks. So, he is saying that this making of the English working class is a political and cultural fact because it builds on what has gone before and is not just the result of the factory system or the Industrial Revolution acting on the mass of unformed humanity (213).
6. See Note 2.
7. Ibid.
8. One vivid example of this is given in the film *The White Ribbon* (2009, by Michael Haneke) in which the son of farmworkers destroys a field of cabbages in protest at an act of cruelty by their landlord. He is scornful of his father, but his father understands that absolute obedience and docility is

necessary because the family is not able to work again because the landlord punishes them all.

9. A Barmecide feast is one at which no food is served. It comes from a story in the *Arabian Nights* in which a rich man serves a beggar an imaginary meal with plates but no food.
10. See Note 2.
11. We are thinking here of work on the intergenerational transmission of trauma that shows the effects on the hormone system (e.g. adrenaline and cortisol production (Yehuda et al., 2001) as well as the neurological effects of continued terror (Yehuda et al., 1995)).
12. See Note 2.
13. Ibid.
14. Ibid.
15. Ibid.
16. Ibid.
17. Ibid.

3   Communal Beingness and Affect

1. The notion of group used by Anzieu and all psychoanalytic approaches does assume a rather general notion of group rather than a situated one, though this work usually refers to therapy groups. However, the notion has been extended to other groups, such as work groups, by the Tavistock Institute (see the three volumes of collected papers, under the general title of *The Social Engagement of Social Science*).
2. I am here referring both to social and unconscious fantasies and not wanting to make a strong distinction between them in the sense that an object can be a material object, operate in the fantasy of the community and also have an unconscious dimension.
3. Fences are also significant in work on the decline of 'traditional' communities reviewed by Savage (2008).
4. There is no room here to develop important issues that explore the relationship between the language of object relations, with its internal and external objects and Deleuze and Guattari's concept of the assemblage, which understands actual physical objects, such as houses, paths and fences, as central to the flow of affect, but also refers to an object relations and Lacanian account of part objects (Guattari, 1989).

4   De-Industrialisation, Suffering, Crisis and Catastrophe

1. In relation to British studies, we can mention Fevre's (1989) *Wales Is Closed*, a study of Port Talbot, which does not discuss the emotional effects of deindustrialisation. A study by Waddington et al. (1991), *Split at the Seams*, about three coal communities after the pit closures, cites Bulmer's (1975) model of a mining community, which he characterises as follows:

    1. physical isolation
    2. economic predominance of mining

   3. a working class majority of the population
   4. daily experience of arduous work pervading the community
   5. industrial conflict endemic
   6. gender roles segregated
   7. leisure public and male dominated
   8. social networks close-knit, overlapping and supportive.

Noting this, the main changes that Waddington et al. witnessed after the closures were as follows:

   1. some people opposing the strike
   2. greater female equality
   3. youth culture
   4. home-based consumer culture
   5. influx of commuters and council tenants
   6. nuclear family replacing kinship system
   7. new movements replacing unions
   8. deskilling.

All of Bulmer's categories, except obviously mining, could be used to describe Steeltown before the closure, and many of the points made about the change by Wyles et al. relate also to what happened to Steeltown.

2. He developed this idea by reference to the work of the German neurobiologist Kurt Goldstein, who argued that the nervous system could be understood as a whole and not as the sum of individual neurons. He called this a network and the individual neuron a nodal point in the network.

3. Note also how Ogden (1986) calls the mind a matrix because it emerges from the relational space of mother-baby.

4. We might also note that the term 'matrix' in a more mathematical sense has been used by Foucault, who argues that power takes the form of a matrix or a 'tightly knit grid of material coercions' in which we are all embedded as 'objects of power' (Foucault, 1980, p. 104). The task as Foucault sees it in relation to his work on biopower is to understand the complexity of the social matrix that gives our understanding of, for example, sexuality, its force. Butler (1997) also uses the term in a Foucauldian sense in her concept of the 'heterosexual matrix'. We can indeed think of a community of affect in this way, but I suggest that we would be quite wrong if we were not to engage with the basic and embodied sense of safety provided by the community and its necessity for the possibility of life for its inhabitants. It is not just a 'grid of material coercions' that is tightly knit for these people. We explore Butler's heterosexual matrix in Chapter 7.

5. Elsewhere, I explore this example in more detail, using it to think about the relationship between 'death' as breakdown and fear of annihilation and its creative potential as developed by Deleuze through his reading of Artaud's work on mania. See Walkerdine (forthcoming).

6   The Next Generation

1. In our first study, we interviewed five young men. One of them was employed in a car tyre manufacturing factory, one was working as an information systems assistant, two were studying and one was doing temporary shop work.

In the second study, we interviewed six young unemployed men. Four of them had previously been made redundant more than once but continued to look for work, especially manufacturing work, which seemed to be their preference. A few had also contemplated the armed forces as a kind of last yet somewhat possible option. One of them had completed one year in the armed forces and was back in his home town but was not looking for work there. He was contemplating instead finding a way of carrying on studying a trade. In terms of their educational background, all of them could at least read and write. Four of them had started other post-school basic training (e.g. basic NVQ in bricklaying, plastering, baking, plumbing and carpentry), but none of them had managed to complete these courses and they were still contemplating completing them at some point in the future. One of them had not managed to complete any post-compulsory education and was also already a father of three children, and was therefore experiencing a lot of difficulty finding suitable work. Another had also only completed basic compulsory education and was not prepared to study any more because he reckoned school was not interesting or relevant to him. He was trying instead to find a job that paid well but that did not require further educational and/or work credentials.

2. The method we used was psychosocial interviewing, informed by relational psychoanalysis (Hoggett et al., 2010; Walkerdine et al., 2002). Because we were interested in exploring the emotional dimension of the participants' lived experiences, we focused on encouraging a dialogue to create an emotional space (third space, mutuality) (Aron, 2006) to explore their emotional responses to redundancy and its aftermath and their associated meanings within a wider social context. This means we see the space of the interview as a space of creation in which a 'third narrative' is produced, which is different from that which either interviewer or interviewee would have produced alone. This co-constructive dialogical narrative interview approach (Hoggett et al., 2006) also allowed us to explore the sets of historically and culturally specific practices that the inhabitants of this community deploy in their coping with the effects of redundancy and neoliberal labour market changes, and to appreciate its psychosocial dimension by highlighting its affective component (Walkerdine et al., 2001); for example, how these sets of practices are also modes of conscious and unconscious relating, leading to a narrative associated with the decision not to take on embarrassing or feminine work.

3. cf. Abraham and Torok's concept of the phantom and Freud's concept of the revenant.

7 Women, Gays and Mammy's Boys

1. These have been identified in mainstream developmental accounts (Bowlby, (1960), Greenson, (1968), Stoller, (1968)) and also in some psychoanalytic work (Wieland, 2000), as well as being commonly understood within feminism.

Bibliography

Aaron, J. (2002) *A View Across the Valley: Short Stories by Women from Wales c. 1850–1950 Anthology.* Aberystwyth: Honno.

Aaron, J. (2007) *The Very Salt of Life: Welsh Women's Political Writings from Chartism to Suffrage.* Aberystwyth: Honno.

Adam, B. (2004) *Time.* Cambridge: Polity.

Adkins, L. (1995) *Gendered Work: Sexuality, Family and the Labour Market.* Buckingham: Open University Press.

Adleman, J. & Enguidanos, G. (eds) (1993) *Racism in the Lives of Women.* New York: Haworth Press.

Agamben, G. (2002) *Remnants of Auschwitz: The Witness and the Archive.* New York: Zone Books.

Ahmed, S. (2000) *Transformations, Thinking through Feminism.* London: Routledge.

Ahmed, S. (2004) *The Cultural Politics of Emotion.* Edinburgh: Edinburgh University Press.

Alexander, J.C. et al. (2004) *Cultural Trauma and Collective Identity.* Berkeley: University of California Press.

Anderson, B. (1983) *Imagined Communities.* London: Verso.

Andrews, M. et al. (2000) *Lines of Narrative: Psychosocial Perspectives.* London & New York: Routledge.

Antonis, B. (2008) In Raphael-Leff, J. & Perelberg, R.J. (eds) *Female Experience: Four Generations of British Women Psychoanalysts on Work with Women.* London: Routledge.

Anzieu, D. (1984) *The Group and the Unconscious.* London: Routledge and Kegan Paul.

Anzieu, D. (1989) *The Skin Ego.* New Haven, CT: Yale University Press.

Arendt, H. (1958) *The Human Condition.* Cambridge: Cambridge University Press.

Aron, L. & Harris, A. (eds) (2005) *Relational Psychoanalysis II: Innovation and Expansion.* Hillsdale, NJ: The Analytic Press.

Arribas-Ayllon, M. (2007) *Unpublished PhD Thesis.* Cardiff: Cardiff University.

Ashurst, F. (2010) *Unpublished PhD Thesis.* Cardiff: Cardiff University.

Avery, J. et al. (1998) 'The Mental Health and Physical Health of Miners Following the 1992 National Pit Closure Programme: A Cross Sectional Survey Using General Health Questionnaire GHQ-12 and Short Form SF-36' *Public Health,* 112: 169–173.

Axelrod, S.D. (1997) 'Developmental Pathways to Masculinity: A Reconsideration of Greenson's "Dis-identifying from Mother"' *Issues in Psychoanalytic Psychology,* 19: 101–115.

Azoulay, E. et al. (2005) 'Risk of Post-Traumatic Stress Symptoms in Family Members of Intensive Care Unit Patients' *American Journal of Respiratory and Critical Care Medicine,* 171: 987–994.

Bailey, D. (2003) 'Globalisation, Regions and Cluster Policies: The Case of the Rover Task Force' *Policy Studies,* 24 (2/3): 67–85.

Bailey, D., & De Ruyter, A. (2007) 'Globalisation, Economic Freedom and Strategic Decision-Making: A Role for Industrial Policy?' *Policy Studies,* 28 (4): 383–398.

Balsom, D. (1985) 'The Three Wales Model' In Osmond, J. (ed.) *The National Question Again.* Llandysul: Gomer.

Banks, M. (1995) 'Psychological Effects of Prolonged Unemployment: Relevance to Models of Work Re-Entry Following Injury' *Journal of Occupational Rehabilitation,* 5 (1): 37–53.

Bar-On, D. et al. (1998) 'Multigenerational Perspectives on Coping with the Holocaust Experience: An Attachment Perspective for Understanding the Developmental Sequelae of Trauma across Generations' *International Journal of Behavioural Development,* 22 (2): 315–338.

Bateson, G. (1972) *Steps to an Ecology of Mind.* Chicago: Chicago University Press.

Bauman, Z. (1998) *Globalization: The Human Consequences.* New York: Columbia University Press.

Beck, U. (1992) *Risk Society: Towards a New Modernity.* London: Sage.

Beck, U. (1998) *World Risk Society.* Cambridge: Polity Press.

Beck, U. (2000) *The Brave New World of Work.* Cambridge: Cambridge University Press.

Beck, U. & Beck-Gernsheim, E. (2001) *Individualization: Institutionalized Individualism and Its Social and Political Consequences.* London: Sage.

Beck, U., Giddens, A. & Lasch, S. (1994) *Reflexive Modernisation.* Cambridge: Polity.

Bederman, G. (1995) *Manliness and Civilisation: A Cultural History of Gender and Race in the United States 1880–1917.* Chicago: Chicago University Press.

Bell, C. & Newby, H. (1971) *Community Studies: An Introduction to the Sociology of the Local Community.* London: George Allen & Unwin.

Bentham, J. (1875) 'Panopticon' In Bozovic, M. (ed.) *The Panopticon Writings.* London: Verso, pp. 29–95, www.carome.org/panopticon2.htm. Date accessed 21 August 2010.

Berardi, F. (2009) *The Soul at work: From Alienation to Autonomy.* Los Angeles: Semiotext(e) Foreign Agents.

Berlant, L. (2000) 'The Subject of True feeling' In Ahmed, S. et al. (eds) *Transformations, Thinking through Feminism.* London: Routledge, pp. 33–34.

Berlant, L. (2004) *Compassion: The Culture and Politics of an Emotion.* London: Routledge.

Bick, E. (1968) 'The Experience of the Skin in Early Object Relations' *International Journal of Psychoanalysis,* 49: 484–486.

Bion, W. (1959) 'Attacks on Linking' *International Journal of Psycho-Analysis,* 40 (5–6): 308.

Bion, W. (1962) *Learning from Experience.* London: William Heinemann.

Blaenau-Gwent Council/The Works Archive (2010), www.blaenau-gwent.gove. uk/theworks/archive, Date accessed 21 August 2010.

Bollas, C. (1987) *The Shadow of the Object: Psychoanalysis of the Unthought Known.* London: Free Association.

Boulanger, G. (2007) *Wounded By Reality: Understanding and Treating Adult Onset Trauma.* Mahwah, NJ: The Analytic Press.

Bowlby, J. (1960) 'Separation Anxiety' *International Journal of Psychoanalysis,* 41: 89–113.

Brod, N.H. (ed.) (1987) *The Making of Masculinities: The New Men's Studies*. New York: Routledge.

Brown, K. et al. (2000) *Rhetorics of Welfare: Uncertainty, Choice and Voluntary Associations*. London: Palgrave Macmillan.

Bulmer, M. (1975) 'Sociological Models of the Mining Community' *Sociological Review*, 23 (1): 61–92.

Bulmer, M. (1986a) *Social Science and Social Policy (Contemporary Social Research)*. London: HarperCollins Publishers Ltd.

Bulmer, M. (1986b) *The Chicago School of Sociology*. Chicago & London: Chicago University Press.

Burchell, D. (1996) 'Liberal Government and Techniques of the Self' In Barry A., Osborne T. & Rose N. (eds) *Foucault and Political Reason*. Chicago, IL: University of Chicago Press.

Burke, P. (ed.) (1991) *New Perspectives in Historical Writing*. Cambridge: Cambridge University Press.

Butler, J. (1990) *Gender Trouble: Feminism and the Subversion of Identity*. New York: Routledge.

Butler, J. (1997) *The Psychic Life of Power*. Stanford: Stanford University Press.

Butler, J. (2004) *The Judith Butler Reader*. Oxford: Blackwell.

Campbell, B. (1984) *Wigan Pier Revisited, Poverty and Politics in the 1980s*. London: Virago.

Campbell J. & Pile, S. (2010) 'Telepathy and Its Vicissitudes: Freud, Thought Transference and the Hidden Lives of the (Repressed and Non-Repressed) Unconscious' *Subjectivity*, 3: 403–425.

Caruth, C. (1995) *Trauma: Explorations in Memory*. Baltimore: The John Hopkins University Press.

Castells, M. (1997) *The Power of Identity*. Oxford: Blackwell.

Cath, S.H., Gurwitt, A.R. & Ross, J.M. (eds) (1982) *Father and Child*. Boston: Little Brown.

Cerutti, S. (2004) 'Microhistory: Social Relations versus Cultural Models?' In Castrén, A.M., Lonkila, M. & Peltonen, M. (eds) *Between Sociology and History. Essays on Microhistory, Collective Action, and Nation-building*. Studia Historica 70, Helsinki, pp. 17–40.

Charles, N. & Davies, C.A. (2005) 'Studying the Particular, Illuminating the General: Community Studies and Community in Wales' *The Sociological Review*, 53: 672–690.

Charlwood, A. (2006) 'What Determined Employer Voice Choice in Britain in the 20th Century? A Critique of the "Sound of Silence" Model' *Socioeconomic Review*, 4 (2): 301–309.

Clare, A. (2000) *On Men: Masculinity in Crisis*. London: Chatto and Windus.

Clarke, J., Critcher, C. & Johnson, R. (eds) (1979) *Working Class Culture*. London: Hutchison.

Cloke, P. & Milbourne, P. (1992) 'Deprivation and Lifestyles in Rural Wales – Rurality and the Cultural Dimension' *Journal of Rural Studies*, 8 (4): 359–371.

Cohen, J. & Arato, A (1992) *Civil Society and Political Theory*. Cambridge, MA: MIT Press.

Connell, R.W. (1995) *Masculinities: Knowledge, Power and Social Change*. Oxford: Polity.

Cross, S. & Bagilhole, B. (2002) 'Girls' Jobs for the Boys? Men, Masculinity and Non-Traditional Occupations' *Gender, Work & Organization*, 9 (2), April: 204–226.

Crow, G. & Maclean, C. (2004) 'Families and Local Communities' In Scott, J., Treas, J.K. & Richards, M.P. (eds) *The Blackwell Companion to the Sociology of Families*. Oxford, UK: Blackwell, pp. 69–83.

Crow, G. & Maclean, C. (2006) 'Community' In Payne, G. (ed.) *Social Divisions* (second edition). Basingstoke: Palgrave Macmillan, pp. 305–324.

Damasio, A. (2000) *The Feeling of What Happens: Body and Emotion in the Making of Consciousness*. London: Heinemann.

Danieli, Y. (ed.) (1998) *International Handbook of Multigenerational Legacies of Trauma*. New York: Plenum Press.

Davidson, J.R.T. et al. (1991) 'Post Traumatic Stress Disorder in the Community: An Epidemiological Study' *Psychological Medicine*, 21: 713–721.

Davoine, F. (2007) 'The Characters of Madness in the Talking Cure' *Psychoanalytic Dialogues*, 17 (5): 627–638.

Davoine, F. & Gaudilliere, J. (2004) *History Beyond Trauma: Whereof One Cannot Speak, Thereof One Cannot Stay Silent*, Translated by Susan Fairfield. New York: Other Press.

De Bolle, L. (2010) *Deleuze and Psychoanalysis*. Leuven: Leuven University Press.

Dekker, P. & van den Broek, A. (1998) 'Civil Society in Comparative Perspective: Involvement in Voluntary Associations in North America and Western Europe' *Voluntas*, 9 (1): 11–38.

Deleuze, G. (1991) *Bergsonism*, Translated by Hugh Tomlinson and Barbara Habberjam. New York: Zone Books.

Deleuze, G. (1994) *Difference and Repetition*. London: Continuum.

Deleuze, G. & Guattari, F. (1984) *Anti-Oedipus: Capitalism and Schizophrenia*. London: Athlone.

Deleuze, G. & Guattari, F. (1987) *A Thousand Plateaus: Capitalism and Schizophrenia*, Translation and Foreword by Brian Massumi. Minneapolis: University of Minnesota Press.

Dempsey, K. (1990) *Smalltown: A Study of Social Inequality, Cohesion and Belonging*. Melbourne: Oxford University Press.

Denham, A. (2008) 'Rethinking Historical Trauma: Narratives of Resilience' *Transcultural Psychiatry*, 45 (3): 391–414.

Department of Children, Schools and Families (DCSF) (2008) *The Extra Mile: How Schools Succeed in Raising Aspirations in Children, Schools and Families*. London: DCSF.

Diamond, M. J. (2004) 'Revisioning Boys Turning Away from Their Mothers to Construct Male Gender Identity' *International Journal of Psychoanalysis*, 85: 359–380.

Dolby, N., Dimitriadis, G. & Willis, P.E. (eds) (2004) *Learning to Labour in New Times*. London/New York: Routledge Kegan Paul.

Dorling, D. (1997) Death in Britain: How Local Mortality Rates Have Changed: 1950s–1990s, Report published by the Joseph Rowntree Foundation.

Du Gay, P. (1996) *Consumption and Identity at Work*. London: Sage.

Edley, N. & Wetherell, M. (1999) 'Imagined Futures: Young Men's Talk about Fatherhood and Domestic Life' *British Journal of Social Psychology,* 38 (2): 181–194.

Elias, N. & Scotson, J. (1994 [1965]) *The Established and the Outsiders: A Sociological Enquiry into Community Problems.* London: Sage.

Engels, F. (1892) *The Condition of the Working Class in England.* London: Penguin Books.

Erikson, K. (1984) *A New Species of Trouble: Explorations in Disaster, Trauma and Community.* New York: W.W. Norton.

Erikson, K. (1994) *A New Species of Troubles: Explorations in Disasters, Trauma and Community.* New York: Norton.

Erikson, K. (1995) 'Notes on Trauma and Community' In Caruth, C. (ed.) *Trauma: Explorations in Memory.* Baltimore: The John Hopkins University Press, pp. 183–199.

Ettinger, B. (2001) 'Wit(h)nessing Trauma and the Matrixial Gaze: From Phantasm to Trauma, from Phallic Structure to Matrixial Sphere' *Parallax,* 7 (4): 89–114.

Ettinger, B. (2006) *The Matrixial Borderspace.* Minneapolis, MN: University of Minnesota Press.

Evans, W. (1974) *Land of My Fathers: 2000 Years of Welsh History.* Swansea: John Perry Press.

Faludi, S. (2000) *Stiffed: The Betrayal of the American Man.* New York: Harper-Collins.

Fanon, F. (2004) *The Wretched of the Earth.* New York: Grove Press.

Fast, I. (1990) 'Aspects of Early Gender Development: Towards a Reformulation' *Psychoanalytic Psychology* (Suppl), 17: 105–117.

Featherstone, M. (1995) *Undoing Culture: Globalisation, Postmodernism and Identity.* London: Sage.

Ferrie, J.E. et al. (2001) 'Employment Status and Health after Privatisation in White Collar Civil Servant: Prospective Cohort Study' *British Medical Journal,* 322 (7287): 647.

Ferrie, J.E. et al. (2002) 'Effects of Chronic Job Insecurity and Change in Job Security on Self-Reported Health, Minor Psychiatric Morbidity, Physiological Measures, and Health-Related Behaviours in British Civil Servants: The Whitehall 11 Study' *Journal of Epidemiology and Community Health,* 56: 450–454.

Ferrie, J.E. et al. (2003) 'Future Uncertainty and Socioeconomic Inequalities in Health: The Whitehall 11 Study' *Social Science and Medicine,* 57: 637–646.

Ferrie, J.E. et al. (2005) 'Self-Reported Job Insecurity and Health in the Whitehall 11 Study: Potential Explanations of the Relationship' *Social Science and Medicine,* 60: 1593–1602.

Fevre, R. (1989) *Wales Is Closed.* Nottingham: Spokesman Books.

Fineman, S. (2000) *Emotions in Organisations.* London: Sage.

Foucault, M. (1977) *Discipline and Punish: The Birth of the Prison.* New York: Vintage Books.

Foucault, M. (1980) *Power/Knowledge: Selected Interviews and Other Writings 1972–1977,* edited by Colin Gordon. London: Harvester.

Foucault, M. (2006) *The History of Madness.* New York: Routledge.

Foulkes, S.H. (1983) *Introduction to Group-Analytic Psychotherapy: Studies in the Social Integration of Individuals and Groups.* London: Marsefield Reprints.

Foulkes, S.H. (1986) *Group-Analytic Psychotherapy Method and Principles.* London: Marsefield Library, Karnac.

Foulkes, S.H. (1990) *Collected Papers of S. H. Foulkes.* London: Karnac.

Frazer, W. (1982) 'Milton Friedman and Thatcher's Monetarist Experience' *Journal of Economic Issues,* 16 (2): 525–533.

Freud, S. (1913) *Totem and Taboo,* Standard Edition of the Complete Works of Sigmund Freud, Vol. X111. London: Hogarth Press and Institute of Psychoanalysis.

Freud, S. (1917) *Mourning and Melancholia,* Standard Edition, XVII (2nd ed.), Hogarth Press, 1955.

Freud, S. (1922) *Group Psychology and the Analysis of the Ego.* London: International Library of Psychoanalysis.

Frosh, S. (2002) 'Racism, Radicalised Identities and the Psychoanalytic Other' In Walkerdine, V. (ed.) *Challenging Subjects: Critical Psychology for a New Millennium.* London: Palgrave Macmillan.

Fyfe, N.R. & Milligan, C. (2003) 'Out of the Shadows: Exploring Contemporary Geographies of Voluntarism' *Geography,* 27: 397.

Gallo, W.T. et al. (2000) 'Health Effects of Involuntary Job Loss Among Older Workers: Findings from the Health and Retirement Survey' *Journal of Gerontology: Social Sciences 2000,* 55B (3): S131.

Gantt, S. & Hopper, E. (2008) 'Two Perspectives on a Trauma in a Training Group: The Systems Centred Approach and the Theory of Incohesion, Part 1' *Group Analysis,* 4 (1): 98–112.

Garland, C. (1999) 'Thinking about Trauma' In Garland, C. (ed.) *Understanding Trauma: A Psychoanalytical Approach.* London, New York: Karnac.

Gee, J. P. (2000) 'New People in New Worlds: Networks, the New Capitalism and Schools' In Cope, B. & Kalantzia, M. (eds) *Multiliteracies: Literacy Learning and the Design of Social Futures.* London: Routledge & Kegan Paul, pp. 43–68.

Giddens, A. (1991) *Modernity and Self-Identity: Self and Society in the Late Modern Age.* Oxford: Polity Press.

Giddens, A. (1998) *The Third Way.* Cambridge: Polity Press.

Giddens, A. (2000) *The Third Way and Its Critics.* Cambridge: Polity Press.

Ginzburg, C. (1993) 'Microhistory: Two or Three Things I know about It' *Critical Inquiry,* 20: 10–35.

Goldthorpe, J. et al. (1968) *The Affluent Worker: Industrial Attitudes and Behaviour* Cambridge Studies in Sociology, Vol. 1. Cambridge: Cambridge University Press.

Gonnick, M. (2002) *Unpublished PhD Thesis.* Ontario: Institute for Studies in Education.

Gordon, A. (2008) *Ghostly Matters: Haunting and the Sociological Imagination.* Minneapolis: University of Minnesota Press.

Grant, J.A. (2004) 'A "Real Boy" and Not a Sissy: Gender, Childhood and Masculinity, 1890–1940' *Journal of Social History,* 37 (4): 829–851.

Greenson, R. (1968) 'Dis-identifying from Mother: Its Special Importance for the Boy' *International Journal of Psychoanalysis,* 49: 370–374.

Greenspan, S.I. (1982) 'The Second Other: The Role of the Father in Early Personality Formation and the Diadic-Phallic Phase of Development' In Cath, S.H., Gurwitt, A.R. & Ross, J.M. (eds) *Father and Child.* Boston: Little Brown.

Griffin, C. (2000) 'Discourses of Crisis and Loss: Analysis of the "Boys' Under-Achievement" Debate' *Journal of Youth Studies*, 3 (2): 167–188.

Guattari, F. (1989) *The Three Ecologies*. London: Continuum.

Hahn, H. (ed.) (1994 [1974]) *Sincerity and Other Works*. London: Karnac.

Hall, S. et al. (1978) *Policing the Crisis: Mugging, the State, and Law and Order*. London: Macmillan Press.

Hall, A., Hockey, J. & Robinson, V. (2000) 'Occupational Cultures and the Embodiment of Masculinity: Hairdressing, Estate Agency and Firefighting' *Gender, Work & Organization*, 14 (6), November: 534–551.

Hamilton, T. & Holdren, N. (2008) *Compositional Power* retrieved from 'Turbulance', http://www.turbulence.org.uk/index.php?s=hamilton+and+holdren. Date accessed 7 November 2010.

Hansard (2001) *Steel Industry* (3 May 2001 Vol. 367 cc962-6) retrieved from www.hansard.millbanksystems.com. Date accessed 22 August 2010.

Hansen, M. (2004) *New Philosophy for New Media*. Cambridge MA: MIT Press.

Hardt, M. & Negri, A. (2001) *Empire*. Cambridge, MA: Harvard University Press.

Harris, C.C. (1987) *Redundancy and Recession in South Wales*. Oxford: Blackwell.

Harris, J. (2007) 'Cool Cymru, Rugby Union and an Imagined Community' *International Journal of Sociology and Social Policy*, 27 (3/4): 151–161.

Head, E. (1842) *Report of the Poor Law Commissioners on an Enquiry of the Sanitary Condition of the Labouring Population of Great Britain* (Somerset House, 9 July), www.sochealth.co.uk/chadwick/Foreword.html. Date accessed 22 August 2010.

Hearn, J. (1999) *A Crisis in Masculinity, or New Agendas for Men? New Agendas for Women*. London: Palgrave Macmillan.

Henderson, H.D. (1955) *The Inter-War Years and Other Papers: A Selection from the Writings of Hubert Douglas Henderson*. Oxford: Clarendon Press.

Henriques, J. (2010) 'The Vibrations of Affect and Their Propogation on a Night Out on Kingston's Dancehall Scene' *Body and Society*, 16 (1): 57–89.

Henriques, J. et al. (1984) *Changing The Subject: Psychology, Social Regulation and Subjectivity*. London: Methuen.

Henson, K. & Krasas, J. (2001) 'Why Marcia You've Changed!: Male Clerical Temporary Workers Doing Masculinity in a Feminised Occupation' *Gender & Society*, 15: 218–238.

Hinshelwood, R. (2002) 'Review of Judith Mitrani: Ordinary People and Extraordinary Protections: A Post-Kleinian Approach to the Treatment of Primitive Mental States' *International Journal of Psychoanalysis*, 83: 287–290.

Hinshelwood, R. & Chisea, M. (2002) *Organisations, Anxieties and Defence*. London: Whurr.

Hirsch, M. (2008) 'The Generation of Postmemory' *Poetics Today*, 29 (1): 103–128.

Hoggett, P. et al. (2006) 'Identity, Life History and Commitment to Welfare' *Journal of Social Policy*, 35 (4): 689–704.

Hoggett, P. et al. (in press) 'Working Psycho-socially and Dialogically in Research' *Psychoanalysis, Culture & Society*.

Hollan, D. (2004) 'Self Systems, Cultural Idioms of Distress, and the Psychobodily Consequences of Childhood Suffering' *Transcultural Psychiatry*, 41 (1): 62–79.

Holland, J. (2007) 'Emotions and Research' *Journal of Social Research Methodology*, 10 (3): 195–209.

Hollway, W. & Jefferson, T. (2000) *Doing Qualitative Research Differently.* London: Sage.

Holmes, B. (n.d.) Guattari's Schizoanalytic Cartographies. Continental Drift, http://brianholmes.wordpress.com/2009/02/27/guattaris-schizoanalytic-carto graphies/. Date accessed 14 December 2010.

Hopper, E. (2003a) *The Social Unconscious: Selected Papers.* London: Jessica Kingsley.

Hopper, E. (2003b) *Traumatic Experience in the Unconscious Life of Groups: The Fourth Basic Assumption: Incohesion: Aggregation/Massification or (BA) I: A/M.* London: Jessica Kingsley.

Hopper, E. (2009) 'The Theory of the Basic Assumption of Incohesion: Aggregation/Massification or (BA) I: A/M' *British Journal of Psychotherapy,* 25 (2): 214–229.

Ingrassia, F. (2006) *What in the Hell Is Bio Syndicalism,* http://www/whatinthehell. blogsome.com/2006/07/27/is-biopolitical-sindicalism. Date accessed 7 November 2010.

Jahoda, M., Lazarsfeld, P. & Zeisel, H. (1933 [1972]) *Marienthal: The Sociography of an Unemployed Community.* London: Tavistock.

Jankowski, M.S. (1991) *Islands in the Streets: Gangs and American Urban Society.* Berkeley: University of California Press.

Jay, M. (2007) "Melancholy Femininity and Obsessive Compulsive Masculinity: Sex Differences in Melancholy Gender". Studies in Gender & Sexuality, Vol. 8 (2): 115–135.

Jimenez, L. & Walkerdine, V. (2011a) 'Melancholic Masculinities' *Gender and Education,* 23(2): 185–199(15).

Jimenez, L. & Walkerdine, V. (2011) ' "Shameful work": A psychosocial approach to father–son relations, young male unemployment and femininity in an ex-steel community' *Psychoanalysis, Culture and Society.* doi:10.1057/pcs.2011.14

Kalil, A. et al. (2010) 'Job Insecurity and Change Over Time in Health Among Older Men and Women' *The Journals of Gerontology Series B,* 65 (1): 81–90.

Kellerman, N. (2001) 'Transmission of Holocaust Trauma – An Integrative View' *Psychiatry,* 64 (3): 256–266.

Kelly, S. (2002) *Simulating Future Trends in Wealth Inequality,* Paper presented at the 2002 Australian Conference of Economists, Adelaide, South Australia, 3 October 2002.

Kenway, J. & Kraack, A. (2004) 'Reordering Work and Destabilising Masculinities' In Dolby, N., Dimitriadis, G. & Willis, P.E. (eds) *Learning to Labour in New Times.* London/New York: Routledge Kegan Paul.

Kenway, J., Kraack, A. & Hickey-Moody, A. (2006) *Masculinity Beyond the Metropolis.* Basingstoke: Palgrave Macmillan.

Kidron, C. (2004) 'Surviving a Distant Past: A Case Study of the Cultural Construction of Trauma Descendant Identity' *Ethos,* 31 (4): 513–544.

Kimmel, M. (1987) 'The Crisis of Masculinity in Historical Perspective' In Brod, N.H. (ed.) *The Making of Masculinities: The New Men's Studies.* New York: Routledge.

Kimmel, M. (2005) *The Gender of Desire: Essays on Masculinity.* Albany: State University of New York Press.

Klein, M. (1986) *The Selected Melanie Klein* (J. Mitchell, ed.). Harmondsworth: Penguin.

Kleinman, A. & Kleinman, J. (1997a) 'The Appeal of Experience; the Dismay of Images: Cultural Appropriations of Suffering in Our Times' In Kleinman, A., Das, V. & Lock, M. (eds) *Social Suffering*. Berkeley: University of California Press.

Kleinman, A., Das, V. & Lock, M. (eds) (1997b) *Social Suffering*. Berkeley: University of California Press.

Latour, B. (1993) *We Have Never Been Modern*. London: Harvester.

Latour, B. (2005) *Reassembling the Social: An Introduction to Actor-Network-Theory*. Oxford: Oxford University Press.

Law, A. & Mooney, G. (2006) ' "We've Never Had It so Good": The "Problem" of the Working Class in Devolved Scotland' *Critical Social Policy*, 26 (3): 524–542.

Layton, L. (2002) *Who's That Girl? Who's That Boy?: Clinical Practice Meets Postmodern Gender Theory*. Northvale, NJ: J. Aronson.

Layton, L. (2006) 'That Place Gives Me the Heebie Jeebies' In Layton, L., Hollander, N.C. & Gutwill, S. (eds) *Psychoanalysis, Class and Politics: Encounters in the Clinical Setting*. Falmer and New York: Routledge.

Lefebvre, H. (2004) *Rhythmanalysis: Space, Time and Everyday Life*. London: Continuum.

Levi, G. (1991) 'On Micro History' In Burke, P. (ed.) *New Perspectives in Historical Writing*. Cambridge: Cambridge University Press, pp. 97–119.

Lewis, J. (1999) 'Reviewing the Relationship between the Voluntary Sector and the State in Britain in the 1990s' *Voluntas*, 10 (3): 255–270.

Lewis, S., Smithson, J. & Brannen, J. (1999) *Young Europeans' Orientations to Family and Work: Annals of the American Academy of Political and Social Science*. Thousand Oaks: Sage.

Leys, R. (2000) *Trauma: A Genealogy*. London: Chicago University Press.

Leys, R. (2007) *From Guilt to Shame*. Princeton: Princeton University Press.

Leys, R. (2009) *From Guilt to Shame: Auschwitz and after*. Princeton: Princeton University Press.

Liepins, R. (2000) 'New Energies for an Old Idea: Reworking Approaches to "Community" in Contemporary Rural Studies' *Journal of Rural Studies*, 16: 23–35.

Lindsay, C. & McQuaid, R.W. (2004) 'Avoiding the "McJobs": Unemployed Job Seekers and Attitudes to Service Work' *Work, Employment and Society*, 18 (2): 296–319.

Lloyd, T. (1999) 'Young Men, The Job Market and Gendered Work'. Work and Opportunity Series. York: Joseph Rowntree Foundation.

Lotringer, S. & Marazzi, C. (eds) (2007) *Autonomia, Post-Political Politics*. Los Angeles: Semiotext(e) Foreign Agents Series.

Lupton, B. (2006) 'Explaining Men's Entry into Female Concentrated Occupations: Issues of Masculinity and Social Class' *Gender, Work and Organisation*, 13 (2): 103–128.

Luthar, S., Cicchetti, D. & Becker, B. (2000) 'The Construct of Resilience: A Critical Evaluation and Guidelines for Future Work' *Child Development*, 71 (3): 543–562.

MacInness, J. (1998) *The End of Masculinity: The Confusion of Sexual Genesis and Sexual Difference in Modern Society*. Milton Keynes: Open University Press.

MacKenzie, R. et al. (2006) 'All That Is Solid? Class, Identity and the Maintenance of a Collective Orientation amongst Redundant Steel Workers' *Sociology*, 40 (5): 833–852.

Maffesoli, M. (1996) *The Time of the Tribes.* London: Sage.

Magnusson, S.G. (2003) 'The Singularization of History: Social History and Micro-History within the Postmodern State of Knowledge' *Journal of Social History,* 36 (3): 701–735.

Malthus, R.T. (1798) *An Essay on the Principle of Populations as It Affects the Future Improvement of Society with Remarks on the Speculations of Mr. Godwin, M. Condorcet, and Other Writers.* London: Printed for J. Johnson, in St. Paul's Church-Yard, www.esp.org/books/malthus/population/malthus.pdf. Date accessed 22 August 2010.

Malthus, R.T. (1820) *Principles of Political Economy.* London: John Murray.

Malthus, R.T. (1827) *Definitions in Political Economy.* London: John Murray.

Marx, K. (1863–1883) *Capital: A Critique of Political Economy. Vol. 3* (edited by Friedrick Engels and completed by him in 1894). New York: International Publishers (n. d.), www.marxists.org/archive/marx/works/1894-c3/index.htm. Date accessed 23 August 2010.

Massey, C. (2005) *For Space.* London: Sage.

Maynard, S. (1980) 'Rough Work & Rugged Men: The Social Construction of Masculinity in Working Class History' In Pleck, E. & Pleck J. (eds) *The American Man.* Englewood, NJ: Prentice-Hall.

McDonald, S., Edwards, J. & Savage, M. (eds) (2005) 'Community, Continuity and Change in the Study of Britain: A Festschrift for Ronnie Frankenberg' *Sociological Review,* 53 (4): 587–621.

McDowell, L. (2000) 'The Trouble with Men? Young People, Gender Transformations and the Critis of Masculinity' *International Journal of Urban and Regional Research,* 24 (1): 201–209.

McDowell, L. (2002) 'Transitions to Work: Masculine Identities, Youth Inequality and Labour Market Change' *Gender, Place & Culture,* 9 (10): 39–59.

McDowell, L. (2003) *Redundant Masculinities? Employment Change and White Working Class Youth.* Oxford: Blackwell.

McFarlane, A.C., Atchison, M. & Rafolowicz, E.P. (1994) 'Physical Symptoms in Post Traumatic Stress Disorder' *Journal of Psychosomatic Research,* 38 (7): 715–726.

Meltzer, D. (1994 [1974]) 'Adhesive Identification' In Hahn, H. (ed.) *Sincerity and Other Works.* London: Karnac, pp. 335–350.

Menzies Lythe, I. (1960) 'Social Systems as a Defence Against Anxiety' *Human Relations,* 13: 95–121.

Mitchell, S. (1988) *Relational Concepts in Psychoanalysis.* Cambridge, MA: Harvard University Press.

Mitchie, J. (2003) *The Handbook of Globalisation.* Cheltenham: Edward Elgar Publishing.

Mitrani, J. (1996) *A Framework for the Imaginary.* Northvale, NJ: Jason Aronson.

Mitrani, J. (2001) *Ordinary People: Extra-ordinary Protections: A Post-Kleinian Approach to Primitive Mental States.* Hove: Brunner Routledge.

Morison, J. (2000) 'The Government-Voluntary Sector Compacts: Governance, Governmentality, and Civil Society' *Journal of Law and Society,* 27 (1): 98–132.

Nava, M. (ed.) (1996) *Buy This Book: Studies in Advertising and Consumption.* London: Routledge.

Neilson, B. & Rossiter, N. (2008) 'Precarity as a Political Concept or Fordism as Exception' *Theory, Culture and Society*, 25 (7): 51–72.

Nixon, D. (2006) ' "I Just Like Working with My Hands": Employment Aspirations and the Meaning of Work for Low-Skilled Unemployed Men in Britain's Service Economy' *Journal of Education and Work*, 19 (2): 201–217.

Nixon, D. (2009) ' "I Can't Put a Smiley Face on": Working-Class Masculinity, Emotional Labour and Service Work in the "New Economy" ' *Gender, Work and Organization*, 16 (3): 300–322.

Nordberg, M. (2002) 'Constructing Masculinity in Women's Worlds: Men Working as Pre-School Teachers and Hairdressers' *NORA: The Nordic Journal of Women's Studies*, 10 (1): 26–37.

O'Donnell, M. & Sharpe, S. (2000) *Uncertain Masculinities: Youth, Ethnicity and Class in Contemporary Britain*. London: Routledge.

Office for National Statistics (ONS) (2010) *Labour Market Profile – Blaenau-Gwent*, www.nomisweb.co.uk/reports/lmp/la/2038432100/report.aspx Date accessed 20 August 2010.

Ogden, T. (1986) *The Matrix of the Mind*. Northvale, NJ: Jason Aronson.

Ogden, T. (1989) *The Primitive Edge of Experience*. Northvale, NJ: Jason Aronson.

Osmond, J. (1985) *The National Question Again*. Llandysul, Dyfed: Gomer Press.

Ouelette, L. & Hay, J. (2008) *Better Living through Reality TV*. Oxford: Blackwell.

Pahl, R. (2005) 'Are All Communities in the Mind?' *Sociological Review*, 53: 621–640.

Payne, S.J. (1985) *Crisis in Masculinity*. Westchester, IL: Crossway Books.

Pearson, G. (1983) *Hooligan: A History of Respectable Fears*. Basingstoke: Palgrave Macmillan.

Pheterson, G. (1993) 'Historical and Material Determinants of Psychodynamic Development' In Adleman, J. & Enguidanos, G. (eds) *Racism in the Lives of Women*. New York: Haworth Press.

Pitchford, S. (2001) 'Image-Making Movements: Welsh Nationalism and Stereo-Type Transformation' *Sociological Perspectives*, 44 (1): 45–65.

Pleck, E. & Pleck, J. (eds) (1980) *The American Man*. Englewood, NJ: Prentice-Hall.

Pocock, B. (2003) *The Work/Life Collision*. Sydney: The Federation Press.

Pollack, W.S. (1998) *Real Boys: Rescuing Our Sons from the Myths of Boyhood*. New York: Random House.

Pomata, G. (1999) 'Telling the Truth about Micro-History: A Memoir and a Few Reflections' *Netvćrk for historieteori og historiografi* Arbedjdspapirer nr. 3 April 2000, Copenhagen: 28–40.

Prugl, E. (1999) *The Global Construction of Gender: Home Base Work in the Political Economy of the 20th Century*. New York: Columbia University Press.

Pusey, M. (2003) *The Experience of Middle Australia: The Dark Side of Economic Reform*. Cambridge: Cambridge University Press.

Puttnam, R.D. (1995) 'Bowling Alone: America's Declining Social Capital' *Journal of Democracy*, 6 (1): 65–78.

Puttnam, R.D. (2000) *Bowling Alone: The Collapse and Revival of American Community*. New York: Simon & Schuster.

Puttnam, R.D. (ed.) (2002) *Democracies in Flux: The Evolution of Social Capital in Contemporary Society*. Oxford: Oxford University Press.

Raphael-Leff, J. & Perelberg, R.J. (eds) (2008) *Female Experience: Four Generations of British Women Psychoanalysts on Work with Women*. London: Routledge.

Rees, A. (1951) *Life in a Welsh Countryside: A Social Study of Llanfihangel yng Ngwynfa*. Cardiff: Cardiff University Press.

Revel, J. (1996a) 'Micro-Analyse et Construction du Social' In Revel, J. (ed.) *Jeux d'Echelles. La Micro-Analyse à l'Expérience*, pp. 15–36. Paris: Gallimard-Seuil.

Revel, J. (ed.) (1996b) *Jeux d'Echelles. La Micro-Analyse à l'Expérience*. Paris: Gallimard-Seuil.

Revel, J. & Hunt, L. (eds) (1996c) *Histories: French Constructions of the Past*. New York: The New Press.

Ricardo, D. (1821) (original 1817) *Principles of Political Economy and Taxation*. London: Dover Publications.

Richards, L. (1990) *Nobody's Home: Dreams and Realities in a New Suburb*. Oxford: Oxford University Press.

Ricoeur, P. (1988) *Time And Narrative Volume 3, Part IV*. Translated by Kathleen McLaughlin & David Pellauer. Chicago: Chicago University Press.

Rivers, W.H.R. (1918) 'An Address on the Repressions of War Experience' *The Lancet*, 2 February, pp. 173–177, www.pb.rcpsych.org/cgi/reprint/20/7/440/pdf Date accessed 28 August 2010.

Rose, N. (1990) *Governing the Soul: The Shaping of the Private Self*. London: Routledge.

Rose, N. (1996) 'Governing "advanced" Liberal Democracies' In Barry, A., Osborne, T. & Rose, N. (eds) *Foucault and Political Reason*. London: UCL Press, pp. 37–64.

Rose, N. (1999) *The Powers of Freedom: Reframing Political Thought*. Cambridge: Cambridge University Press.

Savage, M. (2008) 'Histories, Belongings, Communities' *International Journal of Social Research Methodology*, 11 (2): 151–162.

Seidler, V. (2007) *Young Men and Masculinities: Global Cultures and Intimate Lives*. London: Zed Press.

Sennett, R. (1971) *The Uses of Disorder*. New York: Vintage Books.

Sennett, R. (1997) *The Corrosion of Character*. New York: Norton.

Sennett, R. (1998) *The Corrosion of Character: The Personal Consequences of Work in the New Capitalism*. New York: W.W. Norton.

Singh, A. & Zammit, A. (2003) 'Globalisation, Labour Standards and Economic Development' In Mitchie, J. (ed.) *The Handbook of Globalisation*. Cheltenham: Edward Elgar Publishing.

Skeggs, B. (1997) *Formations of Class and Gender*. London: Sage.

Smith, A. (1988) *Julia Kristeva: Speaking the Unspeakable*. London: Pluto Press.

Squire, C. (2001) 'The Public Life of Emotions' *International Journal of Critical Psychology*, 1: 27–38.

Steedman, C. (1996) *Landscape for a Good Woman*. London: Little Brown Book Group Limited.

Steele, B. (2007) *Farming in Michaelchurch Escley from Medieval to Victorian Times [1500s, 1600s, 1700s, 1800]*, www.ewyaslacy.org.uk/doc Date accessed 22 August 2010.

Stern, D. (1997) *Unformulated Experience: From Dissociation to Imagination in Psychoanalysis*. Hillsdale, NJ: The Analytic Press.

Stoller, R.J. (1968) *Sex and Gender Vol. 1 The Development of Masculinity and Femininity*. London: Hogarth Press.

Stopford, A. (2004) 'Researching Postcolonial Subjectivities: The Application of Relational Psychoanalysis to Research Methodology' *Critical Psychology. Psychosocial Research Issue,* 10: 13–35.

Studdert, D. (2006) *Conceptualising Community: Beyond the State and the Individual.* Basingstoke: Palgrave Macmillan.

Sverke, M., Hellgren, J. & Naswall, K. (2002) 'No Security: A Meta-Analysis and Review of Job Insecurity and Its Consequences' *Journal of Occupational Health Psychology,* 3 (July): 242–264.

Thompson, E.P. (1963) *The Making of the English Working Class.* London: Victor Gollancz Ltd/ Vintage Books.

Tönnies, F. (1955) *Community and Association.* London: Routledge and Kegan Paul.

Tönnies, F. (1880) (2001) *Community and Civil Society.* Cambridge: Cambridge University Press.

Trist, E. & Murray, H. (eds) (1990) *The Social Engagement of Social Science: A Tavistock Anthology, Vol. 1: The Socio-Psychological Perspective.* London: Free Association, p. 625.

Trist, E. & Murray, H. (eds) (1993) *The Social Engagement of Social Science: A Tavistock Anthology, Vol. 2: The Socio-Technical Systems Perspective.* Philadelphia: University of Pennsylvania Press, p. 695.

Trist, E.,Emery, F. & Murray, H. (eds) (1997) *The Social Engagement of Social Science: A Tavistock Anthology, Vol. 3: The Socio-Ecological Perspective.* Philadelphia: University of Pennsylvania Press, p. 718.

Tustin, F. (1981) *Autistic States in Children* (revised edition). London: Routledge.

Urlic, I. (2004) 'Trauma and Reparation, Mourning and Forgiveness: The Healing Potential of the Group' *Group Analysis,* 37 (4): 453–471.

Urwin, C. (2002) 'A Psychoanalytic Approach to Language Delay: When Autistic is not Necessarily Autism' *Journal of Child Psychotherapy,* 28 (1): 73–93.

Van Dijk, Pieter, A. & Brown, A. (2006) 'Emotional Labour and Negative Job Outcomes: An Evaluation of the Mediating Role of Emotional Dissonance' *Journal of Management and Organisation,* www.highbeam.com. Date accessed 3 September 2010.

Van Hoven, B. & Horschelmann, K. (2005) *Spaces of Masculinities.* London: Routledge.

Waddington, D. et al. (1991) *Split at the Seams? Community, Continuity and Change after the 1984–5 Coal Dispute.* Milton Keynes: Open University Press.

Walkerdine, V. (1981) 'Sex, Power and Pedagogy' *Screen Education,* 38: 14–24.

Walkerdine, V. (1990) 'On the Regulation of Speaking and Silence' In Walkerdine, V. (ed.) *Schoolgirl Fictions.* London: Verso.

Walkerdine, V. (1991a) *Didn't She Do Well* (Working Pictures).

Walkerdine, V. (1991b) *Schoolgirl Fictions.* London: Verso.

Walkerdine, V. (1997) *Daddy's Girl: Young Girls and Popular Culture.* London: Palgrave Macmillan.

Walkerdine, V. (ed.) (2002) *Challenging Subjects: Critical Psychology for a New Millennium.* Basingstoke: Palgrave Macmillan.

Walkerdine, V. (2005) Thinking Subjectivity beyond the Psychoanalytic and Discursive Divide, ESRC Identities Programme public lecture, University of the West of England.

Walkerdine, V. (2007) *Children, Gender, Videogames: Towards a Relational Approach to Multimedia.* Basingstoke: Palgrave Macmillan.

Walkerdine, V. (2009) 'Steel, Identity, Community: Regenerating Identities in a South Wales Town' In Wetherell, M. (ed.) *Identities in the 21st Century.* Basingstoke: Palgrave Macmillan.

Walkerdine, V. (2010) 'Communal Beingness and Affect: An Exploration of Trauma in an Ex-industrial Community' *Body and Society,* 16 (1): 91–116.

Walkerdine, V. & Bansel, P. (2009) 'Neoliberalism, Work and Subjectivity: Towards a More Complex Account' In Wetherell, M. (ed.) *Identities in the 21st Century.* Basingstoke: Palgrave Macmillan.

Walkerdine, V. & Jimenez, L. (2006) A Relational Approach to Psychosocial Method, ESRC Idnetities Programme workshop, Bristol.

Walkerdine, V. & Lucey, H. (1989) *Democracy in the Kitchen: Regulating Mothers and Socialising Daughters.* London: Virago.

Walkerdine, V., Lucey, H. & Melody, J. (2001) *Growing Up Girl: Psychosocial Explorations of Gender and Class.* London: Palgrave Macmillan.

Walkerdine, V., Lucey, H. & Melody, J. (2002) *Growing Up Girl: Psychosocial Explorations of Gender and Class.* Basingstoke: Palgrave Macmillan.

Warwick, D. & Littlejohn, G. (1992) *Coal, Capital and Culture: A Sociological Analysis of Mining Communities in West Yorkshire.* London: Routledge.

Watson, I. et al. (2003) *Fragmented Futures: New Challenges in Working Life.* Sydney: The Federation Press.

Welsh Assembly Government (2002) *Cabinet Statements/Corus Anniversary,* www. cymru.gov.uk/about/cabinet/cabinetstatements/2002/130102RMCorus. Date accessed 22 August 2010.

Welsh Assembly Government (2006) *Key Phase of (Steeltown) Steelworks Reclamation Gets Underway,* www.new.wales.gov.uk/newsroom/businessandeconomy/2006/4029818. Date accessed 22 August 2010.

Welsh Assembly Government (2010) *The Strategy for Older People in Wales [2008–2013],* www.new.wales.gov.uk/topics/olderpeople. Date accessed 22 August 2010.

West-Newman, C.L. (2008) 'Suspect Emotions in Social Theory' *New Zealand Sociology,* 23 (2): 104–118.

Wetherell, M. (ed.) (2009) *Identities in the 21st Century.* Basingstoke: Palgrave Macmillan.

Whitehead, S.M. (2002) *Men and Masculinities.* Cambridge: Polity Press.

Whitehouse, G. (2004) 'From Family Wage to Parental Leave: The Changing Relationship between Arbitration and the Family' *The Journal of Industrial Relations,* 46 (4): 400–412.

Wieland, C. (2000) *The Undead Mother: Psychoanalytic Explorations of Masculinity, Femininity and Matricide.* London: Rebus Press.

Wilkinson, I. (2004) 'The Problem of "Social Suffering": The Challenge to Social Science' *Health Sociology Review,* 13 (2): 113–121.

Williams, R. (1973) *The Country and the City.* London: Chatto & Windus.

Williams, G.A. (1985) *When Was Wales?* Harmondsworth: Penguin.

Willis, P. (1977) *Learning to Labour: How Working Class Kids Get Working Class Jobs.* Farnborough: Saxon House.

Willis, P. (1979) 'Shop Floor Culture, Masculinity and the Wage-Form' In Clarke, J., Critcher, C. & Johnson, R. (eds) *Working Class Culture.* London: Hutchison.

Willoughby, R. (2001) 'The Petrified Self: Esther Bick and Her Membership Paper' *British Journal of Psychotherapy,* 18 (1): 3–6.

Willoughby, R. (2004) 'Between the Basic Fault and the Second Skin' *International Journal of Psychoanalysis,* 85: 179–196.

Winnicott, D.W. (1958) 'The Capacity to Be Alone' *International Journal of Psychoanalysis,* 39: 416–420.

Winnicott, D.W. (1971) *Playing and Reality.* Harmondsworth: Penguin.

Wundt, W.M. (1902) *Outlines of Psychology* (second edition). Ann Arbour, MI: University of Michigan Press.

Wundt, W.M. (2009) *Elements of Folk Psychology.* USA: Bibliobazaar, LLC.

Yehuda, R. et al. (1995) 'Low Urinary Cortisol Excretion in Holocaust Survivors with Post Traumatic Stress Disorder' *American Journal of Psychiatry,* 152: 982–986.

Yehuda, R. et al. (1998) 'Phenomenology and Psychobiology in the Intergenerational Response to Trauma' In Danieli, Y. (ed.) *International Handbook of Multigenerational Legacies of Trauma.* New York: Plenum Press.

Yehuda, R., Halligan, S. & Grossman, R. (2001) 'Childhood Trauma and Risk for PTSD: Relationship to Intergenerational Effects of Trauma, Parental PTSD and Cortisol Excretion' *Development and Psychopathology,* 13 (3): 733–753.

Yellow Horse Brave Heart, M. (2003) 'The Historical Trauma Response among Natives and Its Relationship with Substance Abuse: A Lakota Illustration' *Journal of Psychoactive Drugs,* 35 (1): 7–13.

Yellow Horse Brave Heart, M. & DeBruyn, L. (1998) 'The American Holocaust: Healing Historical Unresolved Grief' *American Indian and Alaska Native Mental Health Research,* 82 (2): 56–78.

Young, A. (1995) *The Harmony of Illusions: Inventing Post-Traumatic Stress Disorder.* Princeton: Princeton University Press.

Zippay, A. (1991) *From Middle Income to Poor: Downward Mobility among Displaced Steelworkers.* New York: Praeger.

Index